THE BIRTH
OF THE
BRITISH MOTOR CAR
1769–1897

Volume 1
A NEW MACHINE
1769–1842

By the same author
A Toy for the Lion (Kimber)
Adventurer's Road (Cassell)
The Trailblazers (Cassell)
Five Roads to Danger (Cassell)
The Wild Roads (Jarrolds)
The Age of Motoring Adventure (Cassell)
Car Badges of the World (Cassell)
The Motor Book (Methuen)
The Second Motor Book (Methuen)
Automobile Treasures (Ian Allan)
The World's Motor Museums (Dent)
European Cars 1886–1914 (Ian Allan)
The Vintage Car 1919–1930 (Batsford)
Sports Cars 1907–1927 (Blandford Press)
Sports Cars 1928–1939 (Blandford Press)
Passenger Cars 1863–1904 (Blandford Press)
Passenger Cars 1905–1912 (Blandford Press)
Passenger Cars 1913–1923 (Blandford Press)
Racing Cars and Record Breakers 1898–1921 (Blandford Press)
Sprint: Speed Hillclimbs and Speed Trials in Britain 1899–1925 (David & Charles)
Isotta-Fraschini: The Noble Pride of Italy (Ballantine)
Contributor to G.N. Georgano: *The Complete Encyclopedia of Motor Cars* (Ebury Press)

THE BIRTH
OF THE
BRITISH MOTOR CAR
1769–1897

Volume 1
A NEW MACHINE
1769–1842

T. R. Nicholson

First published 1982 by
THE MACMILLAN PRESS LTD
London and Basingstoke
Companies and representatives
throughout the world

Volume 1   ISBN 0 333 23764 1

Volume 2   ISBN 0 333 28561 1
Volume 3   ISBN 0 333 28563 8
The set   ISBN 0 333 32717 9

Typeset and printed in Hong Kong

Contents

List of Plates

Author's Note

When first written, this book took the form of a Ph.D. thesis for Leicester University entitled *The Origins of the Motor Car in Britain 1769–1881*, together with its continuation *The Origins of the Motor Car in Britain 1882–1897*. The references given in these two places are very much fuller than in the present book. Both are bound typescripts, and both are lodged in Leicester University Library.

Acknowledgements

The writer owes a great debt to all the following for their help and advice so freely offered during the preparation of this work. Especial thanks for their guidance and patience are due to Professor J. Simmons, late of the Department of History at Leicester University, Professor M. Biddiss of the Department of History at Reading University, David Crompton of the Department of Civil Engineering at Imperial College, London, and Dr W. Albert of the School of Social Studies at the University of East Anglia; also to Ronald H. Clark for checking the technical aspects of Parts 1 and 2 of Volume 2, and to Hilda F. Howell, to whom the typing must at times have seemed like a life sentence.

Grateful thanks are due, too, to those individuals and institutions listed below. Literally hundreds of others gave generously of their time and expertise, and the writer hopes that this word of acknowledgement will adequately express his obligation to them all.

The City, Borough, District or Divisional Librarians of Banbury, Bolton, Chelmsford, Edinburgh, Leicester, St Ives, Tameside, Tunbridge Wells and Walsall.

The Librarians or County Archivists of Devon, Gloucestershire, Humberside, Staffordshire, and Wiltshire.

The Librarians, Archivists and other officers of the British Transport Historical Records, the University of Birmingham, Daimler-Benz A.G., David Salomons House, the National Motor Museum (Mr G.N. Georgano), the Glasgow Museum of Transport, the Institute of Agricultural History and Museum of English Rural Life at Reading University, the Institution of Mechanical Engineers, the National Library of Scotland, the National Register of Archives of Scotland, the Royal Agricultural College, the Royal Artillery Institution, the Royal Automobile Club, the Scottish Record Office, and the Musée de l'Armée of Paris.

Dr G. Alderman, Department of History, Royal Holloway College; W.G.P. Arnold; Graham Bannock, Economists' Advisory Group;

Comte Geoffroy de Beauffort; Peter H. Collinson; Anthony Dent; Baron F. Duckham, University of Strathclyde; Peter Garnier; John Hibbs, City of Birmingham Polytechnic; the late Dennis C. Field; A.S. Heal; Jacques Ickx; Geoffrey Kichenside; D.S. Manson; Keith Marvin; Frank Mullineux; Gordon J. Offord; E.A. Olive; John M. Peckham; Barry Peerless; Leon R. Potter; Derek Roberts; Michael Sedgwick; Marylian Watney, British Driving Society.

Note on the Sources

Many of the events, people and machines described in these pages were the subject of more than one contemporary account. These accounts frequently differ, totally or in detail, according to who is telling the story. Inventors, constructors, promoters and politicians tended to offer versions that satisfied their vanity, cupidity, or other forms of self-indulgence; or else that were founded on ignorance of the complete picture.

Where these sources do not contradict one another, but are complementary, a composite picture has been built up from the most likely elements. Where they are inconsistent, the writer has given preference to the most probable story. The opposing view is not given space unless it is in some way significant or relevant.

The sources are sometimes unsatisfactory in that large gaps appear in the knowledge at our disposal. Here informed guesses, based on such facts as are available, have been substituted, and the reader so informed.

Both difficulties arise when, for example, one attempts to unravel the labyrinthine complexities of the coachbuilding Mulliner family. As often happens, they are not so much ill-documented as over-documented, with a mass of scrappy, often vague, often inconsistent material, some of it claiming the status of holy writ. The note on p. 489 represents the most likely picture that can be pieced together without devoting a Master's thesis to the subject.

1

Pure Experiment,
France and Britain, 1769–1826

What is a motor car? Because it has meant different things at different times to different people, any study must begin with a definition; and for the same reason, any such definition must be to some extent arbitrary. Here, it is defined as a working, self-propelled, self-contained road vehicle with three or four wheels, purpose-built as personal, private transport for up to six people, including the driver and any other operators; or for more passengers if intended for carrying small private parties. Its motive power has for practical purposes been confined to steam, electricity, and oil-based fuels. The one essential element is the vehicle's private nature – it is not for public or commercial use.

As a general rule, the activities of foreign vehicles are dealt with only if there is evidence of their being known in Britain, and if there is a possibility that they influenced British construction. An exception has been made in the case of the Cugnot machines of 1769–71. They had no discernible effect on development in Britain. There is no mention of them across the Channel for 60 years, and no detailed description for another 20 years. However, they were the world's first full-sized, working, self-propelled vehicles, and the fact poses a question that must be answered: why did the new machine, invented in France, develop not there but in Britain? Some of the answers are bound up in the nature and history of the Cugnot vehicles, so their story has to be told.

Although they cannot be called motor cars, vehicles designed as coaches or omnibuses for fare-paying passengers, and road tractors for drawing passengers, goods, agricultural equipment or military impedimenta loom large in this study. There are two reasons for this. First, legislation designed to deal with such vehicles also – though accidentally – affected contemporary motor cars. Second, these other vehicles gave birth to the first generation of the motor car, and deeply affected the second. It is natural enough that this should have happened, for it is a cliché that after the first curiosity of the scientist or experimental engineer has done its work, commercial or military competition are among the strongest impulses that have driven man to make technological advances.

The successful evolution of a practical invention is not, however, as simple a matter as that. There are two prerequisities if it is to appear. One, obviously, is adequate technology. The other is a favourable context – a motor car must not only work, it must also be able to do so in its most immediate environment, the road. It is not fanciful to suggest that in the case of the motor car, the two requirements were most intimately linked. France produced the first full-scale, working self-propelled road vehicle in 1769; in the same period as she was acquiring her first modern network of good, scientifically built roads. Britain followed suit in 1802, in the same general context of road improvement. These earliest efforts were abortive in both countries, partly because the roads were not yet good *enough*; but there is something more than inherent probability to suggest that self-propelled vehicles, from their earliest beginnings, were encouraged by better roads and, conversely, discouraged by their absence. Moreover, this was certainly true of horsedrawn traffic. Although the frailer steam carriage demanded still smoother surfaces, it is reasonable to suppose that the same rule applied. Beyond doubt, it was true of the first petrol-engined vehicles in Britain and the United States.

Denis Papin, the first man known to have built a vehicle driven by a reciprocating steam engine (*c.* 1698), was only able to make a working model, for reasons explained later; but even he, limited probably to a smooth and level floor, appreciated the obstacles that would await the then-theoretical road vehicle: "... j'ay fait un petit modèle d'un chariot qui avance par cette force ... mais je crois que l'inégalité et les détours des grands chemins rendrons cette invention très difficile à perfectionner pour les voitures par terre."

Around the end of the 17th century, and for long after, "the unevenness of the main roads" was indeed a discouragement, not only to the hypothetical self-propelled vehicle, but also, to a lesser degree, to existing animal traffic. Conditions in Britain around the time Papin wrote in France were representative, in essentials, of north-western Europe as a whole in 1700. In France some roads were rather better than this at the time; in Britain they would remain as bad for longer.

The pavement of the Roman highways had vanished; roads were, in general, unsurfaced tracks worn across country by the passage of feet, hooves and wheels over the bare ground, and following the easiest way. Where the surrounding land was unenclosed, the roads were broad, beaten wider and wider as travellers tried to bypass the potholes and ruts created by their precursors. Where there was enclosure, by hedges or fences, there was no way around the churned mud and pond-sized puddles of winter, autumn and spring, and the dust and jarring holes and ridges of summer. In marshy ground, heavy clay or forest, the difficulties multiplied.

Road repair – and construction where it took place – were amateurish in the extreme. The normal mode of repair was to throw rough stones into the worst ruts and holes, with or without a covering of gravel, sand or earth, and leave all to be bedded down by the passage of traffic. Little or no repair took place in the winter months. If a new road was to be made, a foundation of large stones was followed by smaller stones and a top-dressing of earth, to form, for the sake of good drainage, a sort of long bank with sharply shelving sides. On either flank might be a stone causeway for pack animals. This was both inefficient and dangerous. The loose material forming the crown of the road, to which traffic kept in order to avoid the steep camber, was soon broken down into ruts and potholes. These collected water, and forced traffic on to the camber, where vehicles frequently overturned.

The growth of industry, commerce and population in the 16th century started by making matters worse, through increasing traffic on the roads. Before the canal boom, the development of inland manufacturing towns depended principally on the roads, which carried all passengers and commodities calling for the relative speed, certainty and security that coastwise shipping could not offer. To pedestrians, horsemen and carts were henceforth added increasing numbers of pack-horse trains, herds of animals – cattle, sheep, pigs – on their way to and from the expanding markets, and, a little later, the great 4-ton stage wagons advancing at a walking pace on their 16-inch rims. Stage coaches added to the crush from the middle 1630s, multiplying after the Civil Wars were over.

Government had been alerted to the strain on inland communication as early as 1555, when an Act was passed that assigned responsibility for the maintenance of the roads in passable condition; the first official intervention in this sphere. They were, said the preamble, "nowe bothe verie noysome and tedious to travell in, and dangerous to all Passengers and Cariages". Each parish was to appoint two unpaid surveyors to decide on and supervise repairs within its boundaries; every parishioner, and every owner of a team or cart, was to provide four (later six) consecutive days of unpaid labour a year. Money could be offered in lieu, but defaulting was punished. This statutory labour system, in force until 1835, was hated and hard to enforce. Attempts were made to substitute a parish rate – in practice the fines levied for failure to provide labour – but these also failed to improve the roads. Nor could the system offer any improvement in efficiency over what had gone before, lacking as it did professional skills at every level from surveyor to labourer.

It seems likely, however, that some improvement was effected in the next 100 years, since the volume of traffic continued to increase without a further marked decline in standards being reported; though any such improvement probably did no more than keep pace with the destruction. The spread of the stage coach from the 1630s was significant: it implied a regular, if still slow, service devoted to passengers, who were more fragile and less tolerant of delay than freight. Indeed, it could be commended for speed too, by the standards of the day. In the mid-17th century, some stage coaches could cover the same distance in a day as a post-boy of half a century before. As against this, the comments of the much-travelled Celia Fiennes, covering the period 1685–1703 and the whole country, point to a situation no different from that facing Mary Tudor. She or her contemporaries told of how a footman with an axe might have to precede a coach to clear encroaching undergrowth; how a traveller could lose his way even on the Great North Road; and how the ladies of Sussex had to go to church in ox-drawn carriages because horses could not cope with that county's muddy horror.

In the early years of the 18th century conditions in Britain and France diverged, France taking the lead. She initiated the first scientific roadmaking programme in north-western Europe since Roman times, when the Corps des Ponts et Chaussées, a body of Crown-appointed road and bridge engineers, was founded in 1716. The German states, too, began to interest themselves in better roads; then Austria, Sweden and Russia. All, like France and unlike Britain, were authoritarian states wedded to central government control. Most had vulnerable land frontiers, and needed good roads to allow easy movement of troops. In France, meanwhile, the Corps des Ponts et Chaussées had a school by 1747. By 1776 half of the country's 25,000 miles of highways were being rebuilt or realigned, and the *routes nationales* had been defined and classified. The roadmaking system of the highway engineer Pierre Trésaguet was being adopted nationwide at the same period. Materials were carefully chosen. The foundation consisted of large stones laid on edge, on top of which were laid and tamped down layers of successively smaller stones, and finally a gravel surface. The road was both well drained and safely cambered. These roads provided an exceptionally favourable environment for wheeled traffic of all kinds. If a steam vehicle was to appear, the best place it could do so was France. The technology was there, too, for any European engineer to see; if at first only on paper.

In its fundamentals, the steam engine of the third quarter of the 18th century was virtually unchanged from Thomas Newcomen's first machine of 1712, which was totally unsuited to propelling a vehicle. Although it was the world's earliest practical reciprocating steam engine, its usefulness and that of its successors was limited to its immediate purpose, which was to pump water from mines, or, less frequently, to pump water to a height sufficient to drive a water wheel. The boiler produced steam at a pressure of, at most, a few pounds per square inch above that of the atmosphere, and the pressure played no part in activating the mechanism. Because it was not required to withstand high pressures, the boiler needed to be no stronger than any tank for holding boiling water. It might, indeed, be made of wood, like much of the rest of the engine. The steam was admitted to the base of a vertical open-topped cylinder at least 6–8 feet tall, 2 feet in diameter, and perhaps weighing several tons; it was then condensed by the injection of cold water (which also cooled the cylinder, leading to heat loss). The resulting vacuum under the piston, retained in the cylinder by a layer of water on top of it, allowed atmospheric pressure to force the piston down. The piston was suspended by chains to one end of a rocking beam, on the other end of which was hung the pump rod. The counterweight of the rod caused the piston to rise, completing the cycle. The Newcomen engine could operate at 12 strokes per minute, but was likely to average 5. At the limit of its development, it would run at up to 18 strokes a minute, with a working speed of 10. The engine in its housing was a piece of architecture as much as a machine, 40 feet high and tied to the earth by stone foundations. It could be made on a small, even model, scale for demonstration purposes,[1] when no useful work was called for, but in practical use, it was severely restricted by size, weight and inefficiency.

The first Newcomen engine in France was set up in 1726, but comparatively few had been built there by 1769, for the French mining industry was not mechanising as fast as Britain's. It seems all the more surprising that the first practical application of a revolutionary advance in steam technology should come in France; but two factors, apart from Europe's best roads, worked in its favour. One was the lack of a powerful vested interest in the established steam technology, as compared with Britain. Engineers and experimental scientists, starting with Papin, had always appreciated the theoretical advantages of high-pressure steam over a vacuum created by steam condensation. The piston would be driven by steam alone, at well above atmospheric pressure. Because a vacuum would be unnecessary, the heat loss from condensation could not arise. The steam, having done its work, would be discharged into the open air. The whole apparatus promised to be more efficient, lighter, and more compact than the low-pressure engine. For these reasons it would also be infinitely more adaptable, for it would no longer be anchored to the ground. In 1725 a design for a two-cylinder pumping engine on these lines was published by Jacob Leupold in Germany.

There remained one formidable practical difficulty –no one had yet built a boiler capable of standing up to pressures considerably above that of the atmosphere. Nor, while the low-pressure engine did its one job reasonably well, was there any irresistible impulse for engineers to develop such a boiler.[2] But, in France at least, there was no active discouragement. Another problem would be to convert the up-and-down reciprocating motion of the pumping engine into the rotary motion necessary to turn a shaft, and thus wheels. It had not been called for so far; but the answer here, too, lay on paper, for Papin in France had devised a ratchet-and-pawl mechanism that promised to do the job, albeit crudely. It seems probable that he used this on his model vehicle.

A third factor, working indirectly, induced the full-sized, working, self-propelled vehicle to appear first in France. This was military necessity. In 1763 France had suffered defeat in the Seven Years' War, and lost most of her overseas empire, partly on account of inefficient and conservative organisation and methods in her army. The Duc de Choiseul, Minister of War, an enlightened man of progressive ideas, was determined to restore the army to pride of place in Europe. One of the objects of his attention was the artillery. General de Gribeauval, whom he appointed France's first Inspector-General of Artillery, drew up plans to reform this arm, and by the time of the Revolution, the artillery of France – like her road system – was the finest in Europe. Choiseul was in fact involved with both, or at least with road transport, for he was also Superintendent of the "Couriers Postes et Relais de France". The military significance of the roads of France was well understood, so it is not strange that one man held both jobs.

In 1769, when new ideas still filled the air, a Swiss officer called de Planta came to Choiseul with a scheme for a steam vehicle. Choiseul told Gribeauval to investigate it. The Inspector-General already had such a design before him, submitted by Nicolas Joseph Cugnot, a 44-year-old French officer from Void in Lorraine, already known in military circles for his originality of mind. He had designed a new type of small arm, and had written three books on fortification. Cugnot's project was at a more advanced stage than Planta's; indeed, he had already begun it "en petit", which might mean the model he is said to have made six years earlier. Planta withdrew, and Gribeauval recommended to Choiseul that a small version of Cugnot's vehicle – not a model – should be built at government expense.

The machine was demonstrated before Choiseul, Gribeauval and others at the Paris Arsenal on 23 October 1769. So, for the first time on record, Leupold's proposals for high-pressure steam were put into practice, and its versatility and potential to a limited extent demonstrated. The vehicle had three wheels. The single small wheel at the front was driven by a two-cylinder high-pressure engine[3] and boiler mounted above and in front of it, on a swivelling forecarriage. The pistons transmitted rotary motion to the driving wheel through connecting rods and Papin's ratchet-and-pawl mechanism.

The same wheel steered. At this time, every other vehicle on the road was steered by the animals that drew it. As the animals changed direction, so the axle carrying the two leading wheels pivoted on its centre to follow suit. On a self-propelled vehicle, a steersman would be necessary. The force he could exert could not turn axle and wheels, so until a completely new steering layout could be devised, the single small front wheel, or ingenious variations on the theme, would have to do, at the expense of stability and controllability.

However, the Cugnot steersman did not have to cope with high speeds as well. It was estimated that with four people on board, the vehicle should be able to average four kilometres an hour over level ground. In fact in its first test it achieved only a quarter of this modest speed. At another demonstration at the Arsenal in April 1770 it did better, but a halt was necessary every 12 or 15 minutes to get up steam again. The boiler was too small, and may have leaked. It struck witnesses as being too weak – the problem that was to dog boilers under high steam pressure. Also, the firebox wasted its heat, and the cylinders were far from steam-tight.

Nevertheless, the spectators were sufficiently impressed to authorise Cugnot to build a second, larger machine similar in layout. This would be required to cover four kilometres in the hour, including stops, while carrying its crew of two – steersman/driver and stoker – and hauling a load of 8000–10,000 pounds. Except by inference, nothing can be learned of the purpose of the experiments while the first machine was being built and tested, but now it becomes clearer. A contemporary witness, Louis Petit de Bachaumont, said that the "chariot à feu" covered about six kilometres in an hour in the grounds of the Arsenal, where it had been assembled, drawing a load of 5000 pounds "servant de socle à un canon de 48" – a heavy artillery piece of about the same weight. The machine, he said, would draw wagons, but would be destined principally for towing guns. Bachaumont went on to specify that it should "monter sur les hauteurs les plus escarpées; et surmonter tous les obstacles de l'inégalité des terrains ou de leur affaisement".

Later, the Marquis de Saint-Auban, an artillery general, bore out Bachaumont's words when he wrote that the vehicle was "pour le transport de l'artillerie". Another test was made in the following summer. On 2 July 1771 Gribeauval wrote to inform the new Minister of War, the Marquis de Monteynard, that the machine was at the Arsenal and ready for trial. In a memorandum with his letter, Gribeauval suggested a test in the Parc de Meudon, private ground near the Avenue de Versailles that could be closed against spectators, and that had a good surface and gentle gradients. It would be a suitable place for the driver to gain experience before venturing on to public roads. Saint-Auban mentions another outing, which was probably later because it was from Paris to Vincennes, a journey of about six kilometres on public highways. The small size of the boiler still called for several stops. On that occasion, a load of 6500 pounds was drawn. No elapsed time is mentioned.

Such is all we know of the Cugnot steamers' performance. So far, the second alone had cost 20,000 livres, about £900 sterling at the time,[4] not counting fuel and wages for the crew; and it can have shown little promise of fulfilling all the requirements. Saint-Auban described it as "heavy and clumsy"; it weighed 5000 pounds unladen, and its turning circle was only 15 or 20 degrees. According to an obituary of Cugnot published in 1804, at some point it demolished a wall. The weight of the machinery bearing down on the front wheel, and the torque exerted by the drive passing to it, cannot have helped the steersman. These stresses should have been counterbalanced when the machine was running laden, but it must have been a handful at any time.

Saint-Auban's summing up was "aussi ingénieuse qu'inutile". Very similar words are said to have been used by a commentator who may have been the Marquis Joseph Florent de Vallière, also a general of artillery, and author of works on siegecraft. Whoever he was, he added sensible technical criticisms, and doubted the vehicle's staying-power on difficult terrain. It is, indeed, hard to see the "chariot à feu" hauling big guns through the mud and broken ground of siege works, or even, with its persistently inadequate boiler, maintaining a 4 k.p.h. average speed on the roads.[5]

Cugnot's second machine was stored initially in the Paris Arsenal, and then, from 1801, in the Conservatoire National des Arts et Métiers, now the Musée National des Techniques, where it is on public view. Once the military had dismissed Cugnot's invention –

rightly, from their point of view – it sank from sight.[6] It had been built for a very specialised and demanding purpose, and had been known only to a restricted circle. Given the state of steam expertise in 1771, and everyone's total lack of experience in building and operating self-propelled vehicles, far too much had been expected of it. When placed in the Conservatoire, where in normal times it might have attracted international scientific attention, Europe was at war. During the brief respite granted by the Peace of Amiens, in 1802, Napoleon ordered it to be taken out and tested, but lost interest with the renewal of hostilities. When, in 1851, General Morin's report to the Academy of Sciences first sparked off international awareness of Cugnot's pioneering role, his device was a museum piece in every sense of the phrase.

Bachaumont had concluded by remarking that, for lack of capital, not even low-pressure pumping engines were in use in France, as they were in England. This was not so in the literal sense; and the implication of general French backwardness in steam technology was belied not only by the Cugnot vehicle itself, but soon by other advances as well, which continued to anticipate developments in Britain. The first successful experimental steamboat was French; the Marquis Jouffroy d'Abbans' 180-ton vessel navigated the Saône in 1783. John Fitch's American boat did not follow for another four years, and Symington's appeared a year after that. It is possible that at least one more full-scale steam vehicle propelled itself along French roads at this time. It is claimed for Thomas-Charles-August Dallery that in 1780, this musical-instrument maker of Amiens demonstrated a machine with a high-pressure engine, a water-tube boiler, and a form of differential. Nothing is known of the vehicle's performance, and its engine was removed to power machinery in Dallery's organ factory.

Still, Bachaumont's strictures held good to the extent that, in comparison with well-capitalised, steam-minded Britain, steam as a means of driving machinery of all sorts was undeveloped. This may account for the slower but surer advances across the Channel, and for Dallery's failure to patent his engine for another 23 years.

Morin was to echo Bachaumont's chagrin, adding that the English had exploited what French ingenuity had created; but in the Britain of 1769, there was as yet little to suggest that his complaint would be justified. That little, however, was important. Britain's roads were improving again, if less quickly than those of France. This was due to the spread of the turnpike trusts, and, to a lesser extent, to growing official concern.

Although unpaid statute labour continued, two new principles came into being – that a stretch of road could be a commercially exploitable commodity,[7] and that its upkeep should be paid for not by the parish but by its users. The more enterprising of the local gentry or townspeople obtained an Act of Parliament giving them the right to charge tolls on one or more lengths of road, totalling on average 10–20 miles, in return for making it good and keeping it in sound repair; or, it may be, for building new roads. To effect initial repairs, the Act permitted them to raise loans, on which interest usually of four or five per cent was payable, from among local people. These embraced a wide spectrum of interests, mostly influential, from landowners and tenant farmers to manufacturers and merchants, and even small tradesmen and craftsmen. At first justices of the peace, and later trustees, anything from 30 to 500 in number, supervised the works and the running of the trust through the officers they appointed – surveyor, clerk, and treasurer. Administrative costs, continuing repairs, and interest were funded out of toll receipts and out of contributions from the parish in lieu of statute labour. In theory, the loans were repaid in the same way. Each Act ran initially for only 21 years, for in law its purpose was only to repair or make a particular length or lengths of road. When the work was done, it was assumed that the loan could be repaid, the trust wound up and the roads returned to parish care. In practice, the trustees always appealed to Parliament for a renewal, more work being needed to keep the road in good order, and the debt still unpaid. These reasons apart, vested financial interests in the trust's perpetuation had been created. In the narrow sense, it was a source of income, and in a wider one, it was seen that better communications were good for business and for agriculture. The interests of the trusts were in powerful hands. High property qualifications were required of trustees, who would include county M.P.s, justices, and landowners. Intelligence and a sense of public responsibility were expected of the ruling classes, and in the absence of universal education, it was generally considered that the best available criterion of these qualities was the ownership of property.

The first turnpike gates were set up on a stretch of the Great North Road in 1663, but no more Acts followed until 1695. The system took its final and effective form only in 1706, when the first body of trustees was appointed, replacing the county justices, who could no longer cope. Trusts began to multiply in the 1720s. In that decade, the mileage under tolls trebled, and 46 new bills were passed. By 1750 the number of acts, including renewals, had reached 146, and the turnpiking of 13 of the main inter-urban routes out of London was almost complete.

There were signs that Parliament and government were taking a new interest in roads. Now, as later, the turnpiking Bills, and their renewals when applied for, were passed as a matter of course. Government-sponsored road legislation was increasingly frequent from about 1700, though it was ineffective, and concerned almost wholly with damage to the roads by loads and wheels, not with improved road repair and construction. Vehicles should be adapted to roads, not roads to vehicles. Select committees on trust management reported in 1763 and 1765. Existing legislation was modified and re-enacted, though not altered in substance, by the Highway Acts of 1766 and 1773. As in France, official interest was spurred by strategic considerations. Jacobite rebellions in Scotland in 1715 and 1719 had led to the construction, between 1726 and 1737, of 250 miles of new Highland roads by General Wade. By 1780 roads in Ireland were vastly improved, Arthur Young found. Statute labour had been abolished there in 1762, and rates efficiently substituted. Poor communications in northern England had hindered the suppression of the "Forty-five" by slowing the lateral movement of troops and artillery. One result was that stone was removed wholesale from Hadrian's Wall to make a better road between Newcastle and Carlisle.

By mid-century road improvement, still patchy but widespread, was becoming noticeable, and was being attributed to the work of the trusts. Daniel Defoe in 1724 is the first recorded commentator to remark on this. By 1752 such sentiments were being heard more frequently. One of Samuel Johnson's "harmless drudges", taking an encyclopedist's-eye-view of the whole country, said that travel was not only safer, easier and faster, it was also more economic – the most telling argument. Carriers were drawing greater weights with the same number of animals, and the cost of carriage by road had declined by 30 per cent, taking tolls into account. Compared with 30 to 40 years before, "the public hath found great advantage from the improvements of the roads."[8]

This was at the beginning of a boom period in trust growth. Between 1751 and 1791, 454 new Bills – roughly quadrupling the mileage of road turnpiked, and not counting renewals – were passed. More than four-fifths of them became law in the first half of the period – the time of the "Turnpike Mania". Violent local opposition to turnpiking, that had flared in the first half of the century, died away in the second. Not only were industry, commerce and population expanding faster than ever before; interest rates were low, and landowners had more money to invest, thanks to prosperity from enclosures and other agricultural improvements, high prices for produce, and high rents.

More travel, more traffic in general, and more public attention being directed to roads brought a much heavier volume of comment than hitherto. Its drift varied greatly, depending on the region described (West Country roads, far from the major centres of industry, were notoriously awful); on whether the particular length was turnpiked or not; on the season (many roads were still impassable in winter); and what the critic was accustomed to. Most important, standards were constantly rising, so conditions that might have been regarded as acceptable a generation earlier were no longer tolerable.

A writer in the *Gentleman's Magazine*, also in 1752, deplores the leakage of sterling abroad, complaining that while the Englishman in Paris had spent £100,000 in the previous year, he avoids his West Country relations – "he thinks no more of visiting them than of traversing the deserts of Nubia." Writing in the same journal in the same year, an overseas visitor bears out this judgement on West Country roads – they were "as God had left them after the Flood". Roads in France, Austria and Switzerland, he says, are far better.

A few years later, writers are becoming lyrical. A contributor to the *Annual Register* in 1761 can say that "the lover can now almost literally annihilate time and space, and be with his mistress before she dreams of his arrival". Six years afterwards, another writer declares that "our very carriages travel with almost winged Expedition between every Town of Consequence in the Kingdom and the Metropolis". In 1782 a German writer, Carl Philipp Moritz, describes the roads around London as very good. Yet Arthur Young, covering those of the whole country in the late 1760s, laces his text with such adjectives as "infamous", "infernal", and "most execrably vile". Occasionally, he is lost for words. At the same time, a careful reading of Young reveals that he is referring in most cases to the "cross roads". These, run mostly by the parishes, linked the main traffic arteries, which were by now largely under trust control. Of trust roads in the north, Young regarded only about one-quarter as being bad. It is clear that he, too, regarded turnpiking and improvement as synonymous. This is borne out yet again in 1794 – except as regards Wales – by the surveyors of the Board of Agriculture, who were concerned with roads insofar as they affected agricultural prosperity.

In this welter of seemingly conflicting evidence, two things are clear. First, the roads were still being administered and repaired by amateurs, on the time-honoured principles of ignorance. After the mid-1770s, there was no outside regulation of any sort over the trustees' activities. This was generally thought right, since they were all men of property, qualifying on this account as natural rulers, and providing their services free. The trusts' surveyors were generally no improvement upon those of the parishes. They could be undertakers, publicans, a former Lloyd's underwriter, or even a bed-ridden old man who had not left his home for several months. They were paid, but poorly. The trusts did not offer salaries that would have attracted professionals, even had they existed. Their labour was equally unskilled, and often obtained on the cheap. The trusts were entitled to a share of free statute labour, or cash in lieu from the parish, and also employed the destitute, who would otherwise be on parish relief. The result, inevitably, was that British roads in the second half of the 18th century fell below the best standards of the time.

Even so, it is equally clear that "by the mid-1770s, an interconnected and fairly comprehensive network of improved roads had been formed".[9] They were very far from perfect, but they were better than they had been, and were constantly improving. The truth of this is suggested not only by contemporary comment, but also by comparing the times taken by stage coaches to cover their routes at different periods.

Coach services flourished on the desire of provincials, especially those in the industrial regions, to draw closer in time to London, the metropolis, the centre of commerce, society and culture. Speed and ease of communication were good for more than just business. Travelling what was alleged to be the 18th-century Scot's fairest prospect, the high road to London, took him 10 days from Edinburgh in 1754, or 12 days in winter. There was only one coach a month. By 1776 the time of the fastest, "flying" coach had shrunk to four days. The 170-odd miles from Exeter to London, traversing part of the notorious west, took five or six days in 1700, but only two in 1764. The time to Bristol, Britain's second port, declined from two days in 1754 to 16 hours 30 years later. Dover, the main link with the Continent, was two days from London in 1751, and one in 1795.

The industrial and manufacturing towns of the Midlands and north were just as well served. Birmingham, Britain's principal manufacturing town, was two days distant from London in 1742, and 19 hours in 1782. The Sheffield coach was three days on the road in 1760, and 26 hours in 1787. Manchester was $4\frac{1}{2}$ days away in 1754, three days in 1760, and 28 hours in 1788. The time to Newcastle in 1734, nine days by the flying coach (three days faster than the rest), had halved within 20 years. Liverpool could not be reached at all by direct coach in 1757, for the road between there and Warrington could only be negotiated on horseback. The complete journey, including the ride, took four days. The first through Liverpool coach ran in 1760, and six years later the time was down to two days in summer and three in winter. A further proof of the road improvement was furnished when, in 1784, John Palmer won the London-Bristol mail contract for coaches from the horsed post-boys. The fast, reliable carriage of the Royal Mail was of prime importance to the Crown. The new mail coaches, with their tight and ruthlessly maintained schedules, and the privilege of exemption from stopping to pay toll, brought London to within 36 hours of Liverpool in 1785. They would later perform still greater prodigies, driving the flying coaches to go faster in order to compete. Only bad weather would check them seriously. Such times were achieved partly by the new practice of driving through the night; but it was also true that the overall average running time on the road of all coaches was cut by half or more in the 80 years from 1750.

Thus, as far as roads were concerned, the overall picture in Britain was one of mild, gradually growing encouragement – by no means as strong as in France – of wheeled traffic of all sorts. Before 1800 there was nothing else that boded well for anyone interested in steam vehicles. The technology was as available, on paper, as it was in Continental Europe, but in Britain it took much longer to appear in the metal. Her poorer roads may have contributed to this state of affairs; also her heavy commitment to low-pressure steam, which may have bred a certain conservatism and lack of interest in high-pressure engines. After 1769 – the year, ironically, when Cugnot's first machine moved – there also appeared more powerful deterrents: the patents of James Watt.

Watt transformed the efficiency of the low-pressure engine. He found the Newcomen engine much improved by John Smeaton, who in the 1770s had doubled the useful work it could do, but Watt left it eight times as efficient. His separate condenser, steam jacket around the cylinder, and stuffing box instead of water seal on top of it minimised energy loss and dramatically reduced fuel consumption. His double-acting engine doubled the power output of any cylinder of given size. These improvements greatly accelerated the spread of low-pressure steam power. Most significantly, by applying rotary motion to it (initially by planetary gearing, a much more efficient method than ratchet-and-pawl) Watt introduced the steam engine into manufacture. His rotative engines had flywheels, to permit smooth operation. When, in 1794, James Pickard's patent for imparting rotative motion by means of a crankshaft expired, Watt and later other engine-builders began to use this system also. Since Boulton & Watt engines were the best, and, thanks to patent protection, the only ones available apart from the obsolescent Newcomen type, they provided the Industrial Revolution in Britain with a powerful boost. Some of their features would also benefit all kinds of steam engine.[10] Finally, it could be argued that if Watt had not brought steam power into general acceptance when he did, the first road steamers in Britain would not have enjoyed even short-lived and qualified success.

When all this is said and done, it is equally true that the onset of the Industrial Revolution was slower than it might have been, because of Watt's opposition to the high-pressure engine. He did his best to prevent its introduction in Britain, and therefore, incidentally, held back the arrival of steam vehicles on British roads. Others could not make or sell high-pressure engines, because Watt's 1769 patent, covering principally his separate condenser, embraced those as well. His purpose in this was not to develop such an engine himself – the reverse was the case – but to protect his investment in low-pressure steam. Watt was clearly aware of the advantages of the high-pressure engine, and feared them. He reiterated his distrust of high pressures, on account of the weakness of existing boilers, but he would hardly have taken the trouble to patent the high-pressure engine if he had thought it would never be practical. The fact was that, with Boulton & Watt's monopoly of engine manufacture, they profited from a standstill in the fundamentals of design. Watt may also have thought that, with low-pressure engines doing so well, it was pointless if not risky to enter unknown territory.

Watt was to reinforce his dominant position up to the final expiry of his patents; though he would have to fight for it. In 1784 he took out another, even more all-embracing patent that tried to cover every possible application of steam, including a full-sized steam carriage. This could only be powered by a high-pressure engine, and he showed no sign of building it. Indeed, in a letter to Boulton, Watt admitted that his steam carriage patent was intended solely to stop others from making them.

Several people were planning to do so, and two actually built successful working models immediately afterwards. One was William Murdock, Boulton & Watt's most brilliant engineer, who produced his advanced little vehicle[11] while supervising his company's pumping engines at Redruth in Cornwall in 1785–6. Watt was angry, and insisted that if Murdock wanted to make a full-scale carriage, it must be under his employers' financial control. Nothing more was heard of this enterprise, nor of James Sadler's paper project of 1786, which Watt is also known to have suppressed. In Scotland, William Symington constructed a working model with a low-pressure engine and ratchet-and-pawl drive[12] that was exhibited in Edinburgh in 1786, but he is said to have dropped any idea of making a full-scale vehicle because of the discouraging state of the roads, and the difficulties of finding sufficient fuel and water in the course of a journey. Here is the first evidence that the roads, though improved, were not yet thought good enough for steam carriages. Other projects, such as that of Robert Fourness and James Ashworth, got as far as the drawing-board at this time, but seem to have progressed no further; the technical and legal pitfalls were no doubt too much for them.[13]

In 1771, the year when Cugnot's invention, seen by few and appreciated by none but its inventor, vanished into the Arsenal, Richard Trevithick, mining engineer and son of a mining engineer, was born near Camborne in Cornwall. In 1800, when Watt's patents finally expired, Trevithick built his first full-scale high-pressure engine, which was installed as a winding engine at a Cornish mine. His cylindrical iron boilers with domed ends were designed, successfully, to withstand high pressures. His engines were nicknamed "puffers", because they exhausted steam into the air, which was a novelty. From the start, Trevithick regarded them as adaptable to all uses. Popular fear of high-pressure steam boiler explosions, fostered by Watt, was a handicap; a long-lived one where steam carriages were concerned, and not without foundation, thanks to human error. One of Trevithick's stationary engines blew up with fatal results as early as 1803, when an inexperienced mechanic fastened down a safety valve. Laymen did not relish sitting on top of what they had been told was a bomb. Boulton & Watt "strained every nerve" to get a Bill passed through Parliament that would put a stop to Trevithick's engines, on the grounds that they endangered the public.[14] Government-appointed engineers came to test them, and the move came to nothing.

Trevithick had already made two working model steam vehicles, between 1796 and 1798, and was building a full-scale one while he was constructing his first mine engine. On Christmas Eve 1801, Beacon Hill near Camborne, with its 1:20 gradient and its memorial to Trevithick, saw the first test of Britain's earliest self-propelled road vehicle. The *Cornwall Gazette and Falmouth Packet* for 20 February 1802 reported, somewhat belatedly, that:

> A carriage has been constructed containing a small steam-engine, the force of which was found sufficient, upon trial, to propel the carriage, containing several persons, amounting to at least a ton and a half in weight, against a hill of considerable steepness, at the rate of four miles in an hour. Upon a level road, it ran at the rate of eight or nine miles an hour.

The "carriage" was in fact only a small three-wheeled locomotive, to which its passengers clung. Various accidents dogged it; one account describes how it turned over in a gulley, another how the boiler burst and the vehicle caught fire after the water had been allowed to boil away. Neither incident reflected on its design, only on the inevitable inexperience of its operators. "Captain Trevithick's

Dragon" was, in fact, a highly sophisticated machine. Its boiler was small, but Trevithick employed various ingenious methods of keeping water and fire hot, and steam up. As in Murdock's model, the cylinder was recessed into the boiler to keep it hot. The exhaust steam was passed in pipes through the feed water to warm it.[15] Forced draught, reinforced by bellows, was obtained by directing the exhaust steam finally up a chimney.

By 1802 Trevithick was experimenting with a pumping engine operating at 145 p.s.i., with a cylinder of 7-inch bore and 38-inch stroke, and a 4-foot-diameter boiler; thus far had efficiency progressed, in terms of power to weight and volume, in a generation. This was exceptional; generally Trevithick's engines ran at under 50 p.s.i. He came to London in the same year to take out a patent for his high-pressure engine, adaptable to many different uses. Figure 6 of the patent was a drawing of another road carriage. In 1803 its deviser shipped its engine and 30 p.s.i. boiler to London. Engine and boiler were installed between the rear wheels, which were driven from a crankshaft through gears at 50 strokes per minute. Gearing-down must have been essential, as the driving wheels were made 8 feet in diameter, to surmount the worst road surfaces. There were two forward speeds. Although change-speed mechanism was not essential in a steam vehicle, and although (as with the later traction engine) a gear-change could only be effected at a standstill, such a mechanism allowed smaller, more economical engines to be used: important considerations in steam vehicle design.[16] The drive to each wheel of the Trevithick coach could be disengaged independently by clutches, providing a differential effect and so avoiding stress while cornering. This became a common feature of road steamers. A sprung coach body capable of holding eight to ten passengers was made and fitted in London by William Felton.

The carriage – another three-wheeler, though lighter than the first – made at least two successful journeys through the streets. Starting from the coachbuilder's shop in Leather Lane, it passed along Gray's Inn Road and by Lord's cricket ground to Paddington, then returned via Islington – a run of ten miles, accompanied by the waves and cheers of the populace. On another occasion, its reception was more mixed.[17] During a four- or five-mile trip along Tottenham Court Road and down City Road, it was bowling along at its customary 8 or 9 m.p.h. when the steersman lost control. The machine charged a garden wall and tore down some railings, to the dismay of spectators. It seems that mechanical trouble only arose when the firebars shook loose, letting the fire fall into the engine below. As the mechanism was unsprung, and London's suburban roads were subject to exceptionally heavy wear, this was to be expected.[18] No mention is made of the purpose of this vehicle, but it is clear from the body style that it was seen as a prototype for a public passenger coach.

Like most of his successors, Trevithick was fundamentally an experimenter, always seeking new applications of his patent, rather than a man who would concentrate on a particular one for commercial or other practical ends. He ran out of money – another parallel with those who came after. His London carriage, in spite of having been run quite extensively through the metropolis, had attracted no publicity, and no demand for it had appeared. It was seen no more.[19]

Trevithick's interest in road locomotion would return in old age, but for the present he turned back to his stationary engines, nearly 50 of which were in use by 1804, and to fields which might be less fraught with difficulty than the road. In 1803 a Trevithick locomotive installed at the Coalbrookdale ironworks in Shropshire became the first railway engine, substituting for horses pulling wagons on a tramway. Two years later, Trevithick made an engine to power the mechanism of a dredger. One of the eminent people who took an interest in this device was the Marquess of Stafford,[20] whose grandson will be seen taking a bigger role in this story later on. Much more significantly, for this study and for his country, Trevithick appreciated the benefits that the versatile high-pressure steam engine could bring to agriculture. In 1812 a Trevithick engine powered a threshing machine, and was an unqualified success, cutting operating costs as compared with horse power by seven-eighths.

In 1811 this brilliant man had gone bankrupt, without having seen steam road vehicles follow high-pressure engines into general acceptance. Nevertheless, he had established a frame for them – a context of practical principles in which improvements could be made, available to the next generation of constructors.

At first, it seemed that, like those of Cugnot and Dallery, Trevithick's carriages were to be a false start, for it was to be 16 years before any more was heard of working steam road vehicles in Britain. Although the technology now existed in the metal, the state of the roads must still have been discouraging. Trevithick is said to have felt this. Boilers and moving parts – sometimes unsprung, even at a later date – would be subjected to continuous jolting and vibration relatively harmless to the stage coach, which had no machinery, and which in Britain had been suspended on metal cee-springs since at least the 1730s. Innovative designers would be encouraged, like Trevithick, to approach elements less destructive of experimental designs and materials – water, and the smooth rail.[21]

In all elements, the capabilities of men, materials and tools were limited. Naturally, no specialists in self-propelled steam machinery existed. As late as 1823, by which time several steam locomotives had been built, George Stephenson would feel compelled to build his own locomotive factory. Only general engineers were available, working largely with hammer, chisel, file, calipers and wooden rule. Until 1775 their sole machine tools had been the water-powered tilt hammer and the treadle-and-crank-operated pole lathe. In that year, an accurate cylinder-boring machine was devised by John Wilkinson, in response to the growing popularity of the steam engine, and Henry Maudslay's all-metal, slide-rest screw-cutting lathe arrived in 1800; but even these few and basic machine tools were seldom found. They were rarer still outside the manufacturing districts.[22] The standard of hand forging was high, and foundry work was adequate. Drilling machines were well developed, but other metal-cutting techniques – shaping, milling and gear-cutting – were not. The standardised screw thread was unknown. Forgings and castings were finished by hand, with consequent inaccuracies and wide and uneven tolerances. Packing with tallow-soaked hemp was the best available answer to leaking pistons: the first experiments with metal piston rings did not come until 1832. Materials and lubricants capable of withstanding high stresses and temperatures were lacking. Steel was made in small batches, to inconsistent standards. Cast iron, the commonest metal, was cheap but brittle. Iron suitable for forgings such as boiler tubes was expensive, as were steel, copper, brass and bronze. For bearings, fragile cast iron was used, or soft brass and bronze, which tended to squeeze out.

In the United States, there was still less inducement to build road steamers. The reserve of experience in steam was small: as late as 1803, there were at most six steam engines of all kinds in the United States.[23] Inland North America at the end of the 18th century depended on its rivers for transport: a fact which tended to encourage the steamboat. John Fitch had made America's earliest working steamboat as early as 1787, anticipating Britain by a year, and three years later initiated the world's first commercial steamboat service on the Delaware River. The roads outside the cities were bad, and did not, as a whole, begin to improve significantly until the 1890s. No one in the period in question is known positively to have built and run a steam road carriage; though there was no lack of enterprise, and of solid achievement in other elements.

In 1791 Nathan Read of Massachusetts patented the high-pressure boiler of multiple fire-tube type, in which water was vaporised by contact with the heated pipes round which it circulated. This kind of boiler was to enjoy complete success on the railway, when used by

Robert Stephenson in his *Rocket* of 1829, but did not affect the first steam carriages. A year earlier, Read patented a steam carriage, of which a model was made and shown, but there is no proof of a full-scale vehicle being built or run. Oliver Evans of Delaware also devised a high-pressure engine. In 1787 he successfully petitioned the Maryland legislature for a 14-year monopoly in the construction and use of steam vehicles in the state, and patented a steam carriage ten years later, but as far as is known, he did not make one. In 1805 Evans, who like Trevithick had made a steam engine to drive dredging machinery, mounted a flat-bottomed dredger on wheels, took off the power of the dredger engine to them, and "drove" the boat for $1\frac{1}{2}$ miles from his workshop to the Schuylkill river, Philadelphia. Evans's aim was to show that his engine was good for propulsion on both land and water; but he did not claim to have created a road vehicle.[24]

In England, meanwhile, continuity in development, which enables a pool of experience to be formed and encourages its dissemination, was lacking. Nor, in this age before rapid mass communications, were there many published records of accumulated knowledge widely available to the working mechanical engineer. The patent, the main means by which progress was announced, was not always taken out, because it could be a challenge to the enterprising innovator rather than a deterrent, as James Watt had learned. The battle to hold off the challenge in the courts, which might or might not succeed, would certainly be expensive. Watt's defences had cost him £30,000. Even patenting an invention was expensive; in 1831 it amounted to the very considerable sum of £360 – enough to put off an inventor of modest means. If a patent was taken out, it was lodged at the Patent Office in London. The inventor could, if he wished, bring it to the attention of potential investors through the press, or by means of broadsheets; but this attracted the predatory eye of possible plagiarisers too.

This situation started to change only when the *Repertory of the Arts, Manufactures and Agriculture* began to appear monthly from 1794. It was a selective assemblage of patent specifications and of descriptions of inventions culled from specialised journals, offered without editorial comment. The *Repertory* was alone until 1820. In that year, the *London Journal of Arts and Sciences*, a record of new patents "such as embrace the most recent inventions and discoveries in practical mechanics", first came out. The *Register of Arts and Sciences*, published from 1824 to 1832, also publicised patents. Both journals also included news, letters and comment, and were generally so similar that they were inevitably rivals.

The *Mechanics' Magazine*, the earliest popular technical journal of the British Industrial Revolution, started publication only in 1823.

Though long-lived itself, it was followed by several ephemerals that lasted only a few issues. The most interesting, because concerned partly with steam on the road, was the *Journal of Elemental Locomotion* and its successor the *Journal of Steam Transport and Husbandry*, of which a mere six numbers appeared during 1832 and 1833. The august *Engineer* was first published in 1856. The more popular *English Mechanic* did not follow until 1865, and *Engineering* a year later.

For all these reasons, an inventor's successes might be as little publicised as his failures. Successful but short-lived early experiments such as Trevithick's might easily fail to become widely known. Still less were men likely to learn from others' failures, which would naturally tend to be hushed up.

Until the 1820s, therefore, trial and error, laboriously repeated, was the rule. For instance, as late as 1825 some engineers held that if power were transmitted through wheels to a road – a very new and almost unexplored concept – the wheels would slip and spin when reaching a hill.[25] Trevithick had proved them wrong – that, to quote his 1802 patent, "in general, the ordinary structure or figure of the external surface of these wheels will be found to answer the intended purpose." But Trevithick's patent was not published in the *Repertory*, and there was to be no well-publicised evidence of anyone else successfully tackling ordinary public-road hills with a self-propelled carriage until 1827. Engineers ignorant of Trevithick's success, or of his patent, had nothing to go on. It should also be remembered that the doubters were thinking of normal carriage wheels with tyres of smooth unyielding iron and 2-inch section, and roads with, at best, loose and sometimes soft surfaces; not modern tyres and tarmac.

So, however impractical their designs were, one should not with hindsight sneer at such men as David Gordon, Goldsworthy Gurney and Walter Hancock.[26] All, emulating William Brunton's idea of 1813 for a "mechanical traveller", fitted, or at one time proposed to fit, their earliest experimental carriages with steam-powered "propellers" or "legs" as well as wheels, to "walk" them up hills. Brunton's "legs" reappeared as late as 1829, on his entry in the Rainhill railway locomotive trials. These arrangements were almost by definition complicated, heavy, frail, wasteful of power, and generally over-ambitious; and progress must have been agonisingly slow. Yet none of these men was an impractical dreamer, and the last two named, soon discarding "legs", were to prove themselves the very reverse.

Still less could engineers of the age be criticised for seeking other, easier ways around the imaginary traction problem. J. & S. Seaward's patent of 1825 and James Neville's of 1827 for spade- or spike-like projections on wheel rims were simple, and would no doubt have been effective. Their major drawback, and that of similar devices, was that they would have the effect of a rotary digger on any road, and of a red rag to a bull on any highway authority. In more practical vein, a carriage proposed by Timothy Burstall and John Hill of Leith in 1825 incorporated an arrangement for coupling the axles on hills, so obtaining four-wheel drive. Burstall summed up the experimenters' universal dilemma in a nutshell when he said: "As to steam carriages moving on common roads, we have nothing but theory to guide us, and experience will discover defects which no skill can anticipate."

Red herrings and all, development in Britain accelerated from 1819. The picture is one of an increasing number of purely experimental vehicles, almost all for carrying passengers, and the majority envisaged as embryo public service vehicles. So much is clear from the accommodation provided. The fare-paying passenger market was the obvious one. It could be lucrative, as the stage coaches had shown, and it was booming, thanks to improving roads. Few built a vehicle small enough to be suitable for personal, private transport – a "motor car" – and none was described as such. Canals and coaches between them monopolised a powerful and growing public interest in transport. The canals had become the country's main inland freight carriers, capable of transporting bulk goods with a combination of economy and speed that would not be rivalled until the railway came. No one made a road steamer designed solely for freight.

Eight or nine steam carriages were designed, and may have been built, from 1819 to the end of 1826; of these, about half will be seen actually running on the public road. Their outings were brief, tentative, and seldom repeated. Although most of their projectors no doubt saw them ultimately as taking passengers from the stage coaches, there were no talk yet of competing, for the speeds achieved in this period were not usually much above a walking pace. This was very far from the overall best average speed of 8–10 m.p.h. over long distances, including halts, being achieved by stage coaches. No single carriage attracted much attention on its own, but together, as a phenomenon, they were becoming noticed in the popular and engineering press. Reports of vehicles that never ran, or may never have been built, contributed to the process. Among them were the projects of William Henry James, an engineer, between 1824 and 1827, and of David Gordon in 1824–5. Gordon's design had three wheels, but they were undriven – the vehicle was to rely on "legs" alone for propulsion. James was the eldest son of William James, the railway promoter. His machine had four-wheel drive by an engine at each wheel, not for the sake of adhesion, but so that a differential effect could be obtained on corners by slowing down engines on one side or the other. The steering was connected to each engine so that the latter could come into operation automatically.

None of this ingenuity bore fruit, but in other cases some useful technical progress is in evidence, and is suggested even where hard detail is lacking. Information about carriages and their expeditions – if any – is extremely patchy at this time, partly, no doubt, because some makers did not want publicity. Most seem to have been built quite independently of one another, for reasons already touched upon, and the causes of their sudden comparative proliferation can only be guessed at.

One was, perhaps, the prospect of roads that might be good enough for steam. The trusts continued to spread in the new century. Between the end of the so-called "Turnpike Mania" and 1812, the number of new trusts almost doubled, to about 1000. Between 1792 and 1815, 173 were formed, and another 139 between 1816 and 1839. In 1812 the trusts and parishes between them spent over £1.3 millions on repairing and administering 95,000 miles of road in England and Wales.

Two other factors contributed to improved roads. One was the appearance, at last, of the trained professional roads surveyor applying his scientific methods country-wide. These men designed roads to suit vehicles; they did not expect vehicles to conform to road conditions. The second factor was increased government support, including Treasury finance for road building and repair in areas too poor to pay for it. John Metcalfe, the blind road contractor of Knaresborough, was Britain's earliest scientific repairer of roads, contemporary with Trésaguet in France, but local in his impact. Between 1765 and 1792 Metcalfe widened, straightened, drained and mended 180 miles of turnpikes for the trusts of Yorkshire, Lancashire, Derbyshire and Cheshire. One of Metcalfe's methods – which varied according to the terrain – was similar to Trésaguet's, and involved superimposing several layers of stone topped by graded, prepared gravel on a solid, built-up stone foundation.

In 1802 Thomas Telford, a civil engineer with an established reputation, was sent to Scotland by the Crown to report on the state of Highland roads and make recommendations for their improvement, as part of a government-supported attempt to halt the economic decline and depopulation caused by the Clearances. Telford was responsible for the Caledonian Canal, but in 18 years he was also to build 117 bridges and 920 miles of new roads in the Highlands, half of the cost being met by the Treasury. Telford's principles of repair had been foreshadowed by Trésaguet and Metcalfe, but now, for the first time, they would achieve nationwide application and fame in Britain.

Telford's work soon showed results; the first stage coach ran between Perth and Inverness in 1806. Moving into the Lowlands, he had rebuilt most of the Glasgow-Carlisle road by 1816, with the help of public money. His greatest work on highways, also subsidised by the government, was the total reconstruction of the Shrewsbury-Holyhead section of the London-Holyhead road, the vital link with troubled Ireland. In north Wales, it was in a state of utter ruin. The importance of the work was first urged by the Post Office, which tried, unsuccessfully, to establish a mail coach service between Shrewsbury and Holyhead in 1808. In 1811 Telford reported to a Parliamentary committee set up to investigate the complaints of the Post Office and of the Irish Members. The task got under way at last in 1815, under the direction of the Holyhead road commissioners, but the link, including the Menai Bridge, was not complete for another 12 years. Towards the end of his life, Telford became a supporter of steam on the road, where he believed it had a brighter future than on the railway.

Although more famous for his roads and their bridges – his friend, the poet Robert Southey, called him the "Colossus of Roads" – than for his canals and harbours, Telford was not the strongest single personal influence favouring road improvement. His painstaking methods were expensive and time-consuming. The Treasury had helped to finance his major works, so their cost did not greatly matter; but the turnpike trusts could not have afforded his services. Even the government found them too heavy a financial burden; Telford surveyed an immensely greater mileage of road between 1820 and 1830 than he actually worked on. He devoted no special efforts to promoting his methods, perhaps because he had so many other interests.

Another engineer, John Loudon McAdam, was ultimately responsible for an incomparably greater mileage of improved road. He was reconstructing Ayrshire roads as early as 1785, but his rise to fame began only in 1816, when he became general surveyor of the Bristol trust, which managed 148 miles or road – the longest mileage of any trust in the country at that time. Soon afterwards, local trust consolidation increased the length to 172 miles. After only 18 months, McAdam could report that all the Bristol trust's roads were good, that their cost of upkeep was reduced, and their revenues augmented. He was an improver of existing roads, rather than – as Telford was – a builder of new ones. His method, in which a single layer of small, graded broken stones was laid directly on the subsoil,[27] was not new. It had already been used in Europe, and in Scotland by the road surveyors Paterson and Lester. The technique was, too, less elaborate than Telford's, and therefore less permanent, but for this reason it was cheaper and faster. It therefore recommended itself to the trusts, to a public increasingly greedy for better roads, and to the state. Both the Post Office and the Board of Agriculture supported McAdam, the latter publishing the memorial he had addressed to them in 1810 concerning his methods.

By 1818 McAdam was able to claim that they had "begun to be generally approved"; bearing this out, a year later he and his sons were consultant surveyors to 34 trusts, which had 328 miles of road under repair and another 300 miles under survey. By 1820 his system had been applied to 1000 miles of roads. A select committee of the House of Commons, reporting on the Highways of the Kingdom in 1819, was eulogistic of McAdam, bringing the man and his work immense publicity. So did the £10,000 voted to him by Parliament partly to repay him for expenses he had incurred demonstrating his system. So, too, did the offer of a knighthood, which he declined. Unlike Telford, McAdam was a skilful, tenacious and single-minded propagandist. His best-known book, *Remarks on the present System of Road-Making*, went through nine editions between 1816 and 1827. By 1824, 147 trusts – about 15 per cent of the whole – were "macadamising" their roads; the word was starting to pass into the language.

To obtain a fair picture of Britain's roads around 1820, it is important to remember that, adding together the mileage of all roads improved by the trusts and the state, with or without the help of the new breed of professional surveyor, the proportion of the whole was still very small. There were now about 125,000 miles of trust- and parish-maintained roads in the country, of which only around 16 per cent were run by the trusts. The cult of the amateur was still the rule, not the exception, in all road bodies. The *Edinburgh Review*, in its issue of October 1819, complained of turnpike trustees that "a business of art and science is entrusted to a promiscuous mob of peers, squires, farmers, and shopkeepers, who are chosen not for their fitness to discharge [their] duties ... but from the sole qualification of residence within a short distance from the road to be made or repaired". The failing was clearly chronic, for the same criticism was repeated in the 1830s. In the 1820s the expenditure of around 1000 trusts on about 20,000 miles of road in England and Wales showed a 53 per cent rise, from just over £1.034 millions in 1821 to £1.678 millions in 1829; but it would be wrong to suppose that all this increase was being spent on repairs. True, the trusts' income had risen in the same period from £1.089 millions to £1.455 millions, but their debts had rocketed from £5.33 millions to £7.78 millions. Nearly £237,000 of their increased expenditure was absorbed by interest payments. By 1833 the cost of renewing a turnpike act was over £400. Having made a small profit overall for their creditors – or, more realistically, their investors – in 1821, they were destined as a whole to be losing money by the end of the decade.

On the other hand, they were still in general solvent and effective, thanks mainly to state aid in various forms. Parliament, recognising that the trusts, whatever their faults, were the most efficient existing road authorities and the strongest force for a better road system, backed them more heavily than ever. From 1817 the Treasury was empowered to make loans to them. Bills to renew trusts, and to allow them to make new roads – about 1000 miles were added to England and Wales between 1818 and 1829 – were still passed as a matter of course. Bills to permit trusts to raise their tolls were accorded the same favour. In some cases, a proportion of their increased income was now going on the employment of professional surveyors such as the McAdams, and on hiring a better class of labour than the parish unemployed provided. Simultaneously, government inquired regularly and diligently, if not very effectively, into the conduct of both trusts and parish vestries. From 1806 the Board of Agriculture set up numerous committees of investigation. Select committees of the House of Commons reported on the state of the roads in 1810–11, 1819, 1820 and 1821. They recommended that Parliament should superintend the work of the road authorities; a suggestion which came to nothing at the time, but which underlined the concern now felt by the state in the matter of roads.

It is true to say, too, that although the improved roads were a small part of the whole, they included the bulk of the most heavily used and most important highways – those, in other words, that were the most attractive to commercial passenger traffic. Also, the publicity attending the improvement of these roads helped to make improvement in general a matter of pressing public and official concern.

The outlook for steam carriages was becoming rosier in another way. There had been recent technical improvements to horsedrawn vehicles. These were adopted patchily or not at all by steam constructors, but their existence was an encouragement to progress in the design of all road vehicles. Obadiah Elliott, a coachmaker, had patented the elliptical laminated leaf spring in 1805. It provided a softer ride than the common cee-spring, and – because it did away with the need for a perch, a pole linking front and rear axles – it reduced weight and afforded a tighter turning circle. In the same year Samuel Miller patented a carriage wheel design that promised much more strength than existing wheels. At their hub ends, the spokes abutted flat against one another for several inches, giving mutual support; and they were further held together by two flat plates of metal or wood bolted together on each side of the hub. This was the origin of the "artillery" wheel common on motor cars of the early 20th century.

Then, in 1818, Rudolph Ackermann the printseller acquired the English licence in Georg Lenkensperger's patent covering steering for horse vehicles. The steering road wheels were mounted on a fixed axle by separate pivots, and linked so that they turned together, independently of the axle. The linkage allowed the inside road wheel on a turn to make a tighter angle than the outside wheel – its natural course. The arrangement further reduced a vehicle's turning circle, and it was safer than centre pivot steering. When eventually fitted to self-propelled vehicles, the advantages of Ackermann steering would become more pronounced. Because steering required less effort, the steersman would find his work much less exhausting; therefore, a self-propelled vehicle could have two front wheels of normal size, the usual distance apart, with much improved directional stability.

Such inventions, when adopted, could help to overcome some of the special disadvantages of early steam as compared with horsed vehicles – fragility, great weight, and difficulty of steering. Burstall estimated that whereas a stage coach could weigh a ton empty, his machine turned the scales at $2\frac{1}{2}$ tons. There were also new, unknown stresses such as those imposed on driven road wheels, where torque was added to the other drawbacks.

To sum up, by the early to middle 1820s the projectors of road steamers could envisage a future in which – thanks to spreading trusts, growing official involvement, the new popularity of efficient roadmaking, and technical progress in the carriage trade – their vehicles were less likely than hitherto to sustain damage on the roads.

The first of the new "wave" of carriages was that of George Medhurst. Medhurst, an enthusiast for compressed air as a means of locomotion, published pamphlets on the subject from 1810 on. His interest in steam was strictly incidental, and it is ironic that while none of his schemes for (among other things) compressed-air road carriages capable of 60 m.p.h. came to anything, he succeeded in making at least one, and possibly two working steam carriages. On two occasions in 1819 he ran a single-seater steamer on the New Road between Paddington and Islington, and repeated the journey on three other days in 1821. A speed of 5–7 m.p.h. was claimed. Judging by Medhurst's description, this machine was of advanced design in at least one respect: fuel and water feed were automatic, as indeed they would have to be, in the absence of a stoker. Some time between 1821 and 1827, Medhurst also built a four-seater carriage.

In 1821 Bramah & Sons, the eminent toolmakers, built a steam vehicle "very ingeniously constructed" for Julius Griffith of Brompton, its designer. Timothy Bramah, one of Joseph's sons, was in charge. He had inherited his famous father's interest in steam power, and had been one of the government-appointed engineers who investigated the safety of Trevithick's high-pressure engines. The Griffith machine was of exceptional size, being 27 feet long, and was envisaged with either passenger or freight wagon bodies. In several respects, it was technically advanced. A change-speed mechanism was incorporated; both body and machinery were sprung, the former on leaf springs; and to save feed water and check steam emission, the exhaust was condensed rather than discharged up the chimney. A differential action was provided, by means unspecified. The final drive was through gears. A speed of little more than 5 m.p.h. on the level was claimed.

The vehicle was tested over a period of two years, but never, it seems, left Bramah's premises in Pimlico. The reason lay in another sophisticated feature of the design, which brought its own snags. Boilers for steam carriages had to be as compact and as light as possible, yet also develop high power, which meant high pressures; and also be capable of getting up a lot of steam quickly. The reason for this was that, like horsed vehicles, they would be constantly stopping and starting, accelerating and decelerating. Town traffic meant progress by fits and starts. Instead of changing horses, halts for fresh supplies of fuel and water would have to be made at least as frequently. If they were public service vehicles, passengers would have to be picked up and set down. The search for maximum boiler efficiency – the smallest possible water content, to save water, combined with the largest possible heating area – brought forth the water-tube boiler, by which the fire vapourised feed water passing through it in pipes.[28] Given reliable components, such boilers could raise and maintain pressures of well over 100 p.s.i. without difficulty, or even, according to some claims, up to 250 p.s.i. The best railway locomotive practice of about 1830, with fire-tube boilers, produced around 50 p.s.i. The water-tube boiler had an added advantage: it was safer than other types. The quantity of steam under pressure at any one time was small and divided up, being confined to the tubes. In theory, an explosion could burst only one tube at a time, damaging no more than that tube and causing no injury.

The Griffith machine had a water-tube boiler, which in this case served only to illustrate the defects of the type. High boiler pressures had always been the weakness as well as the strength of the high-pressure engine, and the problems would increase with the pressures. These put a greater strain on contemporary materials and expertise than they could withstand, in a sense bearing out Watt's warnings. Boiler failure, or inadequacy, was to be the most common of all ailments of the steam carriage, before and after water-tube boilers became general. Contemporary iron tubes could not take the latest stresses, leaking or bursting frequently. They were not formed by drawing: a vulnerable seam ran their full length, butt-welded or at best overlapped. In at least one instance, ordinary gas pipe, not intended to withstand any pressure, was used. The blocking of tubes by deposits caused defective circulation and would also have contributed to bursts. Boiler efficiency was one thing; reliability another. Yet the water-tube boiler was the best available, so designers were to persist with it, and in spite of the failure of the Griffith vehicle, Timothy Bramah continued to take an interest in steam carriages.

Nathan Gough of Salford is said to have tried a carriage on the Manchester-Stockport road about 1822;[29] but there is stronger evidence that two years later, he ran one at a walking pace on the level, with three or four passengers. On its first tentative outing, in Edinburgh in 1825, Burstall and Hill's machine briefly attained 7 m.p.h., but its constructor acknowledged his boiler to be "very defective". Its next trial, in 1826, was conducted at a walking pace. Such low speeds are not to be wondered at, since even a year later, Burstall was thinking in terms of a vehicle weighing three tons with fuel being propelled by an engine with a working boiler pressure of only 25 p.s.i. This machine's next public appearance was in Kennington, London, in the summer of 1827, when owing to safety valve failure, its boiler burst, injuring two or three people, before it had even been set in motion. Samuel Brown's gas vacuum carriage is known to have ascended Shooter's Hill in Kent, which had a maximum gradient of nearly 1:10, in the last week of May 1826. It was not steam-driven – it seems, indeed, to have been the first working internal-combustion-engined vehicle[30] – but it contributed its share to the modest but growing impression that self-propelled road vehicles were making.

By the end of 1826, the age of experiment pure and simple was over. Experiment went on, but, by largely empirical means, a considerable body of experience concerning this new, for the most part unknown world of powered road vehicles had been accumulated, and was now constantly being augmented. Correct answers to the most important problems would soon win general, if not universal acceptance.[31] Carriages which had not yet seen the light of day were being put together, in workshops in Scotland and on London's fringes, by men who saw road steamers as a practical commercial proposition. Some were committing themselves to steam, and some were clever publicists. They were no longer only experimenters. All this was new.

Steam transport was "in the air", for in its other elements it had already passed from the experimental to the commercial context. In 1812 on the Clyde, the *Comet* had operated Britain's first commercial steamboat service, and steam packets carrying passengers and mail were now regularly plying the Irish Sea and the English Channel. The steam locomotives of the Stockton-Darlington Railway had been hauling freight, if not yet passengers, amid considerable publicity since September 1825, and their initial success had led to the passing of 18 new railway Acts in 1826.

Not all this publicity was favourable. Inevitably, once steam transport became "news", opposition to it sprang up. After the Stockton and Darlington Railway Company obtained an Act in 1823 to allow it to use steam locomotives instead of the horse traction originally proposed, and to carry passengers, a pamphlet appeared that forecast a hair-raising future for steam railways.[32] It asked the reader to see himself in a situation in which "we proceed a few miles from London, and in crossing the Great North Road, at the novel railway speed of 12 miles an hour, a sudden explosion unkennels the passengers, parboils the pilot and attendants, and scatters the luggage all abroad like that of a vanquished army." Expert witnesses before the House of Commons Committee on the Liverpool and Manchester Railway Bill of 1825, among them John Rastrick and George Stephenson, both locomotive constructors, found that questioners harped upon possible danger to the public from boiler explosions. They were also asked if locomotives frightened horses, and denied it. Such doubts arose in part from genuine concern, now that the general public was to be exposed to high-pressure steam for the first time, and were in part inspired by ulterior interests – in the case of the railways, the canal proprietors, who feared the new freight-carriers. The doubts expressed, and the mixture of motives behind them, were to become all too familiar to road-steamer promoters also.

However, neither they nor the railway men were deterred. It would indeed have been surprising if, in the combination of circumstances favouring it, steam on the road had not moved out of the purely experimental context. When it did – when it came to affect more people and more interests than just a few experimenters and the engineers and craftsmen they employed – it would take on a new dimension. Once commercial motivation and a usable, if still imperfect, machine joined forces, the latter would begin to touch outside financial interests, and otherwise make itself felt publicly. When that happened, the road steamer, like the railway, would enter politics too.

An unspectacular, not to say insignificant, byproduct was the first appearance on Britain's public roads of a handful of undoubted "motor cars". To understand why these machines appeared, and so account for their character and history, an examination in depth of the public passenger-carrying road steamer will be necessary.

2

Hope Deferred:
the Rise and Fall of
Goldsworthy Gurney, 1827–32

By the end of 1826 only one ingredient – speed – was still lacking from the brew of circumstances favouring the commercial road steamer and its final progeny, the first motor car. Within a year, adequate speed, and the steam coach as competition for the stage coach, were being spoken of in almost the same breath. It cannot have been coincidence – without the first, the second could never have happened.

But experiment continued alongside commercial endeavour. All known vehicles were still imperfect in important respects. Most projectors of road steamers were prudent enough to refrain from allowing the public to be carried for payment. A few did so, claiming readiness and even perfection; or at least announced their intention of doing so. Of these, still fewer were justified by events. Enthusiasm and ambition, together with gaps in their mechanical knowledge, blinkered the rest to the shortcomings of their machines, and put exaggerated claims and expectations into their mouths. They would use the public, in effect, as fare-paying guinea-pigs.

One such was Goldsworthy Gurney; but his total dedication to road steamers had an appealing and a constructive side. He was a genuine enthusiast as well as a seeker of legitimate profit. He was not easily discouraged, and had a flair for attracting and organising publicity. These factors, combined with the fact that his machines worked better than most, if not as well as the best, meant that Gurney was for nearly four years (1827–31) far and away the most prominent steam carriage promoter. His was the name the public knew; he was the pace-setter and the standard-bearer of the movement. For this reason, his progress forms the theme of those years; the rest in that period were also-rans.

Gurney, a Cornishman like so many steam pioneers, was – in contrast with most – no professional engineer. His training was as a surgeon, as a physician, and as a chemist. Michael Faraday admitted

33

his debt to Gurney's lectures on the elements of chemistry, delivered before the Surrey Institution in 1822. But his true inclination lay towards the practical applications of science. As an engineer, he was a self-taught, self-confessed amateur, so it is all the more surprising, and creditable, that he achieved what he did. Indeed, even the finest professional engineers, like the Bramahs, could find themselves, like Gurney, hamstrung by ignorance. At best, men learned laboriously and expensively by error – their own and that of others.

As an inventor, Gurney showed himself both versatile and practical, well before he dedicated himself to steam carriages. He invented limelight (a fusion of lime and magnesium), and conducted experiments in its use in lighthouses for Trinity House. He also invented the oxy-hydrogen blowpipe – the forerunner of modern torch equipment for welding and the first safe apparatus of its kind. His touch was less certain when he left applied chemistry behind and tried mechanical engineering.

Gurney's earliest work on road steamers is known almost entirely from his own accounts alone, which are often imprecise, sometimes contradictory, and occasionally obviously inaccurate. For one reason or another, one approaches them with caution. He claimed, as a boy, to have seen Trevithick's first carriage suffer from wheelspin, which persuaded him to fit his first series of vehicles with "legs", or "propellers", as well as driving wheels.[1] Gurney's first factory was in Oxford Street, London. His earliest full-scale machine, he said, was completed by May 1825. It weighed 4 tons empty. Its creator suggested, without corroboration, that it moved in public: "This weight was severely felt, in consequence of its effect on the roads." The next vehicle – by implication the first, rebuilt – was able, Gurney said, to climb Highgate Hill during 1826. There is independent witness now that a Gurney machine was indeed moving, but none, yet, of any public demonstration.[2] In fact, the date of this climb was 1827, for in his claim Gurney describes an accident that is known to have occurred in the latter year. In any case, the lack of contemporary corroboration of both the 1825 and 1826 dates is suggestive, since he and others publicised his known public excursions very thoroughly.

It is uncertain whether Gurney claimed other hillclimbing feats – Windmill Hill on the Edgware Road, Stanmore Hill, Brockley Hill ("some of the steepest hills in the neighbourhood of London, than which there are few steeper on the ordinary turnpike roads in England") – for this period or later, so vague is he about dates. The strong probability is that they all belong in the four years, 1827–31. Gurney now, and others later, emphasised their vehicles' hillclimbing ability in order to show them in a favourable light compared with the laden four-horse stage coach. To the latter, gradients of more than about 1:20 were unacceptably steep.

In the same year of 1826, Gurney opened new, expensively equipped workshop premises in Regent's Park, behind his home in Albany Street. About April 1827, an independent source says that Gurney "has contrived to GO, and that at times with considerable speed",[3] but gives no details at all; and about two months later more or less contradicts itself – *all* road steamer projects "have either failed altogether, or have not been pursued with sufficient energy". At about this time or earlier, Colonel Francis Maceroni formed a business association with Gurney. Maceroni, born of an Italian father and an English mother, was a retired professional soldier, an inventor (though a less practical one than Gurney), and a skilful publicist. There was also a self-destructive side to his character, as Gurney and others later became aware. Gurney offered to lend Maceroni part of his workshop, where the colonel worked on his own account. Although he later began to work on Gurney's carriages instead, Maceroni's most important role was to help Gurney raise capital to develop his machine. Just how much was obtained through Maceroni's good offices is uncertain; he claimed to have persuaded his friends to part with £22,000 in one five-month period. As his commission, Maceroni was to receive $\frac{1}{4}$d per mile run by Gurney-built carriages. Towards the end of 1827, Gurney advanced the chronically insolvent Maceroni £150 on account of this commission. Gurney was by then ready to make his first known public bid.

The fog surrounding Gurney's work begins to disperse in September 1827. A writer in the *Literary Chronicle* speaks of seeing his "new improved steam coach" – a "beautiful machine" – in motion at 7–8 m.p.h. The place is not specified; it may have been Gurney's own workshop yard, or the barrack yard of the Life Guards in Regent's Park, both of which he used for trials later. But it was certainly level, for the reporter adds: "We have not heard if the carriage has yet been tried in hilly ground."

Although the vehicle was probably another rebuild of the first – its boiler had been "at work every day for two years"[4] – some hard facts start to emerge, by direct statement, illustration, or inference. They are mingled with unprovable, downright misleading or dubious claims. Because coke only was burned, said the *Literary Chronicle* account, the coach made no smoke. For this reason, most steam carriage builders preferred coke to coal, although the latter was cheaper, more widely available, and raised steam more efficiently. It was said, too, that the machine vibrated less than a stage coach, and ran without noise. No strictly contemporary evidence contradicts the second assertion, but Gurney himself casts doubt on the first. Speaking a little later of his vehicles in general, he felt bound to qualify his claim that "there is no annoyance either from smoke or steam" with the words "when the engine is perfect" – that is, running properly Another claim, that the Gurney design was completely immune to dangerous explosions because of its water-tube boiler, was simply untrue.

Other snags, unmentioned for obvious reasons, also existed. An independent witness said at a slightly later date that "the smell of oiled iron, which makes steamboats so unpleasant" was an obtrusive feature of this vehicle.[5] There is no reason to suppose that it was absent in September 1827; and some later Gurney machines were said to suffer from the same complaint. Furthermore, "there was something to repair every moment." It is probable that this "something" was usually a ruptured boiler tube. Colonel Maceroni, a commentator who sometimes gave Gurney credit for a great deal, said later of his trips in general that he "scarcely ever went out without some derangement or other occurring, either to his machinery, or to his boiler, or both". Maceroni had an acid pen, and ran down other men's carriages to boost his own; but Gurney himself bore out his criticisms up to a point, admitting that "the rending or opening of the tubes has often occurred."

Of his designs in general, Gurney said that his ordinary means of braking – a shoe drag to check one wheel, as used on stage coaches – could be reinforced by "reversing" the engine, so that from 8 m.p.h. the coach could stop in 21 feet or less. Such a stopping distance, from the equivalent of a trot, could perhaps be achieved by a coach and four in ideal conditions; but the method imposed severe strains on imperfect mechanism, especially at higher speeds. When applied to one of Sir Charles Dance's carriages on the Brighton road in 1833, at a speed of 16–17 m.p.h., it broke a connecting-rod.[6] Since the braking effect of horses pulling up was absent on steam carriages, there was much official concern about their ability to stop, and great anxiety on the part of their builders to dispel this. Unlikely, or even impossible, claims were not uncommon.[7]

As with most designs to date, the transmission of power from the engine to the rear wheels was direct, by a crankshaft that formed the axle; and only the body was sprung. Thus the mechanism was exposed to every shock from the road surface, and transmission and wheels took both the full driving stresses and the whole weight of the engine. Furthermore, the forging of the axle to bend it to its function as the crankshaft weakened it in both roles. These were crudities that

Trevithick and Griffith had avoided; but there was no overriding reason for Gurney to do so before his first vehicle actually ran. Such over-simplification of construction was until then bad only in theory – it could not show its drawbacks until it was put to the test. The superiority of indirect drive, by gears or some other means, and of sprung mechanism was sound in principle, but had yet to be proved in practice by broken crankshafts and other common failures. It is possible that Gurney and others considered Griffith's gear drive, and rejected it on the grounds that on rough roads and under driving stresses gears would be vulnerable to breakage and rapid wear, and might not even stay in mesh.

Public concern about wear and tear on the roads, caused by heavy vehicles with narrow tyres, persisted as strongly as ever. This had meant primarily the stage coach, whose need for speed demanded narrow tyres to lessen resistance. The *Literary Chronicle* writer claimed that Gurney's steamer did only one-sixth as much damage as a horsedrawn coach, because no horses' hooves were involved. That hooves caused more damage than any wheels was accepted, at least by expert opinion; but no proof was offered for the figure given. Gurney said that, initially, his tyres were at least as wide as those of a stage coach – 2 inches – and were $3\frac{1}{2}$ inches broad on his later vehicles. This seems to have been the most favoured maximum; although Gurney claimed that a breadth of up to 6 inches was possible without excessive drag being set up. Indeed, a reasonably broad tyre was a help to traction on powered vehicles, though a hindrance to the horsedrawn. They gave a greater area of grip; conversely, the "digging-in" action of narrow tyres inhibited traction as well as harming the road.

Steam carriage promotors were particularly sensitive to suggestions that their machines caused disproportionate damage to roads. A laden stage coach with its four horses could weigh four tons, but the weight was evenly spread, not concentrated only on the wheels where they met the road. Also, driven wheels were said to be more destructive of the unbound surfaces than undriven, because of the traction they exerted. But "Mr McAdam" – probably John Loudon – was quoted in Gurney's promotion as saying that "were the wheels broad instead of narrow . . . more good than harm would be done [by steam carriages] to the roads." Later, Thomas Telford and John Macneil, his assistant engineer on the Holyhead road, both subscribed cautiously to the same view.

The *Literary Chronicle* account, which reads for the most part like an inspired "puff", is quoted in the *Courier*, a few columns from a

rather more objective story of the vehicle's first real test. It describes
how, at 5.30 on the morning of 8 September, "the first [steam coach]
that has been brought fairly into action before the public" proceeded
along the Camden Town Road and through Kentish Town to ascend
Old Highgate Hill. Although it was carrying nearly a dozen passengers, and the gradient, generally 1:12, steepened to 1:9, the
propellers were found unnecessary.[8] The wheels spun only when too
much power was applied. But on descending the hill, at a cautious
walking pace, the coach ran away. One wheel mounted a kerb and
came off. The crippled machine had to be towed away by a horse.

The accident underlined the unwieldiness and consequent vulnera-
bility of some steam coaches. Gurney's was 20 feet long, and wider
than a stage coach. Contemporary illustrations confirm its bulk. Among
the figures given for its weight, the most likely are two or three tons,
which are in line with the given weights of other steam coaches.

Gurney's steering arrangements were an improvement on the
simple single-wheel layout. The coach itself had four wheels, the
front axle and its wheels turning on a centre pivot as usual. Projecting
from the front axle was a beam carrying two small wheels on their
own pivoting axle. When the axle of this pilot forecarriage was turned
by the steersman, the front axle of the coach turned with it. The
forecarriage bore only enough of the coach's weight to give purchase
on the road. The pilot forecarriage idea had been a feature of an 1826
design by Frederick Andrews, and such a layout would provide
lighter steering. In the presumably smooth confines of Gurney's yard,
at low speeds, it was said that a child of five was able to steer. Much
was made of ease of control in steam carriages, which was contrasted
with the undoubtedly tenuous authority exercised over his horses by
the driver of a stage coach travelling fast. But on a rough road,
"considerable difficulty" was experienced with Gurney's first vehicle.
Gurney's daughter Anna, not usually one to cast any doubts on the
quality of her father's work, said that before the carriage was
"perfected", "perhaps the greatest difficulty . . . was to control the
immense power of the steam and to guide the carriage" – this still in
the workshop yard.

Perhaps as a result of its accident, Gurney's coach disappeared
from public view until the end of the year. But behind the scenes, its
creator was working hard and successfully to raise the capital that
would enable him to start manufacture on a commercial scale. As
early as 1825 or 1826, on the strength of seeing what must have been
a very unfinished mechanism in motion, John Ward had obtained a
licence from Gurney to operate it on the London–Manchester and
London–Manchester and London–Liverpool roads. At some juncture

he gave Gurney £500 by way of an advance payment on a coach, and agreed to pay 6d a mile royalty when his service was running.

In September 1827, Captain William Augustus Dobbyn of Wells acquired the exclusive licence for the London, Bath and Bristol road, and Gurney agreed to build him eight coaches. In payment, Gurney received a total of £6000 – before any service had run, or any of the coaches had been built – and would get 1d a mile in addition. Dobbyn had been introduced to Gurney by Maceroni. Also at about this time, Colonel Sir James Viney, a native of Gloucester, bought a share in Gurney's patent and the licence for the Gloucester–Cheltenham road for £5000. He had an amateur interest in steam technology; two years later he patented a boiler of his own design with firing by gas or oil, not solid fuel.

By October the licence for the London–Southampton road had been sold, forestalling, it was said, an application from the operator of the *Telegraph* and *Union* stage coaches that ran on that route. In November there followed a licensing agreement for the London to Exeter and Plymouth, and Bristol to Exeter and Plymouth roads, with William Hanning of Dillington Park, Somerset. Hanning, a prominent agriculturalist and wealthy capitalist, had "an immense interest in in-land transport".[9] He had been introduced to Gurney either by Dobbyn or by Maceroni direct. Hanning too, ordered eight coaches. He paid Gurney £700 – the first of several substantial sums, which included a share of Gurney's patent. He would pay 6d a mile on top of this.

News had already reached the newspapers, in October, that the coach was "shortly" to begin a regular London–Southampton service. Early in December there was confirmation, although the service had not yet started.

These were highly significant portents. Granted that Gurney must now have been under pressure to show results, having taken other men's money, never before had a steam carriage constructor announced publicly that he had a vehicle in existence which he thought fast and reliable enough to compete with stage coaches on a commercial route. If Gurney's confidence was new, so too was that of his backers. It is clear that the coach's performance, inconclusive though it was, and aided no doubt by its builder's promotion, had impressed wealthy businessmen sufficiently for them to disgorge very large sums in hard cash on the strength of future promise. It really did seem, at the end of 1827, that the steam coach had joined the steamboat and the steam railway as an acceptable field of investment for forward-looking financiers who did not mind taking big risks with their money.

On land, the steam coach seemed at first sight a more attractive proposition than the railway, for either a self-financing projector or for a capitalist. As it needed no specially built road, it demanded a small fraction of the capital required for a railway. This meant that an enterprising investor could control, or gain a major interest in, such an enterprise without needing access to or risking vast resources; and that the return on his investment should come much more quickly.[10] Furthermore, if the formation of a joint stock company to raise capital was not necessary, there was no need for a Bill, with its attendant expense, delay, and danger from hostile or merely conservative interests in Parliament.

The prospects for steam in the apparently imminent contest on the London–Southampton road must have seemed fair. Six coaches were running daily between the two cities at about this time, taking from eight to ten hours for a distance that varied between 75 and 78 miles depending on the route used. The steam coach was to average 10 m.p.h. – a not impossible objective if the highest speeds attributed to it were accurate, and as fast as the fastest stage coaches. Different estimates, some of them independent, gave the Gurney coach speeds of up to 15 m.p.h. on the level, during the runs described, and also on the Finchley Road and Edgware Road. Highgate Hill had been climbed laden at between 3 and 5 m.p.h.[11] – a better performance than that possible from a stage coach on such a gradient.

It was implied that stops for fuel and water would be fewer than those necessary for changes of horses. This may have been true of the fastest stage coaches, which exhausted their animals the soonest. The Gurney vehicle could carry fuel for one hour. There was room for 60 gallons of water, also enough for one hour, or 10 miles by implication.

Six inside and 15 outside passengers could be carried. No record of the fares proposed has survived, but they were to undercut the competing stage coaches, several of whose proprietors were said to have reduced their fares in reply – one to 10s inside and 5s outside. An example of a normal fare charged for an inside seat on the route in 1828 was £1 12s 0d. Such drastic undercutting hurt the coachmasters, but would have been no novelty. It was common when a new stage coach set up as a competitor on a popular road, and led to price wars, which the strongest won.

In fact, the coachmasters need not have been so precipitate, for the steamer never went into service, and its true performance was never tested in a commercial context. Its three months' total absence from the public eye, coupled with the nationwide expectation and rumour of imminent steam coach services that Gurney had largely set off, but never satisfied, drove the normally sober and sympathetic *London Journal of Arts and Sciences* to capital letters and multiple exclamation

marks: "THERE IS NO STEAM COACH IN EXISTENCE!!".
Gurney's was out of order, and invisible: "No steam coach is at present
capable of being applied to public service."

The judgement was premature, and not entirely just. Gurney's
coach is mentioned as having moved in public on 6 December, in
Regent's Park. At that time it had been "in operation" – which
presumably means running again – for two weeks; although another
source denies it. The story, in the *Observer*, was accompanied by
engravings and a key. It is identical with one appearing in *Bell's Life in
London* on the same day, and both are clearly based on the same
"handout". The Gurney publicity machine was in gear once more.
There is confirmation of a *Times* report that "several experimental
journeys are projected", probably to Windsor, for a demonstration
before the King, and to Bristol. The emphasis is back to experiment –
there is no more talk at this juncture of starting a service.

In mid-January 1828 *The Times* again mentions a trial in Regent's
Park, with corroboration from a foreign visitor, Prince Ludwig von
Puckler-Muskau. In a letter dated 16 January, he reports that "the
new steam carriage" has covered five miles in half an hour in the park.
The Prince, an independent witness, took a ride on the vehicle; though
was less impressed with it at close quarters. Then silence descends on
Gurney's efforts for over 18 months – a reflection, perhaps, of the
Prince's comments. The need for experiment was clearly far from past.
There is no solid evidence to say why Gurney succeeded, if only for a
while, when others before had failed. Gurney used a water-tube boiler
with a normal working pressure of between 70 and 120 p.s.i., so the
theoretical efficiency was there; but Griffith had employed one too,
and had shown that it did not by itself, guarantee success. Anna
Gurney claimed that her father's carriages owed their speed to his
"steam blast". A specially powerful forced draught was obtained by
compressing the exhaust steam into narrow jets running up the
chimney – a device pioneered by Timothy Hackworth's *Royal George*
locomotive in 1827, on the Stockton-Darlington railway. The earliest
contemporary reference to a "steam blast" in Gurney's vehicles occur
in relation to his 1831 vehicles. He and his supporters thereafter made
much of it. No mention of it is made in descriptions of his first publicly
demonstrated coach, so it is reasonable to suppose that the "steam
blast" was not used in 1827–8.[12] In any case, "steam blast" did not, by
itself, increase speed; used alone, it only improved steam-raising
ability. So that was not the answer either.

All that can be offered is less an explanation than a statement of the
obvious. Gurney's machine was far from perfect, nor even very
practical as yet, but it worked, up to a point. Its builder seems to have

achieved his limited success because, in his boiler and other components, he made fewer mistakes than his predecessors. In this, he had much in common with the railway pioneers. Even this was eventually to be expected, given the publication of accumulated experience that began in the 1820s.

Gurney's attempt to bring the road steamer into public service looked like a flash in the pan. Early in 1828 the *Mechanics' Magazine* reviewed the state of the art, pouring scorn on its lack of success. On the first occasion it thought the steam carriage worth an entire editorial, it used the space to condemn efforts to date. In September the *Register of Arts* was less censorious, but had the feeling that "the several attempts to construct steam carriages have terminated in failure." W.H. James's latest rebuild was said to be ready but not yet run in public, while David Gordon's "proceedings have been temporarily terminated". Only Gurney is making "frequent experimental excursions"; but there is no other evidence for them. Gurney again amended his coach towards the end of 1827, or in 1828 – mainly, it seems, by arranging for forced draught by fan. This may have been the form in which it ran in December and January. If he made later excursions, it was without publicity, which would have been very out of character.

Although Gurney had occupied the centre of the stage, he was not alone. Unaffected by his alternate leaps into the limelight and retreats into the shadows, projectors of road steamers old and new continued their work in the background in an entirely experimental, never commercial, context. When they finally brought their vehicles out into the light of day, beyond the specialised pages of the technical press, they helped contribute to the public's growing familiarity with the subject. Burstall and Hill had done so more dramatically than even Gurney would have wished. At the end of 1827 the *Observer* carried a prominent description and engraving of "Mr David Gordon's new steam coach", reprinted from the *Register of Arts and Sciences*; but these did no more than describe a model he built in 1825. The machine itself was no nearer the road. It seems to have been first run publicly in the summer of 1828. By now it had a tubular boiler of Gurney type, but its engine was too small, and after a few hundred yards on the Kingsland Road, on London's north-eastern fringe, its connecting-rods broke when negotiating a turn. Not long thereafter, David Gordon and his engineer son Alexander, who worked with him, suspended what Alexander called their "proceedings", discouraged by the expense, and by the relatively much greater success of Gurney's vehicle.

Like Gordon, W.H. James did at last get under way, if not for long. He had gained financial backing from Sir James Anderson, and built a

3-ton coach that was tested on a run to Epping Forest in March 1829, with up to 24 passengers on board at various times. It attained 15 m.p.h., but it had a water-tube boiler, and, as usual, a tube burst. It was said that the coach was to start carrying the mails in October; but after the one abortive trial, it was dismantled. If this was the vehicle advertised in a James Adcock print published in April 1828, long before it took to the road, it had four wheels, with the steersman in charge of the front pair. The problem of control with such a layout and centre pivot steering was attacked by providing indirect steering. The lower end of the steering column, which at its upper end was furnished with a double-handled bar for maximum leverage, was connected to the centre pivot of the front axle by a horizontal endless chain. In this way the steersman was insulated to some extent from road shocks. The idea had also been found on a model by Burstall and Hill shown some years earlier.

Another old hand, Nathan Gough, is said to have reappeared in Manchester during 1829, but achieved no more than 7 m.p.h. Burstall, who had transferred his activities back to Scotland after his boiler explosion in London, was still trying too. At Leith, in October 1828, his coach, experimental as ever, achieved speeds of up to 8 m.p.h. with 15 people on board. This was better than his earlier performances, but then he vanished from sight again.

The first road steamer from Scotland to work satisfactorily was that of James Nasmyth. It was one of this celebrated engineer's earliest achievements. At 19, while still a student at Edinburgh University, he made a working model and exhibited it before the Society for the Encouragement of the Useful Arts in Scotland. In March 1828 the society subscribed £60 to enable Nasmyth to build a full-scale machine, most of which was put together at Leith. In four months it was ready, and shown to the society. Starting in the second week of September, "many successful trials" were carried out on the Leith-Queensferry Road, over a period of three months. "Eight passengers sitting on benches about three feet from the ground" – regarded as temporary, mock-up bodywork – were taken for non-stop runs lasting for up to $1\frac{1}{2}$ hours. The vehicle averaged 6 m.p.h., and reached 8 m.p.h. A complaint that horses were being frightened was made to the sheriff, but his officers did not find it justified.

Apart from the fact that, as usual, exhaust steam directed up the chimney helped to create draught, nothing is known of the vehicle's technical aspects. It belonged to the society, and was intended for no useful purpose beyond experiment. The society attached no commercial value to it, and presented it to Nasmyth when the experiments were over. The carriage being only a side interest of his, he broke it up and sold the parts for £67. It is ironic, in view of what happened to others involved with steam carriages, that Nasmyth should have made a profit unintentionally. It seems that he had the recipe for reliability from the start, and it is tempting to speculate on the outcome had he found a commercial backer. As it was, Nasmyth went to work for Maudslay, Sons & Field, the marine engineers, whose name will reappear in this story.

Perhaps inspired by Nasmyth's efforts, another brilliant young Scots engineer turned for a while to road steamers. After making the boiler and engine castings for the *Comet*, David Napier from 1818 went on to build steamboats for the Irish Sea and English Channel crossings. Then, in 1829, he built a pier, hotel and houses at Kilmun on the north shore of Holy Loch, from where four of his steamers plied to Glasgow. He also put steamers on Loch Eck (between Holy Loch and Loch Fyne), and (connecting with Inverary) on Loch Fyne; then he made a road between Kilmun and the southern end of Loch Eck. He planned to put one steam coach on this road and another on the road between the northern end of Loch Eck and Strachur on Loch Fyne. Napier thus proposed to create a new route, served entirely by steam, from the Clyde to Inverary and the western Highlands.

In the end, only one Napier coach appears to have been made. Little is known of its construction: only that one single-cylinder engine drove each driving wheel, the engines being mounted vertically over the cranked axle and driving it direct. Although Napier said that he ran the road steamer at half the expense of a stage coach, this part of the enterprise was abandoned before the date on which the service was scheduled to start – 1 June 1829. The road was too hilly and its surface was too soft, and, besides, Napier could not get the speed he expected, because of his ignorance of the construction of boilers for use on roads. As a witness at Kilmun put it, "the roads were of no account at that time, and the motor was not a success." Stage coaches were therefore substituted.

Relatives of David Napier – another David, James and William – patented a "drag", or tractor to tow a passenger trailer, in 1831; but there is no record of their having built it. Napier's own interest revived briefly, but he built nothing; henceforth, like others before him, he forsook the roads and devoted himself to steamboats alone, which were no longer so experimental, and were less fraught with difficulties.

Much more significant was the quiet arrival on the scene of the man who would supplant Gurney, after 1831, as the most prominent steam-carriage builder. Walter Hancock was a professional engineer, who had trained as a watchmaker and jeweller and therefore had the standards and experience of a precision mechanic. He was the best-equipped of all that strangely assorted bag of amateurs and professionals who built road steamers. Moreover, he shared the inventiveness of a brilliant brother. Thomas Hancock was a central figure in the birth of the rubber industry. In 1821 he devised the rubber masticator, the machine which allowed the manufacture of rubber in block and sheet form, so permitting rubber to take its place as a material for manufactured goods. Hancock became a partner of Charles MacIntosh, who pioneered practical rubber-coated garments. In 1844 he patented the rubber vulcanisation process in Britain, which made moulded products possible, and two years later introduced the solid rubber tyre.

Walter shared his brother's interest in the possibilities of rubber, and joined to it a preoccupation with steam. The two were combined in a remarkable engine that he built in 1824 at the works at Stratford, east of London, where he made rubber manufacturing equipment for his brother. Two flexible, rubber-coated canvas boilers alternately filled with steam and emptied, thereby providing reciprocal motion that was transmitted to a crankshaft, without need for pistons. The initial purpose of this device was to drive rubber-forming machinery. It was a failure. Next, prompted by a print he had seen of the Griffith carriage, Hancock made a water-tube boiler, but did not find this type efficient enough to satisfy him. In 1827 Hancock patented his own design of boiler. Its aim was the same as that of the water-tube boiler – to expose the least possible amount of water to the greatest possible heating surface, in a light, compact and safe format – but its construction differed in that its water circulated through box-section pipes forming a homogeneous element like a honeycomb, surrounded by fire. Hancock claimed that this design was lighter and more efficient than the water-tube boiler, producing more heat from a given area of metal and amount of water. In fully developed form, his boiler could raise 200 p.s.i. pressure in 20 minutes. Steam was kept up with the aid of familiar features such as fan-induced draught and pre-heated feed water. The normal running pressure was 60–100 p.s.i.

Having properly given priority to producing the most effective boiler he could devise, Hancock next built a steam carriage. He had an experimental vehicle on the road by 1829, or possibly early 1830. This was a small four-passenger, three-wheeler test-bed, with primitive running gear that recalled Cugnot's work. The engine, which was situated above the single, unsprung front wheel, drove it direct by crank. The front wheel also steered. Yet, thanks no doubt to its efficient boiler, this machine is said to have made expeditions from Hancock's factory at Stratford that totalled hundreds of miles, visiting Epping Forest, Hounslow and Croydon, as well as places nearer to hand. The vehicle was not intended for public use, so Hancock refrained from drawing public attention to it, and at no time gave a detailed description of it. Nothing else, therefore, is known about it.

While Hancock and the rest were experimenting, Goldsworthy Gurney returned to the fray with his customary *élan* and telling effect. By July 1829 he had built an entirely new machine. This was not a self-contained coach, but a "drag" or "tug" that towed a passenger carriage – a road tractor, in fact. It was true that some turnpike trusts charged double toll in such a case, but the arrangement had three major advantages. By isolating the passengers from the boiler, it was intended to lull the fears of people who were concerned about explosions in steam vehicles. The idea was not new – Trevithick had drawn passengers in open carriages when demonstrating his railway locomotive "Catch Me Who Can" on a circular track in 1808. Although there was no universal prejudice against self-contained vehicles – Hancock would soon prove that – general approval was expressed. Then again, by spreading the weight of the complete unit over eight wheels, those who feared that the weight of steamers disproportionately damaged the roads were to be placated. Separate tractors scored in another way, too. When running any service, it would be necessary to have vehicles in reserve, in case of breakdown. A fleet of tractors and separate trailers would be more economical and flexible than self-contained coaches, for only a tractor need be sent to the rescue of the passengers; and whether broken down on the road or in the depot, the tractor alone would be out of use.

In its motive power, Gurney's 1829 tractor differed little from his earlier machines. Basic boiler design was unchanged, although the fan was dropped. Direct drive was retained, and the vehicle was still unsprung. There was no flywheel, which should in theory have added to the vibration, but there are no recorded complaints of this; and as the passengers rode in a separate, sprung carriage, they were comfortable enough. The steering was radically altered. The pilot forecarriage had gone; the tractor had four wheels only, the front pair steering. In an attempt to overcome the resulting problem of control, Gurney introduced rack-and-pinion steering, which is said to have answered well. Just before the famous Arctic explorer, Captain John Ross, left for his epic voyage of 1829–33, he took control of the tractor and, without any previous experience, drove it about for half an hour.[13] One of Gurney's passengers also testified to the apparent ease with which he kept control at speed.

Both steering and adhesion were no doubt helped by the fact that 80 per cent of the vehicle's weight was over the rear wheels. The tractor, a compact 10 feet long, had various weights attributed to it. If one accepts the weight of Gurney's 1827 coach as 2 or 3 tons unladen, figures of $1\frac{1}{2}$ or 2 tons, with fuel and water, given for the new machine sound reasonable.

On 22 July 1829 the tractor was on view at the home of Sir Charles Dance, a retired Life Guards officer, at Bushey near Watford. One of those present was Sir James Willoughby Gordon, Quartermaster-General of the Army. On the following day he drew up a highly favourable report at the Horse Guards. During a demonstration at Bushey, he said, the vehicle performed for half an hour at up to 10 m.p.h., uphill and around corners, with a barouche in tow. It made little smoke, and no more noise than a two-horse carriage. General Gordon said without qualification that it could stop "instantly" – a layman's exaggeration that would shortly be disproved. The machine might frighten horses – the only drawback the general foresaw – but this and all others could be overcome by "time, practice, and ingenuity".

Whether or not road steamers frightened horses was a profitless and never-ending argument. The balance of evidence is that they did, so the accusation was justified; but it was equally true of any other vehicle, or any strange or sudden sight or sound however caused, depending on an animal's temperament. Significantly, even a prejudiced London coachman involved in an accident with a steam carriage freely admitted that his animals were always frightened by horse buses, and that, in general, "you are never safe with any horses." This was a fair summing-up of the situation.

Now, for the first time, official interest was being openly shown in Gurney's work. General Gordon, in his capacity as Quartermaster-General, was in charge of the equipping and movement of the whole army. Gurney had had military contacts at least since his first association with Colonel Maceroni, but until now, soldiers or ex-soldiers had merely invested in, or otherwise shown interest in, his work as private individuals – or allowed him the use of the Regent's Park barrack yard for his experiments. The new, strong official interest would soon come to a climax.

Meanwhile, with encouragement from such unprecedentedly high quarters behind him, Gurney gained public attention again by attempting the first major road journey by steam – major in the sense that it was going to follow a busy stage coach route, that from London to Bath, from start to finish. In 1834, the route was served by 26 coaches daily, making a total of 176 journeys every week, leaving out of consideration local services. Furthermore, the route lay along the London–Bristol road, which was second in national importance only to the London–Holyhead road. Gurney could scarcely have chosen a more prominent locale for his demonstration.

Unlike the abortive London-Southampton project of 1827, this was a comparative success, marred by circumstances that were partly beyond Gurney's control, and none of them the fault of the vehicle. The aim, as on the previous occasion, was to demonstrate, for the benefit of public opinion in general and Gurney's actual and potential backers in particular, that long-distance journeys by steam carriage were practicable.

A procession that had assembled at Cranford Bridge, well clear of London's western fringes, on 27 July left at first light the following morning. In the lead was an "advance phaeton", its passengers including William Hanning, Sir Charles Dance and William Bulnois. The last two named had either already expressed interest in the commercial future of Gurney's work, or would soon do so. On the tractor were Gurney, and James Stone and Thomas Bailey, two of his engineers. In Gurney's private carriage, which was attached to the tractor, were his brother, Sir James Viney, Captain Dobbyn (who held the licence for the road) and two mechanics. Bringing up the rear was a hired post carriage containing David Dady, Gurney's works' foreman, another mechanic and a reserve of coke. At General Gordon's request, Dance kept a detailed journal of the expedition. So, too, did Dady. As a result, the most ambitious steam-carriage expedition to date was exceptionally well documented.

The steamer quickly took the lead from both horsedrawn vehicles. Then, on the bridge over the Coln at Longford, it met the Bath and Bristol mail head-on. Trying to avoid the oncoming vehicle, which filled the bridge, Gurney swerved – and in doing so struck the mail coach a glancing blow and ran into a pile of bricks by the roadside. An axle shaft was broken but the carriage was backed out, and continued on its way more circumspectly, on one driven wheel. The broken component was sent on ahead to Reading for repair. In view of this accident, claims of an average speed of 14 m.p.h. for the first 14 miles of the journey to Maidenhead were impossible. More realistic was the time of 4 hours 10 minutes to Reading, including stops for fuel, water and turnpike gates, which was recorded by Dance. The damaged machine's best pace on this leg was 10 m.p.h.

After a night spent at Reading, the steamer restarted on the 29th. This was a long day. By 8 p.m., Gurney had got only as far as Melksham, 12 miles from Bath. Although hills were no problem, and he sometimes went so fast that the horses of the post carriages had to gallop to keep up, his average speed of 6 m.p.h. told another story. Near Newbury, the travellers were stuck in newly laid gravel. As was pointed out by a contemporary authority, "a newly made macadamised road presenting a surface of loose broken stones offers a resistance several times greater than the same road when its surface is worn smooth." The repair to the axleshaft does not seem to have been effective, as at this point the passengers had to get off and push.

Clinkers inadvertently left uncleared in the grate slowed the machine further. So did the necessity to refill the water tank every half-hour, and coke supplies were often lacking. This meant that the carriage had twice to be refuelled with coal, which made smoke and spat sparks into neighbouring crops. Gurney's inclination to rush into ambitious and important enterprises without adequate preparation, already demonstrated in 1827, shows up again now in the absence of any prearranged fuel and water depots; this in spite of the fact that such depots were envisaged at the time of the Bushey demonstration.

At Melksham in the evening, disaster struck. It was the day of the fair; the streets of this little country town were jammed with farm labourers, and local artisans and tradesmen. The steam carriage was forced to a crawl. According to Gurney some years later, the trouble started among Melksham's weavers. Somewhere in the crowd there were cries of "We are starving already, let's have no more machinery!" and "Knock it to pieces!" Power loom and steam carriage – both were machines, which was all that mattered. It was particularly unfortunate that the Gurney expedition should encounter handloom weavers, who were suffering worse from accelerating mechanisation than any other class of artisans. The number of power looms multiplied about tenfold between 1823 and 1835, and within about the same period, the handloom weavers' wages fell by over 25 per cent.

Abuse was followed on Melksham bridge by a shower of stones and blows from "brutal fellows". A "violent scuffle" ensued as the party defended themselves. Bailey was knocked unconscious. Others of the party were injured, and knocked off the vehicle into the road. The carriage suffered little – those parts that were not too hot to handle were too strong to break. A doctor had to be called to Bailey, who was rushed to Bath by post carriage. The steamer was locked for the night in a brewer's yard, guarded by constables summoned by a magistrate. On the 30th, still under escort, it was hauled to Bath by horses, so as to avoid any more disturbances.

After the vehicle's capabilities had been demonstrated in Bath, it started back to London, exactly a week after setting out. It was once more horsedrawn as far as Melksham. Not surprisingly, "no persuasion or offers" could induce the engineers to pass through the town under steam. The party slipped through by night, and steam was raised a mile beyond. The return was uneventful, if slow. At Devizes, in contrast with Melksham, an enthusiastic welcome awaited the travellers, and on the Marlborough road beyond, riders accompanied them at a gallop. A large crowd waited at the top of a hill outside Marlborough, where stage coaches often needed six horses, to see how the new machine would climb it. Its crew fearing an ambush, the steamer rushed the hill at 8 m.p.h. Stops for water could take a quarter of an hour, because when it was needed, it had to be fetched from a distance by bucket, instead of being pumped up from roadside sources through the flexible hose carried. With depots, water and fuel replenishment should not, it was thought, take more than two minutes. However, the 84 miles from Melksham to Cranford Bridge were covered in 12 hours, including all stops. Another elapsed time quoted, $9\frac{1}{2}$ hours, sounds much more like the running time, for it does not square with an estimated running speed of 12 m.p.h., the only one given. The best speed on the return was 14 m.p.h. If most of the time spent at fuel and water halts on this journey could be discounted once depots were set up, the speed of the new carriage would be competitive in public service. In 1828 the fastest of the London-Bath-Bristol coaches took $12\frac{3}{4}$ hours for the 106 miles as far as Bath, via Devizes; an average speed of $8\frac{1}{2}$ m.p.h. Both first-hand accounts of the journey agree that, with the understandable exception of the animals of the Bath and Bristol mail, no horses had shown fright, in spite of General Gordon's fears.

This was the first road steamer for which detailed fuel consumption figures were recorded. No such record had been called for; or if any builder had made one, he had not made it public. The first Gurney tractor burned a total of 104 bushels, or about 5000 pounds, of fuel in the round trip of 168 miles. With coke at about 6d a bushel in the London area, this gave a fuel cost per mile of a little under 4d. Fuel-carrying capacity was enough for one hour's steaming, or about 10 miles. The vehicle's heavy fuel and water consumption was about average for road steamers of the period. It was due partly to lack of valve gear providing a variable cut-off, which led to a wasteful use of steam, and partly to the absence of condensers.

In his report to General Gordon, Sir Charles Dance was enthusiastic – "I consider this first experiment decisive of success." During 1830 he bought the interest in the Gloucester–Cheltenham road from Sir James Viney, and those for the Birmingham–Bristol, London–Birmingham and London-Holyhead roads from Gurney. For the latter, Gurney received an advance of £600. William Bulnois appears as the new owner of the licence for the London to Portsmouth, Worthing, Brighton, and Southampton roads. Bulnois, another of Maceroni's introductions, had a wide interest in the design of public transport. He patented a horse cab design, and later financed Aloysius Hansom, inventor of the hansom cab. He paid £600 to Gurney as an advance on one carriage to be built, and agreed to pay 6d a mile royalty once it was in service. Gurney had lost none of his ability to charm money from investors' pockets.

Nor had he lost any of his promotional flair. The dramatic trip to Bath was widely reported, but the best possible publicity attended Gurney's next outing. On 12 August, he exhibited his carriage at Hounslow Barracks before the Duke of Wellington, Prime Minister and national hero, at the latter's request. No doubt the Duke had seen General Gordon's report. A number of "military and scientific gentlemen", including Sir Charles Dance, were also present. Its barouche full of ladies and gentlemen, the tractor circled the loose sand and gravel of the barrack yard at speeds of up to 17 m.p.h. Next it towed a wagon-load of 27 soldiers, reflecting, perhaps, the purpose General Gordon had in mind for it. The Duke was quoted as saying that "it was scarcely possible to calculate the benefits we should derive from the introduction of such an invention as this." Gurney could hardly have had a higher recommendation.

John Herapath was an engineer, and like Gurney, was an active publicists on behalf of steam locomotion. He rode at Hounslow with Gurney, and started writing lyrical letters to *The Times* and other journals eulogising Gurney's work, but like some other steam enthusiasts, overstated his case. He ventured on unsafe ground when he claimed that the vehicle would stop "in a yard or two" from 20 m.p.h., and had attained between 20 and 30 m.p.h. Such a short stopping distance would not have been attainable from that speed, and there is no evidence that the maximum speed quoted was ever reached. Herapath must have made his case seem weaker still by declaring that 50 m.p.h. or more was possible with road steamers – a visionary prospect even for railways in March 1830, when the claim appeared in print.[14]

In September it was said that the carriage was no longer experimental, and that a London-Bath service would begin on 1 October. "Surely", asked the *Literary Gazette*, "among all the efforts, something efficient will be done." But it was not to be. Once more, a combination of practical demonstration and sensationalism was followed by 18 months' almost complete silence from Gurney. In February 1830 Herapath said that his tractor, drawing another carriage or an omnibus, had been working in snow and ice in the London area. "Three or four" vehicles had been built; a remark for which there is no supporting evidence whatever. By March, Herapath foretold, services would be in operation; but in that month all he had to report was Gurney's departure to south Wales, to experiment with his tractor on an ironmaster's tramway. The ironmaster was William Crawshay; his works were at Cyfarthfa. A Gurney machine was still drawing loads there, locomotive-wise, as late as January 1832. Another machine, or perhaps the same one, was reported in June 1830 as having run about in Regent's Park for an hour and a half. It was not now drawing a trailer; it had been modified to carry an open carriage body, in which 10 people rode.

Gurney was back to experimenting. There is no evidence, this time, that his invention was as yet unready to be used in public. Rather the reverse was true; it had acquitted itself well. The reason for Gurney's failure to meet his obligations to build carriages commercially may have been an obsession with tinkering, or lack of funds, or both – the first, perhaps, leading to the second. Gurney may have miscalculated the manufacturing costs of his vehicles; certainly his estimate of £600 per machine fell far short of the £1100 apiece that was the actual cost of some other men's public service steamers.

There was a straw in the wind. Dobbyn and Viney had made their contributions of capital late in 1827. Since than, William Hanning, now described as "the only monied man in the party", had become Gurney's financial mainstay, providing more cash than anyone else. After the spring of 1830, this fact, combined no doubt with Gurney's failure to deliver any of the carriages ordered, had begun to irritate him. Henceforth he progressively lost interest in Gurney's projects. It is possible that his financial support slackened in proportion, and Gurney's principal source of funds started to dry up.

During 1830, however, other steam carriage builders continued to pursue their experiments, perhaps encouraged by the wide publicity and official support Gurney had obtained. More vehicles were making relatively sustained and impressive performances on the public road, as lessons were learned. Among these was the coach of two newcomers – Nathaniel Ogle, an amateur enthusiast and publicist, and William Alltoft Summers, who contributed engineering expertise to the team. Ogle claimed that his first coach undertook experimental journeys in the latter part of 1830.[15] In principle, the water-tube boiler sought efficiency in the same way as a Gurney or Hancock boiler, and Ogle's claim to have achieved ten times the heating surface and power output of any other design was an exaggeration typical of the man.

The boiler's normal working pressure was 250 p.s.i. The weight of the empty vehicle was $2\frac{1}{2}$ tons. On top of that would be the weight of ten passengers, 60 gallons of water, and about 500 pounds, or ten bushels, of fuel. This water and fuel capacity was sufficient for a stage of eight miles, or rather under an hour's steaming. The average speed laden was 9 m.p.h. Possibly in 1830, the coach ran from the workshop where it was made, in Cable Street, Whitechapel, to within $2\frac{1}{2}$ miles of Basingstoke, where it broke its axle. From there it ignominiously returned to London by barge. Ogle and Summers regarded its engine as too small and underpowered. It also used fuel twice as fast as Gurney's 1829 tractor. There is no record of this particular vehicle being seen again.

The Heaton brothers of Birmingham, too – John, William, George and Reuben – had thrown their hats into the ring. In mid-October 1830, a Heaton tractor called the *Enterprise* was seen hauling a large iron press along Bath Street, Birmingham. There is no evidence of its pulling a passenger trailer at this time, though obviously it was capable of doing so. The report remains the earliest proof of freight haulage by a road steamer. In November the brothers lodged a patent for a gear-driven tractor.

Walter Hancock, too, had been busy. His second machine was ready about August 1830. This vehicle, which he christened *Infant* because it was the first of his fully-fledged creations, was very far from the crude test-bed on wheels that preceded it. There was no tall, exposed chimney as on other vehicles. This unsightly feature, Hancock realised, was unnecessary; the combination of fan and channelling waste steam up a short, concealed chimney or exhaust pipe created enough draught on its own. There were four wheels. The steering was on the pattern of that of Burstall and Hill, and W.H. James – by horizontal chain from the steering column to the centre pivot. It was combined with Hancock's own slipping-clutch device for dampening road shocks further. Weight was about three tons, with fuel and water.

The vehicle was set apart as the most advanced on the road in its day by its boiler, and by the refinements of its running gear. Two rear-mounted engines drove the rear wheels by endless chains – an idea envisaged in Nathan Gough's patent of March 1828, and in another proposal of the same year for a private steamer. It was far ahead of its time. Dionysius of Alexandria in the third century B.C. and Leonardo da Vinci 1800 years later had drawn driving chains of remarkably modern type; but until the early 19th century chains were made not to take driving stresses but to act as a means of anchorage. The transmission of power from engines to machines in factories was generally done by belts. Although chains in conjunction with toothed wheels would obviously be much better able to withstand and transmit powerful forces than belts on pulleys, in 1830 the modern, strong bush roller chain of Hans Renold, with its considerable load-bearing surface, was almost half a century in the future. It is remarkable, if it is true, that up to August 1831 Hancock's chains broke only once.

Chain drive allowed the vehicle's axle to move in relation to the frame, so helping to insulate the engines from road shocks. Further protection was provided by full springing for mechanism and body, and radius rods to take the driving stresses off the springs and frame. Because drive did not go direct to a cranked axle shaft, the back axle took only the vehicle's weight, not the driving stresses as well. Chain drive was superior to gear drive, too, for gear wheels, which were hard to make accurately, were easily thrown out of mesh or damaged by severe jolting. There were no flywheels; but no complaints of engine vibration are recorded.

Hancock still regarded his carriage as experimental,[16] testing it for several months and some hundreds of miles, mainly on the eastern fringes of the City, and successfully climbing Pentonville Hill to the cheers of the populace. Ten passengers could be carried, all inside an omnibus-style body. This was a feature that showed that Hancock now had his eye on a commercial use for the machine, and spotlit the particular market he had in mind.

George Shillibeer was a London coachbuilder who had moved to Paris, and there in 1825 built two horse omnibuses. By 1829 he was back in London, and in July announced the start of an omnibus service. Two of his 22-seat vehicles would ply for hire, five times a day in each direction, from the "Yorkshire Stingo" public house in the Marylebone Road, Paddington, to the Bank of England, via the New Road and the City Road. The fare was 1s for the whole distance, or 6d for any intermediate stage. The omnibuses would stop anywhere on demand, and would run full or empty.

Both fares and *modus operandi* made the omnibuses an instant success with the public, who thronged the roads concerned in increasing numbers. The New Road from Paddington to Islington had been opened in 1757, and the City Road three years later, forming a northern orbital road outside built-up London. Its aim was to relieve congestion in central thoroughfares such as Fleet Street and Holborn, caused by herds on their way to market, and by growing commuter traffic between residential Bloomsbury and Westminster and the City. From the early 19th century, City-bound businessmen from the growing western suburbs such as Paddington and Notting Hill were also using the New and City Roads. Paddington's population expanded from less than 2000 in 1801 to over 25,000 40 years later. Other built-up commuter areas were spreading along their length on both sides. One was the former village of Islington, of which the population grew from 5065 in 1811 to 37,316 20 years later.

The New Road, intended as the northernmost boundary of building in London, had been swamped by urban spread; but its original status was still reflected in law. Omnibuses working on the principle of a continuous traffic in short-distance journeys had proved profitable in the heart of Paris, but they were not allowed to ply within the limits of building in central London, where the hackney coachmen enjoyed a statutory monopoly of short-distance hire. However, there was an increasingly lucrative traffic on the roads technically outside the limits. Until 1829 it was catered for by short-stage coaches. They were thickest on the Paddington to City route, where, in 1825, 54 coaches made 158 return journeys a day. They were allowed to carry a maximum of 13 passengers, seven of these outside in the weather. They charged up to 2s for the complete journey for an inside seat, and only 6d less outside; and they would wait about trying to collect a full load before setting off.

By early 1830 Shillibeer had opened other routes, and had 12 buses operating; by May, he and his emulators were working 39. The short-stage coaches were driven off the roads. Omnibuses were further encouraged by the abolition in January 1830 of tolls on the New Road and some other thoroughfares (though not the City Road), and the removal of tollgates on them – a measure designed to speed up the remorselessly increasing volume of traffic. Hancock regarded the 1s toll he had to pay at the gates on the City Road as onerous, perhaps because the heavily used roads around London were very bad; but it was the same toll that was demanded on all the roads of the Metropolis trust[17] for a four-horse stage coach, so he had no real cause for complaint. This was the context in which Hancock was making his plans. In 1830 he was not quite ready to join in the scramble for the omnibus travellers' custom, but he had signalled his intentions.

In the north, the steam coach of John and George Hanson of Huddersfield was reported in June to be running experimentally on the Huddersfield-Manchester road.[18] Before it retired from the scene with a broken crankshaft, it had attained speeds of up to 18 m.p.h. with a load of 10 passengers.

Three paragraphs below this story was another stating that on 15 September, the Liverpool and Manchester railway was due to be opened. It was a portent of ruin for all trunk road passenger traffic.

But the railway threat was a long time developing, and was at first unrecognised by the interests that would suffer from it. Indeed, on the years on either side of 1830, both the stage coaches and the turnpike trusts seemed entrenched in positions of great strength, with little to fear. As we have seen, the growing financial unsoundness of the trusts was masked,[19] and to a considerable extent alleviated, by government support, due to their importance as the nation's foremost provider of good roads. The coaching industry had an almost complete monopoly of the fastest, and therefore most lucrative, inland passenger traffic, and it reached the height of its wealth and power in the middle 1830s.

A four-horse stage coach ran about 100 miles a day. Given stages of between eight and ten miles, a single coach called for about 50 fresh horses every day – or twice as many, an average of one fresh horse per mile run, on the fastest and most punishing routes. Over 150,000 horses were used in coaching; their value, with that of their stabling and harness, was more than £3 millions.[20] There were about 700 mail coaches on the road, and rather under 3300 stage coaches. Each cost about £200 to build.[21] The industry provided direct employment for over 30,000 people. The leading operators were captains of industry. William James Chaplin, the biggest of all, had a personal fortune of £1½ million, and owned or leased 106 coaches. Two years later, in 1838, when he had begun to hive off his coaching interests in the face of railway competition, Chaplin still horsed 68 coaches with a stable of 1800 animals, employed 2000 people, and turned over £250,000 per annum.[22] His nearest rivals, Benjamin Worthy Horne and Edward Sherman, respectively horsed 92 and 77 coaches in 1836.

In 1836 London was the heart of coaching. The ten biggest proprietors of stage and mail coaches running to and from the capital together owned or leased 466 coaches. Every weekday 601 coaches left London. In central London alone – the City and West End – 408 inns and coffee houses were coaching establishments. Immediately outside London, at Hounslow, was Britain's greatest staging point. Here coaches converged on London along all the roads from the west, to change their horses for the last time. Two hundred stage and mail coaches passed through Hounslow every day, and stabling for 2500 stage, mail and posting animals had to be provided. There were other major staging centres at Whetstone, Finchley, Barnet and Purley, where coaches to and from the north and south were horsed by the coachmasters. Barnet handled 194 coaches daily – an average of one every 7½ minutes throughout the 24 hours.

If the capital invested in coaching was immense, so were the profits on it when the weather was fine, encouraging travel, and the coaches fully laden. But the constantly increasing pressure for more and more speed, in order to remain competitive with coaches on the same road, was driving the industry to the limit of its capabilities in several respects.

High speed was inordinately expensive. An increase from 8 to 10 m.p.h. in running speed – a mere 2 m.p.h. – doubled expenditure on horse-flesh. At this rate, the useful life of a coach horse was two or three years. Each animal cost between £23 and £37 or more to replace. Mail coach horses, which were driven hardest, died at the rate of two on every three journeys of 200 miles.

Then again, high speed was dangerous, and contributed largely to overturning incidents. Coaches were top-heavy when laden. With horses harder and harder to control at speeds over 10 m.p.h., racing a rival was an invitation to disaster. The drivers were highly skilled men, but had no margin for error. Drunkenness, which was common, or momentary negligence was enough to tip the balance. There was no systematic record of accidents, but it is known that a great many fatalities and countless injuries occurred between 1832 and 1838.

Finally, regardless of the limits imposed by expense and safety, the four-horse stage coach had obviously reached the maximum speed of which it was physically capable. The average speed expected of the fastest stage coaches, which had crept up to 11 m.p.h. by 1831, was "very near the utmost limits which nature has prescribed for animal exertion".[23] A year earlier, some London–Birmingham coaches were timed to cover the 110 miles in eight hours, at a mean speed of $13\frac{3}{4}$ m.p.h. This speed was the highest consistent average ever recorded. Any form of inland passenger conveyance that could match even 11 m.p.h. would be potentially competitive, and any that could surpass it significantly, regularly and economically, charge the same or lower fares, and not fall down too badly in other respects, would sooner or later sweep rivals away.

Expense and danger were the price of speed accepted by the coachmasters. Since the price had been climbing inexorably, they may have been more relieved than worried by the fact that speed had reached its limit, for most of the significant competition came from other coaches, suffering from the same limitations. Different and newer forms of transport were nibbling at the coaching monopoly around 1830, but were not hurting it as a whole.

Coastwise or river passenger steamer services had offered competition to coaches on parallel routes from their inception. As soon as Henry Bell's *Comet* started operating on the Clyde in 1812, four Glasgow to Greenock coaches were taken off. Passenger steamers had been operating between London, Gravesend and Margate from 1816, and between Hull and London from 1817. A Leith–London route opened in 1821, with 100-passenger vessels. Within five years, there were 24 east coast steamboats in service. Steamboats were safer, more reliable and more comfortable than stage coaches, only marginally slower, and a lot cheaper. A traveller from Maidstone to London could go by coach to Gravesend for 2s 6d and take the steamer on to London for 1s 6d. If he rode by coach all the way, the fare was 6s. About 1836 an inside seat on the London–Newcastle coach cost £4 10s 0d,

while one of the best cabins on a steamer between the two cities
was only £3. The coachmasters who suffered from the steamboats
regarded their competition as unfair because the boats did not have to
pay duty, as they did; but they felt that once they were placed on
an equal footing in this respect, they would be able to compete
effectively. There was no thought of being driven out of business.

Even more localised in effect were the canal passage or packet
boats. These appeared soon after 1830.[24] Passengers had been carried
on canal boats at least since 1772, but at no greater speed than freight.
The innovation of the passage boat was its high speed, for which its
hull was specially designed. Experiments on the Paisley and Ardrossan
Canal in 1830 had shown that water resistance decreased as hull speed
increased, contrary to general expectation, and that the banks were
not damaged. Average speeds of 8–10 m.p.h., including the
negotiation of locks, were normal, with two horses hauling each boat in
4-mile stages. Speeds of up to 15 m.p.h. were known. Passage boats
could accommodate up to 110 passengers each, and took precedence
over all other traffic. Services spread in the 1830s to the Union Canal
and Forth and Clyde Canal in Scotland. In England they were
found on the Preston, Lancaster and Kendal Canal, the Wolver-
hampton-Birmingham Canal, the Leeds-Liverpool Canal, and
elsewhere. Passage boats were smoother and more comfortable than
stage coaches, and they were cheaper than either coaches or railways.
Where stage coach routes ran parallel they must have suffered –
though there is no recorded evidence of this.

Most limited of all, in 1830 and for years afterwards, was the
competition offered to stage coaches by the steam passenger railway.
Its future in any context had been doubtful until 1827. Only in
September of that year – at the moment when Gurney was launching
his coach – did steam freight haulage become economic on the
Stockton and Darlington Railway, with the introduction of Timothy
Hackworth's *Royal George* locomotive, which was more powerful
than its predecessors. Steam haulage of passengers would have been
still less profitable, for the first steam trains could not match the speed
of the stage coach. The Stockton and Darlington's locomotive *Active*,
running without a load, once raced a stage coach between the two
towns, and in spite of its name, won by only 100 yards. George
Stephenson estimated that a 20-ton Stockton and Darlington train
would be good for no more than 8 m.p.h.

Although the first Act of Parliament embodying the Liverpool and
Manchester Railway, passed in May 1826, envisaged the carriage of
passengers, no regular steam passenger service existed until exactly
four years later, when the Canterbury and Whitstable Railway was

opened. Locomotives were used on only one short section of the track; the highest speed recorded for a train so hauled was 8 m.p.h. The rest of the line was served by stationary engines and horses.

A much greater impression was made on the public at large by the Rainhill trials of October 1829, which produced the *Rocket*, capable of hauling a 14-ton passenger train at up to 29 m.p.h. The successors of this harbinger of evil for the stage coach went into public service on the Liverpool and Manchester Railway on 17 September 1830. The fare between the two cities was half that of a stage coach, which took more than twice as long – four hours against an average of $1\frac{1}{2}$ hours. Immediate ruin was the fate of the coaches – before the railway opened, there were 29 on the road; within five months, four were left.

But it is important to remember that the Liverpool and Manchester Railway was only 31 miles long, and that it was almost alone. Until 1838, when the London-Birmingham railway was opened throughout its length, only half a dozen local passenger-carrying lines, widely scattered and all local, had been constructed; and all of these carried freight as well, or even depended on it. In 1835 the average length of all steam railways built was less than 24 miles. The concept of trunk passenger railways taking over the function of stage coaches had yet to be realised. In the evidence before the Lords select committee on turnpike returns in 1838, railways are not included among the troubles afflicting coachmasters. Warning notes begin to sound in 1836, but they are few and scattered. Benjamin Worthy Horne expressed open concern publicly after the construction of the London-Birmingham railway had begun, but coachmasters as a class were as yet little affected.

As for the steam carriage, in 1830 there was no public service in operation anywhere – competition from this quarter simply did not exist. There is no evidence, now or later, of coach operators fearing road steamers, or of taking action against them. The reverse was true. Asked in 1836 – admittedly long after the few inter-urban steam coach services had been taken off – if there was hostility among coachmasters towards steam carriages, Horne replied that there was none, and that he actually preferred road to rail steamers, "for the competition of rail is greater . . . . I only hope that steam carriages will be on the high road instead of being on railroads." He was convinced that they frightened horses, and thus endangered travellers, and had instructed his coachmen to stop when they approached; but he admitted that he had had no experience of accidents to steam carriages, and that much of his opinion was based on hearsay. His only unqualified complaint was that road steamers, like steamboats, were unburdened by duty.

Even when the main road services were running, physical opposition directly attributable to coaches was slight. One piece of evidence for it comes from Thomas Harris, a Gurney engineer who went to work on Sir Charles Dance's Gloucester–Cheltenham route in 1831. He said that "a stage coach would sometimes drive so as to prevent our passing". Another case of baulking was reported after a trip to Brighton by Dance in 1833.[25]

The experiences of Hancock, on London's crowded and competitive streets, were very different. His first test vehicle was greeted with "hootings, yellings and hissings", "the grossest abuse", wilful obstruction, and exorbitant charges for, or the withholding of, facilities for running repairs. Hancock specifies neither the source of nor the reason for this hostility. Thronged streets with many horses and little room for manoeuvre must have seen more incidents than occurred on the open road – the reason may be found here. If so, men and horses seem to have quickly got used to the steamer, for the opposition died down for a while.

It revived in much more purposeful and identifiable form once Hancock omnibuses started running services in direct competition with horse buses on the same roads. In April 1833 he reports the "malignant efforts of some of the drivers of the horse vehicles to impede and baffle the course of the new competition". In May, John Hall, driver of Paddington omnibus no. 3926, was fined £2 and costs for "driving against, and wantonly damaging" Hancock's steam bus *Enterprise*. After this, there was less interference for a time, but by 1836 Hancock was again complaining of "a great deal" of baulking by horse buses.

The lack of response to steamers in the coaching industry as a whole was certainly not due to lack of opportunity – after all, they ran, or proposed to run, on the same lines of road. Nor was it due to steam-carriage promoters keeping a "low profile". They, like the omnibus and stage-coach drivers, were not above a little baulking. When Hancock's omnibus *Infant* went to Brighton in 1832, one of its passengers criticised the driver for showing lack of consideration to coach drivers by hogging the crown of the road – "Steam conductors must conciliate". Significantly, he was appealing for realism, rather than for courtesy for its own sake.

The verbal challenge of steam's supporters was vociferous, insistent and unambiguous, especially in the days of Gurney. As early as 1827 an explicit threat to the mighty stage coach found its way into the popular press. Sounding as if it was inspired by Gurney or his supporters, it refers to "the curiosity excited throughout the country by the rumours of the intended substitution of steam carriages for those drawn by horses ... a speculation in the success of which so many interests are involved." "Scientific and practical men of all ranks" were convinced that steam "must, from its economy as compared with the expense of horse power, become almost universal .... Many prejudices will, of course, have to be combatted, but ... individual interests must give way to the public good."

This opening battle cry was followed by a more explicit and ominous challenge. Horses had to be fed and looked after when not in use, incurring unproductive fodder and labour costs. John Herapath's motives in favouring steam, as expressed in his letters to *The Times*, were very elevated, and were shared by undoubtedly disinterested people of high repute. In an open letter addressed to the Duke of Wellington in October 1829,[26] Herapath declared that steam, on road or railway, was a remedy for national distress. He reminded his readers of Adam Smith's dictum that every horse consumed enough food for eight people. Steam transport would allow the land devoted to growing hay as fodder to be turned over to human foodstuffs. Steam's speed and economy compared with the horse would raise profits, reduce prices, increase employment, and expand home markets. Finally, the lives of working horses, cruelly cut to a third or a quarter of their natural span by heavy labour, would be prolonged.

This was the first occasion on which a public appeal to national interest had been made on behalf of the road steamer, and was timed, no doubt, to coincide with recent official notice of it. Herapath did not confine himself to generalisations. He insisted that a steam carriage could be run for a third of the cost of a stage coach – Gurney said a fifth – and that fares, too, would need to be only a third as high. One steam coach in constant use, he said, could do the work of 200 stage coach horses.

Such assertions came very close to home; and their implications did not lack publicity. The *Sickle*, a journal representing the interests of Essex agriculturalists, responded sharply to a proposed London–Colchester service. It underlined the "certain and immediate evils" that would, in its view, flow from the introduction of steam on the road – not only the danger of explosions, but also a reduction in the value of horses and in demand for fodder, and massive unemployment. This was an exactly opposite view to that of Herapath, and was just as incapable of proof. That pro-steam propaganda had little discernible effect on coachmasters must have been due to a "wait-and-see" attitude on their part. They were not worried before steam services were established; and if they were concerned while these were in operation, neither service nor worry lasted very long. The steam promoters' more exaggerated claims were never borne out by events; but such very public hyperbole, designed no doubt to attract investors, was doubly foolish. However unproven, it may have helped to create the most formidable of the steamer's antagonists; and combined with the vehicle's many false starts, it made fools of the perpetrators.

Progressive journalists, engineers and public servants might favour innovation, but grass-roots public opinion was conservative by nature, and ignorant. Then as now, the mass of the people, of all classes, preferred the technology they knew because they knew it. They were ignorant of, and wary of, innovation. If they had suffered like the handloom weavers, they were hostile, and with good reason. Between a sort of sporting curiosity at best, and physical violence at worst, lay the most usual reactions – suspicion or mockery.

The London print sellers knew well how to reflect popular sentiment. From early 1828 numerous prints depicting steam carriages started to appear. Only a handful in the period to 1830 were promotional, perhaps commissioned by the builders – one published by James Adcock in April 1828 depicts the still-conjectural machine of W.H. James; another shows Gurney's 1827–8 coach, optimistically inscribed "London and Bath" – maybe to please Captain Dobbyn.

All prints were either satirical or promotional. The great majority were satirical. More often than not, they did not attack road steamers specifically, but steam power and novelty in general. They made serio-comic predictions of the conquest of the road, and even of the air, by steam within a few years. It is clear from their number that their publishers felt the investment justified by public interest.

The earliest traceable print to feature a steam carriage appeared as early as 1825, no doubt in response to the growing number of unfulfilled promises that a working vehicle was on the way. Most of the rest are not dated, but such dates as there are, plus internal evidence and inherent probability, suggest that none was published before Gurney brought road steamers into the public eye. Among those that bring steam vehicle fantasies into more general political and social satire are *The March of Intellect* (G. Humphry, January 1828); another print of the same title published by Thomas McLean about May 1829; *Heaven and Earth* (1830); and the undated *John Bull's Plight*.

More relevant are the prints aimed specifically at steam. Two S. & J. Fuller publications entitled *The Progress of Steam* (one dated February 1828), G. King's *Going it by Steam* (1829), and a McLean print called *Locomotion* between them forecast, by 1830–31, roads filled with hypothetical steam coaches, private carriages, delivery vans, tricycles, steam "horses", and even steam "legs" for attaching to the body. Coke "filling stations" serve the needs of the new mania.

In the sky above, steam aircraft fly about, or crash out of control.

The road steamers are vomiting steam and smoke, overturning, or blowing up spectacularly. These bad habits were not, unfortunately, mere flights of fancy. The most serious and understandable public fear was that of explosion. Leaving aside ruptures of individual tubes, only Burstall and Hill's carriage had burst its boiler so far; but high-pressure stationary and steamship engines blew up frequently and disastrously. Tubular or cellular boilers might be less likely to explode – Burstall and Hill's was a conventional single-chamber design – but the public could not be expected to appreciate that.

No horses are visible in these prints – they have been made obsolete. The point is rubbed in by *The Horses "Going to the Dogs"*, in which four horses are shown wondering at a passing Gurney coach, while dog spectators look forward with relish to cheap meat when steam has driven all coach horses to the knacker's yard. This prediction was nearer the knuckle than any other. No fun is made of the steamer; the horses are the only victims, and they are without hope. The implications of that did not need stating to a public accustomed to having virtually all its inland transport and haulage tasks performed by 1.4 million horses. Behind the satire was the reality of a Gurney vehicle working, if only temporarily, and the possibility, if no more, of a transport revolution in the foreseeable future.

Thomas Hood, a journalist and poet whose finger was just as firmly on the pulse of popular taste and prejudice, also knew that steam made good "copy". He fastened unerringly on the two aspects of the steam-carriage question which dominated his readers' minds when they thought about it. Out of 37 poems on every conceivable subject in the 1830 volume of Hood's *Comic Annual,* two are devoted to steam coaches. One, the *Sonnet on Steam,* is a lament by an under-ostler who foresees imminent redundancy for himself and for coach horses: steam is "A-turning Coches into Smoakey Kettels", and "Helps and Naggs will sune be out of Vittels". Hood's punning poem *Conveyancing,* a play on legal terminology, offers the prospect of both unemployment and immolation:

> Instead of *journeys,* people now
> May go upon a *Gurney,*
> With steam to do the horses' work
> By *powers of attorney;*
> Tho' with a load it may explode,
> And you may all be *un*done;
> And find you're going *up to Heav'n*
> Instead of *up to London!*

Far more significant than these squibs, or even the odd half-brick,

was the reaction of the turnpike trusts. It was slow in coming, and was
not at first, or ever wholly, hostile. The reason was certainly not
ignorance. Tidings of the new arrival on Britain's roads, heralded so
extravagantly by promoters, press, print sellers, and even the Iron
Duke, could hardly fail to become common knowledge very quickly –
the more so since most of its outings took place around London. Events
in the capital were reported country-wide. The London newspapers
reached the furthest provinces by means of the coach, and local papers
copied them. Trustees became aware of steam carriages from the time
they first appeared on the roads; this is clear from the fact that toll
schedules in turnpike road Acts mention them from 1828 onwards.

None of the Acts for 1827 takes note of road steamers –
understandably, since all were made law before Gurney's coach burst
upon the public. Of the 62 Acts that became law in 1828, only four list
tolls payable by steamers. Only one discriminates against steam, and
that marginally. On the Mildenhall-Littleport road, 1s 6d is asked for
a steamer, as opposed to 1s 4d for a four-horse stage coach. In 1829
there are still only six Acts covering steam, out of 62 passed; and again
only one, covering the Blue Vein and Bricker's Barn roads in Wiltshire
and Somerset, loads its tolls against steam.

In this instance, however, 6d per horse compares with a swingeing
1d per hundredweight for steamers. It is perhaps pertinent that one
of the trust's roads coincided with the Chippenham loop of the
London–Bath–Bristol coaching route that had been Captain
Dobbyn's prospective preserve since 1827, and that they met the
route at several points.

Still, one swallow does not make a summer, and it cannot be said
that the turnpike trusts were yet taking the steam coach seriously. It is
in the Acts of 1830 that steam begins to attract significant notice, and is
to a lesser extent attacked. It is not hard to see why.

The trustees must have been concerned primarily for their toll
income. With the arrival, however tentative, of a new vehicle on the
road, and with the promise of more to come, it was natural that the
trusts should react first by making sure that the newcomer should not,
through absence from the scale of tolls, avoid payment at the gates.
Evasion by other traffic was already a constant drain on income, which
the trusts could afford less and less as their debts increased. Legal
exemption was burden enough. The freedom from tolls in some areas
of vehicles carrying farm produce or agriculturally useful materials
such as lime and chalk, and of mail coaches throughout England and
Wales, severely reduced the trusts' potential income. The former must
have accounted for a high proportion of local traffic; and the trustees,
mostly agriculturalists themselves, must have been in two minds about

them. Mail coach exemption, however, aroused widespread resentment.

In strict law, no charge could be made for steamers at gates where there was no provision for them. Some gatekeepers nevertheless expected payment, either agreed or arbitrarily imposed, and the more sensible steam coach operators were prepared to pay a toll equal to that for a 4-horse stage coach.[27] A *modus vivendi* was possible and advisable; but the more assertive and short-sighted operators went out of their way to antagonise the trustees. The *Observer* publicised an unendearing remark from Gurney's early propaganda: "As to turnpikes . . . it is intended, in order to avoid dispute, to pay the trusts one-half toll" – that is, half of the sum payable on a 4-horse stage coach. Nathaniel Ogle had an even more cavalier way with gatekeepers, "throwing one man a shilling, and another two, being too much occupied to trouble myself about the matter". Francis Maceroni behaved in a similar manner.

But, until 1829, road steamers made no real impact. If the trusts thought about them at all, they clearly felt that there was no reason to take notice of them, let alone attack them. Then, in the second half of 1829 and the first half of 1830, Gurney's reappearance attracts unparalleled publicity, both for and against. His propaganda, echoed by popular satire, repeats the prophecies of boom for steam and doom for the horse. These have been familiar since 1827, but must now be taken more seriously, for the army and the Prime Minister, as well as more and more money, are lining up behind the new invention. Not only must the trusts now take greater account of road steamers in their toll schedules; there may also have seemed a danger that steam would drive out the stage-coach, while leaving no other source of income to replace it to the same extent.

This would harm the trusts on the roads affected, for the stage-coach was their biggest single source of income. On the London–Brighton road, one of the busiest in the country, 23 coaches ran daily in each direction in 1828.[28] At about the same time, each coach contributed £1 4s 6d every day to the trusts along the route. One gate collected £2400 in a year, of which two-thirds was from coaches. On the London–Liverpool road, with 11 coaches in each direction plying every day, each coach produced £5 4s 7d a day the year round. In 1836 the *Wellington* alone, running 364 days, paid £2537 in tolls. Country-wide, stage coaches probably covered 1 million miles a week between them, much of it on trust roads[29] subject to tolls. By the end of the decade, the point had been proved. When the stage coaches on a main road were ruined by a parallel passenger railway, the trusts on that road suffered grievously. Tolls on the Warrington and Lower Irlam road raised £1680 in 1829, the year before the opening of the Liverpool and Manchester Railway, and £332 in 1834; while the toll income on the London–Birmingham road declined by about 50 per cent between 1836 and 1839.

It is reasonable to suppose that the trustees were already aware of the escalating costs of running stage coaches competitively; and that a further challenge might tip them into insolvency. Passenger-carrying steamboats were a reality long before 1829–30. Steam passenger railways and canal passage boats were a less obvious threat, but from the time of the Rainhill trials the writing was on the wall for all who cared to read it – the steam locomotive drawing passengers had suddenly achieved a more than competitive speed, amid the greatest possible publicity. The coachmasters in their position of apparent strength might not yet feel threatened by the encroachments of modern technology, but turnpike trustees were starting to worry on their behalf. The most obvious answer was to impose tolls on steamers high enough either to discourage them, or, if this failed, to make up for the revenue lost by their displacement of stage coaches.

Nor were only the stage coaches involved. If the coachmasters failed, their employees would probably go to the wall as well. Related interests might suffer too: the landowners and tenant farmers who grew fodder; the chandlers who dealt in it; the horsebreeders and traders; the innkeepers and their servants who tended the thousands of coaches, horses and passengers; the stable proprietors; the coach-hiring and coach-building establishments; the second-hand-coach dealers; harness makers; coach makers – the "snowball" effect could be overwhelming. In fact when the railway came, only the trunk road coaching interests suffered immediate disaster, and as will appear, the horse trade actually boomed; but this could not be foreseen. Although there is no direct evidence, it is safe to assume that all the interests mentioned did their best to influence the trusts against the new invention, if and when they felt its threat.

Some individuals were in a uniquely strong position to do so, for they themselves were of the classes from which trustees were drawn – local men of substance, who owned property on or near the line of the road involved, and who in some cases undoubtedly had one financial interest or another in the coach traffic along it. It is easy to envisage meetings of trustees at which more than the trust's own revenues exercised the minds of those assembled.

Undoubtedly, trustees had other worries too. One was the damage caused by fast, heavy vehicles to their roads, and the consequent expense of repairing them. The macadam roads most subject to this kind of traffic cost £372 per mile per annum to keep in order, and had to be renewed completely, at a cost of £2000 a mile, every 10 years.[30] Stage coaches were the most damaging class of traffic. There is little direct evidence of trust concern specifically over the weight of road steamers at this time: but the constant insistence of their promoters that such machines were less harmful than stage coaches, and their anxiety to convince famous and influential road engineers, suggest that the opposite view was widely held, even if ill-founded. It is unlikely to have been a criticism of steam carriages *per se* – what the trustees would have feared was the addition of yet another indisputably heavy and fast vehicle to the traffic.

The amount of damage steamers caused to the roads was arguable; but in another way, they were certainly a danger to property. Every spark they threw out threatened the crops of the men who farmed alongside the road, and many might well be trustees, who were "immediately connected with land and with agricultural pursuits".[31] Burning coke emitted fewer sparks than coal or wood, but coke still produced some, and the other fuels were used, of necessity, when coke supplies were not available.

So these arguments, too, came down to money. Given the "scare" tactics of Gurney, enthusiastically taken up by the press and the print sellers, it is surprising that when the reaction finally attained significant proportions, it was still so muted and inconsistent, and failed to become universally clamorous even after 1830, when commercial services began to operate for appreciable periods of time. Setbacks invariably followed apparent success: this may have moderated concern among trustees, as among coachmasters.

Out of 67 turnpike Acts in 1830, 23 imposed tolls on steam carriages; and 14 of these discriminated against them. In a typical instance, on roads in the Derby and Mansfield area, 2s 6d was levied on a steamer, and 4½d per horse, or 1s 6d for a 4-horse coach. On the Bolton-le-Moors to Blackburn road, a stage coach was charged 1s and a steamer 2s 6d. There are only three cases of tolls clearly designed to exclude all steamers. On the roads in the Ashburton-Totnes area, 5s per wheel would be asked, as against 9d per horse. The toll could thus be as high as £2, for a 4-wheeled tractor and its trailer, but only 3s for a stage coach. On the roads around Glasgow, 9d per horse was also charged. On steam coaches, the toll was based on weight, starting at 2s for the first ton. For a steamer weighing 4 tons laden, £1 0s 11½d would be demanded. On roads in the Tiverton area, a steamer weighing 4 tons laden would be charged 8s if it had 4 wheels, or 16s if eight, as compared with 2s for a 4-horse coach.

It may be more than coincidence that all these three tolls were levied on roads in areas directly threatened by steam. One of the

Ashburton and Totnes trust's roads coincided with a section of one of the two Exeter to Plymouth roads on which William Hanning held a Gurney licence. In September 1828 it had been reported that a steam carriage was due to start a Glasgow–Edinburgh service within two weeks, running at an expected speed of 12 m.p.h. Nothing happened; then early in 1830, the United Steam Carriage Association for Scotland issued a prospectus and offered shares – the earliest recorded joint stock company involved with road steamers. By June, it was said, four steamers would be in service between Glasgow and Edinburgh, each carrying 23 passengers over the distance in three hours, at a running cost less than half that of the existing stage coaches. These vehicles did not appear either; but the challenge was clear. In 1836 the three trusts on this road collected £2993 from two coaches alone. The trustees were unlikely to let such an income slip. Finally, Hanning's Bristol to Exeter and Plymouth roads coincided with one of the Tiverton trust's roads near Exeter.

It may also be significant that nine of the trusts practising discrimination penalised Gurney-type carriages – a tractor and trailer – more than self-contained steamers, either by charging by the wheel, or by levying toll on trailers as well as on towing vehicles. This was to be expected. Most trusts that were hostile to steam had marked the type of machine that was the most prominent.

This was one side of the coin. On the other, almost two-thirds of the Acts ignored steam. Of those that did not, four made no distinction between stage and steam coaches in any shape or form, and five actually favoured all steam. For example, the Malmesbury–Dauntsey Oak and Derbyshire roads trusts proposed to charge steamers 1s, and coaches 6d a horse; while on the Great Yarmouth–Acle road, 1s for a steamer was matched by 4d a horse.

The very limited conclusion to be drawn is that in 1830, the presumed danger to the financial interests of the trusts and of the trustees had to be on the doorstep before they attempted exclusion; but only a minority did so even then. Several other trusts were threatened with steam services on their roads; yet these were among those that made no mention of steam in their acts. Most surprising of all was the Stony Stratford–Rockcliffe trust, in Bedfordshire, which lay on the main road from London to the north-west, with branches to Birmingham, Manchester, Liverpool and Holyhead. Steamer services were said to be imminent on all these routes, yet no measures were taken to profit from, let alone exclude, the new machine. All in all, it is understandable that no word of complaint about excessive tolls is heard from steam promoters prior to 1831.

Eighteen thirty-one was the year in which commercial steam

Plate 1   A semi-serious, semi-satirical print of Goldsworthy Gurney's original steamer in the form in which it first took to the road in 1827. The picture implies the existence of an inter-city service with a stable of vehicles: in fact there was never more than one of this type, and it made only experimental runs in London's immediate vicinity.

Plate 2   Gurney's 1827-type coach climbs Highgate Archway Hill. The Archway is crowded with spectators. This scene depicts an actual event of September 1827, though it exaggerates the gradient.

The Mirror

OF

LITERATURE, AMUSEMENT, AND INSTRUCTION.

No. 391.]   SATURDAY, SEPTEMBER 26, 1829.   PRICE 2*d*.

GURNEY'S IMPROVED STEAM CARRIAGE.

Plate 3   Gurney's drag or tractor, as illustrated on the front page of the
Mirror for 26 September 1829. It had recently received wide publicity for
its London–Bath and Hounslow demonstrations.

BURSTALL & HILL'S
PATENT
Steam Carriage Model,
MAY BE SEEN AT WORK IN
THE BLACK BULL HALL,
ENTRANCE BY VIRGINIA-STREET,

On Monday, the 7th January, 1828, and Following Days,

From 11 to 4, Afternoon, and by Gas Light, from 7 to 9.

Admittance, One Shilling.

A, Water Cistern.—B, The Boiler.—C, Steering Wheel, with the Conductor.—D, Steel Frame which carries the Boiler.—E, The Curved Steam Pipe to supply the Engines.—F, Hand Pump and Pipe to fill the Boiler.—G, Safety Valve.—H, Notice Cocks.—I, Eduction Pipe to take the Steam from the Engine to Chimney. —K, The Crank.—L L, Pan for the Cinders.

N. B.—The Model is constructed on a scale of 3 inches to the foot, is 5 feet 6 inches long, 16 inches over the wheels, and 1 foot 10 inches high, the middle or propelling wheels being 13 inches in diameter.

The Full Size Carriage will be about One Foot longer than a Two Horse Stage Coach and Horses, Seven Feet Four Inches high to the Roof, the Wheels being the common breadth apart. It will be retarded or stopped in running down hill by a powerful Lever and Friction Break, which acts on the two fore wheels, within reach of the Conductor, at the same time, by a Crank and Rod, the Throttle Valve is closed, which shuts off the Steam; the Engineer behind can likewise at pleasure stop the Engine.

Plate 4 Back to the drawing board: an advertisement for a demonstration in Glasgow of a model of Burstall and Hill's coach. A full-scale machine had blown up in London in 1827.

A CORRECT REPRESENTATION OF

MESSRS. OGLE AND SUMMERS'S STEAM-CARRIAGE.

A. Helm by which the carriage is guided.
B. Seat for the conductor.
C. Coupé, like French diligences, for four persons.
D. Seat for outside passengers.
E. Hand-pump for filling tanks.
F. Seat for engineer.
G. Pipe for surplus steam.
H. Jigger by which furnace is fed.
I. Flue or chimney.
J. Boiler.
K. Furnace.
L. A blower worked by strap round the axle.
M. Water-tank.
N. Break to check speed, regulated by a lever to the conductor's seat.
O. Carriage for eight insides.
P. Wheels very strong; the spokes not here marked.
Q. Springs on which the machinery rides.
R. Springs on which the carriage rests.
S. Frame connecting the whole.
T. Machinery under the carriage.
U. Ash-box under the furnace.
V. Pump by which the engine forces the water into the tank.
W. Piston for working the pump.

Some notice has been taken by the public press of the arrival of a steam-coach at Birmingham, from Southampton, on the 4th ult. We have since been favoured with some particulars by a gentleman, whose zeal induced him to become one of the party in this novel and successful experimental journey. This coach is the invention of Messrs. Ogle and Summers, of Southampton, who, after a most serious expenditure of time and money, have at length accomplished the desideratum of a moving power, by which carriages can be propelled on the common roads of the country with speed and safety, and without smoke. The first attempt was from Southampton to Oxford, and then from Oxford to Birmingham. During its first progress there was considerable difficulty in regulating the speed down hill, the machine having, in one instance, hurried down a declivity at a most enormous rate, probably 50 miles an hour. Captain Ogle, by his nerve and management, steered it, notwithstanding, with perfect ease. This has been amended, and the vehicle was seen leisurely proceeding down long Compton-hill at a steady rate of about seven miles an hour; a rate slower than that with which it ascended Leveridge-hill. Through the tortuous windings of Shipstone, too, it proceeded at about ten miles an hour with the greatest precision.

Perhaps a finer sight has rarely been seen than its starting from Oxford. The intention had been known previously, and it being the day of St. Giles's-fair, the town was thronged with thousands of visiters; and as the ponderous machine was preparing to start from the Star-inn, the description of the car of Juggernaut rushing on its votaries was strongly brought to mind. It commenced at about ten miles per hour, accelerating its speed to about 14 miles at the utmost. On the whole line of its journey it suffered delays from the badness of quality, or actual want of coke, and the time taken up in charging the tank—matters of detail, which a regular establishment will easily correct.

When the country through which the experiment has been made is considered, as regards irregularity of level and variety of material of which the roads are composed, it must be thought a most successful attempt. It singularly happened, that the coke was expended and the steam down at the very moment it reached the entrance of Birmingham; the zeal of the populace, however, supplied the want, and it was hauled with cheerings to the Hen and Chickens, where its 22 inmates took up their quarters.

When its speed, security, power, and freedom from smoke are considered, as well as the road it has travelled, we may boldly assert, that the invention of Messrs. Ogle and Summers is worthy of the highest support, and this we trust it will receive. It is a common observation with engineers, that "steam is still in its infancy;" and truly does this essay corroborate the truth of it.

We believe that the patent boiler of Messrs. Ogle and Summers is the main cause of their success, as containing the greatest possible heating surface within the smallest possible space, and without any danger; although worked at 200 lbs. on the square inch, and capable of bearing 294lbs; in fact, this boiler presents 398 feet of heating surface, and at the pressure of 200 lbs. to the inch, exhibits upwards of nineteen millions of pounds of pressure, without the slightest danger!

The cylinders are 2¼ inches diameter, with metallic pistons; and the whole of the machinery is carried horizontally under the body of the carriage.

This information we think worthy the attentive consideration of merchants in general, and particularly the great coach proprietors of the United Kingdom.

Plate 5 Ogle and Summers' coach of 1832, as seen in the *Dublin Literary Journal* after it made its ill-starred journey from Southampton to Liverpool.

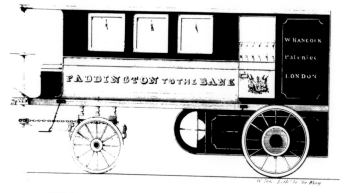

THE TRIUMPH of MECHANICS in 1832.
(Hancock's Road Steam Carriage.)

PROSPECTUS

OF

The London & Paddington Steam=Carriage Company.

THE importance to a commercial country of rapid and economical internal communication is so great, that for many years unceasing and successful endeavours have been made to improve it. By giving our lines of road a more direct course, levelling hills and filling up the vales, and also by giving them a more firm, durable, and permanent surface, our horses are enabled to travel on them with greatly increased speed; but the great cost and danger attendant on such increased rates of speed, with such expensive and wayward animals, has for a long time caused the attention and energies of scientific men to be directed to the attainment of the safe and economical application of Steam Power for the propulsion of carriages on our already formed excellent roads, so as to insure to us, in its fullest extent, the greatest expedition which the unlimited power of Steam could command, and the equally important requisite of the most perfect degree of safety.

These important advantages, so difficult in their attainment, yet so much to be desired, have at length been secured to us by the talent, ingenuity, and perseverance of Mr. Walter Hancock, (as will be seen by a reference to the subjoined extracts from the Report of a Committee of the House of Commons on Steam Carriages); and there no longer exists any obstacle to the instant adoption of Steam Carriages, for the conveyance of passengers and goods on all our common roads, thus insuring to the Public the greatest degree of economy, expedition, and safety that science can command.

For the purpose of facilitating so desirable an object, and of investigating Mr W. Hancock's plans and terms in all their bearings, a meeting of gentlemen was convened at Mr. Thomas Spring's, Macclesfield Arms, City Road, on the 2nd February, 1832, Charles Toplis, Esq. in the chair: which meeting, after due consideration, was adjourned until the 9th of February, 1832, for the purpose of further personal inquiry as to terms, and of trial and inspection of Mr. Walter Hancock's experimental Steam Carriage; which inquiries and inspection proved so satisfactory to all, that, at the more numerously attended adjourned meeting, Robert Hills, Esq., in the chair, the following Resolutions were drawn up, proposed, and unanimously adopted.

RESOLVED—That to this meeting it appears from the statements made, and from documents produced and read, that there is a fair and reasonable promise of commercial profit to be derived from working on the public roads Steam Locomotive Carriages for the conveyance of passengers and luggage for hire.

Plate 6 The front page of the prospectus for the first company floated to use Walter Hancock's steam buses, 1832. The machine shown was a project only; no bus was completed and in service before 1833, and it differed in detail from the illustration.

Plate 7 "The Century of Invention": a satirical print from *Everybody's Album* for 1 February 1834. In the foreground it is announced that "a cast iron parson will preach by steam"; a "hydrogen gas sale" and the last live horse are advertised; and an itinerant barber and a carrier go about their business. In the middle distance the "Steam Guards" pass by; beyond them a "Travelling Bazaar", among other attractions, is on the move by rail. As a result of all this activity, spectators comment that the coal mines of the North are "nearly exhausted". In the sky above, a balloon race is in progress.

Plate 8 "Going it by Steam": an etching by Robert Seymour, 1829. Steam engine explosions did take place, prompting satirical prints like this.

Plate 9 "The Horses 'Going to the Dogs'": another public fear (or to be exact, a fear felt by the interests with something to lose) was of redundancy for the horse. Here, in a Cruikshank forecast of 1829, the sight of Gurney's coach amazes horses, and causes dogs to look forward to a feast when the knackers have had their way.

NARRATIVE

OF

TWELVE YEARS' EXPERIMENTS,

(1824—1836,)

DEMONSTRATIVE

OF

THE PRACTICABILITY AND ADVANTAGE

OF EMPLOYING

STEAM-CARRIAGES

ON

COMMON ROADS:

WITH

𝕰ngrabings and 𝕯escriptions

OF

THE DIFFERENT STEAM-CARRIAGES CONSTRUCTED BY THE AUTHOR,
HIS PATENT BOILER, WEDGE-WHEELS, AND OTHER INVENTIONS.

[STEAM PHAETON.]

BY WALTER HANCOCK, ENGINEER.

London:

PUBLISHED BY JOHN WEALE, ARCHITECTURAL LIBRARY,
HIGH HOLBORN:

AND J. MANN, CORNHILL.

1838.

Plate 10   The first of many? Walter Hancock's steam phaeton of 1838, also called a gig or a cabriolet. Britain's earliest properly authenticated, purpose-built motor car, it may have evolved from a Hancock vehicle of three years earlier. This, the only known reproduction, comes from the title page of Hancock's book.

services got under way in two areas of the country, and when the road steamers was more prominently in the public eye than ever before. Sadly and ironically, it was also the year in which the man who had fought harder than anyone else for the new machine rose like the last rocket in a public pyrotechnic display, then fell abruptly spent.

The year began well for Gurney, and for Sir Charles Dance. To Dance belonged the distinction of being the first of Gurney's clients to take delivery of steamers he had ordered. He received three identical machines, so as to allow a continuous service on the Gloucester–Cheltenham route he had taken over from Viney. A story has gained currency among historians to the effect that Gurney did not himself build these machines in London, but that they were put together in Gloucester by persons unknown. Gurney's unattractive tendency to blame others for his vehicles' real or alleged deficiencies was responsible for this. When told that the tractors were heavier than he intended, he said that if this were so, it was because they had been built "principally under the superintendence of another person" – no doubt meaning one of his engineers, not Dance. The latter had no mechanical knowledge. When one carriage suffered a broken axleshaft as a result of running through thickly laid road metal, it had been "upset by Sir Charles Dance", and when the machines frightened horses, it was because of the design of the bodywork, for which Gurney also disclaimed responsibility. The trailer may have been built at Gloucester; there is nothing to suggest that the tractors were, and there was one positive indication to the contrary. On 29 January the *Gloucester Journal* reported that "two of Mr Gurney's steam carriages are now in this city", which suggests recent arrival.

If the Dance steamers were to be economic, they would have to be worked hard, for the route did not promise outstanding profits. Traffic on it was "very limited".[32] Purely local traffic had in fact been declining. Leaving aside through services on the road, in 1828 there had been at least nine return stage-coach journeys every weekday. By 1836 the number would drop to seven. The total daily capacity of the coaches, in both directions, was 162 passengers. In 1825 one of the two trusts concerned farmed the toll on the road for £1590; by 1833 the figure had declined to £1325. However, the road was "beautiful and perfectly level, for the most part on the border of a canal",[33] and neither of the two trusts, which administered the road from Gloucester towards Cheltenham and Tewkesbury and roads radiating from Cheltenham, made any mention of steam carriages in their toll schedules.

Dance's vehicles were developments of Gurney's 1829–30 tractor design. They were the first of his machines known positively to have had the "steam blast" or "steam jet" exhaust up their chimneys, but this was rather a disadvantage than otherwise. For the first time, Gurney's machines were criticised for being noisy. Indeed, they were said to make a noise "like the barking of a dog". On the other hand, the tractor's boiler and body, if not its engine, were at last sprung – partly, perhaps, because it was now designed to accommodate fare-paying passengers as well as hired men. The trailers used were closed coaches. Between them, tractor and trailer could carry up to 38 passengers. There seems also to have been a fail-safe mechanism, in that the steam valve had to be held open while the engine was running, rather like a "dead man's handle".

Trials began on the Gloucester–Cheltenham road on 1 February 1831, and there were demonstration rides at Montpellier Spa in Cheltenham from the middle of the month; on the 21st, a twice-daily service in both directions was inaugurated – four journeys a day.[34] Steamers left Commissioner's Yard at Cheltenham at 10 a.m. and 2 p.m., and the Spread Eagle Inn at Gloucester at noon and 4 p.m. Early in March, their motion was described as being "remarkably smooth, regular and agreeable"; and "no accident has hitherto occurred of any description." On average, the service was about as fast as the London–Cheltenham mail, usually taking about 50 to 70 minutes,[35] as against one hour for the coach, over the distance of $9\frac{1}{4}$ miles. Estimates of the time saved vary, but in an age when speed was the principal selling point of a public passenger service, an ability – even if seldom demonstrated – to do the journey in 40–50 minutes was a considerable asset, proudly quoted. The steamers' most economical running speed was 12 m.p.h. A price war – the common accompaniment to the introduction of a new service – also began. The 4-horse coaches (which were the fastest) charged 2s 6d for the journey, and the 2-horse coaches 2s. Dance set his fare at 1s. In reply, the coaches reduced their fares to the same level.

Several engineers who had worked for Gurney ran the service for Sir Charles Dance – providing skilled personnel must have been part of Gurney's contract with him, for no one else could have done so. James Stone was designated manager, at the considerable salary of £1 per day, and appeared to be in overall charge of operations. Thomas Bailey was the senior engineer, responsible for keeping the vehicles running. Another Gurney engineer who worked for Dance was Thomas Harris. He and Bailey were probably among the four men, other than Stone, described as drawing £3 a week from Dance. Clearly, Dance's service would not lack such expertise as was available.

Over the ensuing four months, Dance's three machines ran for a total of 3644 miles, or 396 journeys, and carried 2666 paying passengers. According to Harris, boiler tubes burned out five or six times in a 3-month period, or once every 66 journeys on average – if true, a remarkable record, given that this was the Achilles heel of every steamer with a water-tube boiler. There were additional delays owing to such factors as the inexperience of a new stoker. Dance himself said that there were "sometimes delays", owing to "defective pipes in the boiler". Maceroni, on the other hand, claimed that "such was the frequency of derangements, especially in the bursting of one or more tubes of the tubular boiler, that it required the utmost exertions of an engineer ... and four men ... to keep one of the three coaches in moving order."

There was no corroboration for the last assertion, and in any case, the engineers' efforts must have paid off handsomely, for their charges' running record, which was never challenged, was an impressive one given the pioneering context.[36] If one divides the total number of journeys accomplished by the number of days the service lasted, the result is an average of $3\frac{1}{4}$ completed journeys a day, out of four scheduled. The running record covers 92 days to 1 June, on 16 of which there was no service. Like the stage coaches, the steamers usually ran on Sundays, so the lack of a service on these 16 days was due to other factors. It could have been that all three steamers were out of commission, but there were other possible explanations. In any case, five out of every six scheduled journeys were started and completed. On one occasion the time taken was as high as 160 minutes; otherwise it never rose above 82 minutes. The truth is probably that a good many "derangements" did occur; that most, as was generally agreed, were due to ruptured boiler tubes; and that as a rule, this delayed without halting a steamer. A burst tube usually brought a steamer to a halt for half an hour while the tube was cut off and plugged, or closed off with an iron clip. For the rest of the journey speed was reduced.

Stone reported that "the old ladies of Cheltenham offer a formidable opposition to any innovation. Whenever we are a few minutes after our time, it is regularly reported that we have either blown up, or broke down, or both." In view of the climate of public opinion, none of this can have come as a surprise. In fact, the steamers' safety record was good. An accusation that horses were frightened was probably true; but then, it was generally admitted that anything frightened them. The steam carriages were apparently involved in only one accident, when a phaeton drove out of a lane into the main road and overturned, owing, said Stone and Harris, to the carelessness of the coachman.

Then, on 22 June, the service came to an end. The reason given by
Dance was that a Bill imposing a prohibitory toll on the road was
imminent. But a look at the circumstances surrounding the event
suggests that there may have been more to it than that.

First, the figures tell a story of their own. The average number of
paying passengers per journey was fewer than seven – the service was
running at only about one-fifth of its capacity. Stone and Bailey
confirmed that the carriages sometimes ran with only three or four
passengers, occasionally with none. The maximum number normally
carried per journey up to 1 June was 28; a fuller load was very much
the exception. Dance's steamers doubled the number of places
available on public transport between Gloucester and Cheltenham, at
a time when traffic on the road was actually declining. He must have
counted on attracting all the stage coaches' existing trade, as well as
generating new business. The Liverpool–Manchester railway had
done just that; but Dance did not. His average "catch" of fewer than
28 passengers a day must have fallen far short of his ambition.
Furthermore, added Stone, "we took a large number who did not
pay". The only possible excuse for this economic folly was public
relations.

Receipts came to £202 4s 6d, which squares more or less with the
number of fare-paying passengers, with a little over, no doubt for
parcels and so on. The total expenditure is impossible to establish, but
although it was said by some to be less than half that on a 4-horse coach
service, it must still have exceeded income. The cost of coke was £78,
one-third spent on trials and the rest during service, which suggests a
fuel consumption much on a par with that of the 1829–30 vehicle.[37] No
other figure is given. But if Maceroni's figures are accurate, the five
senior men he mentions must alone have run up a wages bill of at least
£324 (£18 a week for 18 weeks). Dance himself said that a steam
carriage operation employed more men than stage coaches –
expensive skilled mechanics in particular. In addition, there would
have to be taken into account repairs, depreciation, and possibly rent
for premises.

Thomas Bailey confirmed what the figures implied: that the
business was running at a loss. He attributed this to lack of passenger
traffic on the road, rather than to public unwillingness to travel by
steam carriage; and he was right. In its first four months, the steam
service had gained a certain clientèle, probably attracted by its
(sometimes) higher speed, and its novelty. Gurney said of it that "the
public was rapidly becoming converts in its favour", and this was true
as far as it went. The running records to 1 June show a steady increase
in patronage, from 169 in the first 10 days to 357 in the middle 10 days,

and 463 in the final 10 days. But the custom was not increasing nearly fast enough to make the service economic. Dance's basic problem was that passenger traffic on the road was insufficient – had it been heavier, a minority of the travelling public might have been enough.

Another factor that may have influenced Dance – although it can hardly have been unexpected – was the hostility of the local trustees. It is probable (there is no evidence) that they were alarmed by the inroads that the steamers must have been making into the declining revenues of the coachmasters, however small the actual number of passengers involved. The trustees saw their main source of revenue suffering, a situation exacerbated by Dance, who, furthermore, took full advantage of the absence of a toll on steam. Not for him the informal, diplomatic payments made in similar circumstances by other operators. It is not difficult to imagine the reactions of the trustees.

At a meeting specially called on 25 June – ironically, after the last steamer had run – the trustees of the Gloucester trust resolved that Dance's machines were a public nuisance, and that if the nuisance were not "abated" by 6 August, the clerk should begin legal proceeding against its perpetrators. A copy of the resolution was sent to Dance. Later, the trust's surveyor defined what the trustees had meant by a nuisance. The tractors were said to make "a very great noise". They shed "red hot coals" on to the road (resented, no doubt, because of the fire hazard). They frightened all but a few animals, often forcing riders to take to the fields, and they had caused a carriage to overturn. Some of these accusations were exaggerated, but all probably had more or less truth in them. The surveyor concluded by declaring that the steamers' activities had caused the road to be deserted by all other traffic – a remark suggesting anxiety over lost revenue.

Stone saw the argument from his side, but it seemed true that "we are surrounded with prejudiced people – agriculturalists, coach proprietors, coachmen, stable boys, and others directly or indirectly connected with them". Dance agreed, adding in a letter to Gurney that these people feared that his steamers would destroy the road, ruin the farmers and coach proprietors, and cause unemployment.

How much further the Gloucester trust's hostility went was a question obscured then and since by acrimony and special pleading. It was a fact that over a period of five days in the second half of June, road gravel was found laid so thickly at one point on the road[38] that mail coaches, carriages and wagons were brought to a full stop. Estimates of its depth varied from 14 to 18 inches. The day when it first appeared is uncertain. Stone, writing at the time, said 22 June, and that the Dance steamers on the same day successfully negotiated the obstacle three times, though not without difficulty and delay. His own passengers were called upon to help push a stage coach out of the gravel. Five years later, Harris claimed that the steamers passed through the gravel some 20 times over four or five days, and that it was laid thicker and thicker over successive days. The same may, perhaps, be said of his testimony. Stone's story is strictly contemporary, and more plausible. Both accounts agree that after the last time of passing, an overstrained driveshaft broke, and the carriage limped home on one driven wheel.

How the gravel came to be there was, and remains, a mystery. On the one hand, it was accepted, without suggestion of ulterior motives, that when roadstone was freshly laid it might be thick enough to inconvenience all traffic until the latter's passage compacted it.[39] The *Mechanics' Magazine*, which took a strong interest in the progress of steam on the road, saw nothing sinister in the Dance incident. Dance and his employees, who were on the spot, thought differently. Dance, Stone and Bailey all referred to "unusual quantities" of stone. Dance added that the road had been "in excellent order", and "required no repairs", and Bailey agreed. Stone said that gravel was "laid down upon that part of the road that was always the most difficult to pass over". Alexander Gordon, a consistent supporter of Gurney's enterprises, pointed out that the season was wrong for laying new road metal – this was usually done in the spring.

There were more direct accusations, too. Bailey said he had overheard workmen breaking roadstone suggest knowingly that it was all laid at once in one place with a definite aim (unspecified) in mind. According to Gurney, a turnpike gatekeeper told one of Dance's engineers that if "filling up" the road failed to stop the steamers, the trust would "get a tickler down from London" – meaning an Act that would do the job. Stone commented darkly, "there is no doubt who has been at the bottom of it." It was not, he said, the coach proprietors. Their coachmen might obstruct the steamers, but "though interested men" their employers "are far too respectable for an act of this kind". More to the point, they stood to suffer as well.

It was probably impossible to show where legitimate gravel-laying ended and obstruction of the king's highway began, and the hints and hearsay allegations were neither substantiated nor disproved. Logic suggests that the obstruction was not deliberate policy. Why should the Gloucester trust take such a drastic step, involving illegality, expense, and inconvenience for other payers of toll, before complaining to Dance and threatening legal action? It sounds like a last, not a first resort. And why should the Cheltenham trust do so, when a "tickler" was, as we shall see, already on its way?

Whatever the truth of the matter, the trustees got their wish. The broken steamer was the only one on the road at the time; the others were laid up with burst boiler tubes. So, the service was perforce suspended. The axleshaft was mended, but none of the vehicles ran again on the Gloucester-Cheltenham road. Dance claimed to have been undeterred by the gravel incident, and to be determined to carry on; what made him give up, he said, was the prospect of penal tolls being imposed. "In the course of the following week [after the service was suspended] I learned that a vast number of turnpike Bills had passed, and that more were passing . . . and that the Cheltenham trust was one of their number."

In the end, the "tickler" had come from the Cheltenham trust, controlling roads radiating from that town. Within its jurisdiction fell the road from Cheltenham to Coombe Hill, part of which formed the last leg of Dance's Gloucester-Cheltenham route. The Cheltenham Roads Bill, which received the royal assent on 30 July, effectively set a toll of 5s 6d on a Gurney-type steamer on both the outward and the return journey (3s for the tractor and 2s 6d for the trailer), as compared with 2s 8d for a 4-horse stage coach. Additional tolls, unspecified, would be imposed in the winter months, when the road would be softer and more liable to damage. A certain amount of unanimity between the trusts on the subject of Dance's carriages was to be expected, if only because they shared many of the trustees. The Cheltenham trust had done the job for both of them. At the same time, there is nothing (beyond the coincidence of dates, and the alleged remark of a toll gatekeeper) to suggest that an Act was obtained specially in order to suppress Dance's activities. The existing Cheltenham Act did not need renewal, being only seven years old; but new Acts for extending or otherwise altering a trust's powers could be, and were, obtained at any time. The stated purpose of the new Cheltenham Act was to build several new roads and deviations of existing ones, for which purpose – as the Act's preamble reminded its readers – fresh legislation was necessary.

The Act took the normal form of a renewal, with an extension of the toll schedule to cover steamers. It is quite likely that this clause was designed to exclude them, but most unlikely that the entire Bill, its real intention heavily camouflaged, was introduced for the purpose. The trustees simply took the opportunity presented to them to counter-attack a man who refused to pay them anything.

It is easy to understand how, given the losses Dance was already sustaining without any toll burden, the new imposition served as the final discouragement. It was not nearly as savage as some other discriminatory tolls, and was only a shade over double the stage coach figure, but it was as effective as the most monstrous of its kind.

Meanwhile, at the other end of Britain in that spring of 1831, another of Gurney's enterprises had been showing signs of reaching fruition. At about this time, John Ward, his very first client, had broadened his interests beyond the London–Liverpool and London–Manchester roads. He acquired from Gurney an option on all Scottish roads, and on the road from Liverpool to Edinburgh. He agreed to pay Gurney £15,000 in instalments of £5000 for Scotland, and £2000 for the connecting road from the south; but Ward had learned his lesson, and parted with no money for the option. His was the *modus operandi* of the stock market speculator. He had no intention of laying out money himself, or of running steamers on his own account; he had a buyer waiting, he said, to whom he expected to dispose of the Scottish option for £32,000, upon which he would pay Gurney and make a cool 113 per cent on the transaction. Gurney may have agreed to this arrangement because Ward had had no return so far on his original £500 outlay, or because of the temptingly large sum in prospect – more, even, than he had got from William Hanning.

But before Ward could bring off his *coup*, he had to prove that he had something of value to sell. In March, Gurney accompanied a tractor, "a very light and elegant carriage", to Edinburgh by sea – the first of six that Ward intended for the Edinburgh-Glasgow road. From there, it undertook experimental runs in Scotland's Central Valley. One account credits it with a single successful expedition – out from Glasgow and back, via Paisley and Renfrew, with nine passengers, at speeds of up to 10 m.p.h. All Ward's other outings were failures. Ward later told Maceroni (who was a party to his schemes) that the steamer took three days to cover the 45-odd miles from Edinburgh to Glasgow, "hooted and laughed at" the while.

After this experience, Gurney returned to London, leaving the tractor in Glasgow in a damaged condition. His engineer followed, having first taken measures (such as removing the safety valve) to prevent the local interested parties getting the machine on the road again in their absence. The Scottish backers, no doubt disappointed, did their best – with disastrous results. During a demonstration in the square of the Glasgow cavalry barracks early in June, the tractor blew up, seriously injuring two boys. Gurney fumed, blaming "unwarrantable experiments", but his Scottish enterprise was over. Ward paid him nothing, no doubt because his deal with his own clients fell through. The reasons Ward gave for his withdrawal were Gurney's constant experiments, which had resulted in a vehicle that was never ready for the road, and the spread of prohibitive tolls on the routes in which he had an interest.

He had reason to feel aggrieved, particularly as far as his Scottish roads were concerned. The trust controlling the Water of Almond-Bathgate-Baillieston road, part of the main Edinburgh-Glasgow road, had obtained an Act in March which entitled it to demand £1 7s 0d every time a tractor and trailer passed. The toll was levied by weight, and shows that a loaded Gurney equipage weighed 4 tons or a little over. A 4-horse stage coach was charged only 1s 3d. The Stirlingshire roads trust did not take in any part of the Edinburgh-Glasgow steamer route, but the Act it obtained in the same 1831 session boded ill for Ward's monopoly of Scottish roads in general. A Gurney-type vehicle would be charged £1 6s 3d as opposed to 5s for a stage coach.

Even more threatening was the Turnpike Tolls (Scotland) Bill, before the Commons that summer. Its purpose was laudable – to impose uniformity of tolls on all Scottish roads outside the Highlands. But it singled out steam carriages for specially heavy charges. The flat rate of 3s up to a weight of 24 hundredweight, and 2s per hundredweight thereafter, meant that a loaded Gurney-type vehicle would pay 12s 4d at every tollgate in the area covered – roughly treble the toll generally asked for horse vehicles of the same weight.

Joseph Dixon, M.P. for Glasgow, opposed the Bill in the House as being prohibitive of steamers. He declared that "the country suffered more from ignorant legislation than from any other cause", and that "to put a stop to such legislation was of more importance than the Reform Bill itself". Sir George Clerk (Edinburghshire) and Robert Cutler Ferguson (Kirkcudbright Stewartry) made the extraordinary claim that the toll scale was suggested by Gurney himself, "the inventor of the steam carriage", who regarded it as fair. Be that as it may, no more was heard of the Bill after August.

Ward's other roads, too, had suddenly become hostile places. From March, the Liverpool-Preston trust was free to demand 16s from a Gurney steamer weighing about 4 tons laden. It charged per wheel, on a rising scale tied to weight. A stage coach could pass for 2s. This trust lay on the Liverpool-Edinburgh road; but before a steamer from London got that far, it would have to run the gauntlet of the Liverpool-Prescot trust, on the London-Liverpool road. From July, this trust would be able to ask 1s 6d per horsepower for the tractor and 6d for the trailer. Since Gurney claimed only 12 nominal horsepower for his machine, he resented the trust's expressed intention to levy £1 8s 0d; but there was no universally accepted way of calculating horsepower, so the gatekeepers' charges would necessarily be arbitrary. Even the figure based on 12 h.p. – 10s 6d – was more than enough, compared with 6s for a 4-horse stage coach. From March, too, the Coventry-Over Whitacre trust, also on the London-Liverpool road, could exact 5s for eight wheels, compared with 1s for a stage coach.

In spite of all this, Ward professed continued confidence in the future of steam on the road, so long as prohibitory tolls were lifted. As late as 1833 he said that capital was ready and waiting in Scotland for a demonstration of the practicability of steam.

But it was Dance's defeat which lay at the root of the troubles now to overwhelm Gurney. Ward's retreat – the explosion, even – were apparently much less damaging to him. Ward's enterprise was so abortive that it may have been regarded simply as yet another Gurney setback of the long-familiar sort. The eyes of all interested parties were on the Gloucester-Cheltenham road, where an altogether more serious and successful trial of the Gurney steam carriage was in progress. When it ended in discomfiture for Dance, Gurney suffered a far greater misfortune, for Dance's retirement precipitated a general desertion from his ranks.

Bulnois withdrew when Dance did so; or rather, he lost interest and wrote off his investment – he never actually received any vehicles. Dobbyn pulled out too, and to him Gurney had to return £2000. Dobbyn and Stone subsequently crossed the Atlantic to try to interest the Americans in steam carriages.

Probably the worst financial blow to Gurney was the further disenchantment of William Hanning, his heaviest backer. Three of the eight carriages Hanning had ordered were tested prior to delivery, in incomplete form. They ran three or four times a day on the Finchley Road for three or four weekends, and beat the *Bedford Times* coach up Highgate Archway Hill. Then came the influx of hostile turnpike Bills. The stream of money that Hanning had been pouring into Gurney's coffers – said to be £10,000 in all, though declining since 1830 – now fell to a trickle.

A complete list of the reasons for the panic, admitted and otherwise, would probably be a lot longer. No doubt some of Dance's fellow-entrepreneurs were disheartened when they saw a service of the kind they hoped to imitate given a fair trial, and fail. How, then, could they succeed? No doubt, too, they were all impatient with Gurney,[40] and anxious (unless they were resigned) about their money. But the only reason given by anyone in the summer of 1831 was the "vast number" of discriminatory Acts passed or in the pipeline, and it is worthwhile seeing how well-founded it was. Ward had plenty of excuse for a persecution mania, but what of the others?

The 1830 figures showed a (so far) very limited and inconsistent attempt to discourage steam. The two sessions of 1831 offer a markedly different picture. Between December 1830 and August 1831, 76 turnpike Bills became law. Of these, 47 took cognisance of steam carriages – nearly two-thirds of the whole, or double the proportion and more than double the number of the previous year. This sharply increasing awareness of steam among trustees should not by itself have surprised the advocates of steam, or caused them resentment.

Far more significant was the proportion of these 47 Bills that discriminated against the new machines – or rather, against Gurney 8-wheeled tractor-and-trailer combinations in particular, which were the relevant vehicles. All but five of the 47 came under this heading. To put it another way, as far as Gurney's backers were concerned there were three times as many discriminatory tolls imposed in 1831 as in 1830. Of the 42, six including those on the Bathgate, Stirling, and Liverpool-Prescot roads, were clearly intended to be prohibitory by any standard, charging between £1 and £4 5s 0d for a Gurney-type steamer, as against 1s 3d to 6s for a 4-horse stage coach. These two figures were respectively for the Teignmouth-Dawlish roads trust and the Pucklechurch (or Lower District) roads trust. The Teignmouth-Dawlish trust administered roads leading into and out of Exeter that were on Hanning's London to Exeter and Plymouth route. The Pucklechurch trust administered part of Dance's route from Birmingham to Bristol. The sixth of these monstrous impositions was laid on the Laggan Bridge in Belfast, where there was no discernible threat from steam carriages. Five more trusts asked between 8s and 16s for a steamer, or four to eight times the toll for a stage coach. A total of 30 trusts out of 47 doubled or more than doubled the sum asked for a stage coach, when imposing tolls on Gurney-type vehicles.

The methods they used varied widely. The Liverpool–Prescot trust was unique at the time in charging by horsepower – an elastic yardstick that perhaps reflected public ignorance of steam rather than deliberate encouragement to gatekeepers to overcharge.[41] A Scottish trust made no bones about it – the toll was left to the gatekeeper's discretion, but the steam carriage driver had the option of paying 1d per hundredweight – a most confusing situation.

A few trusts betrayed their anxiety over road damage by gearing toll partly or wholly to weight. Some trusts specifically mentioned trailers as well as tractors; others dealt with them by charging by the wheel, or by levying toll on every vehicle propelled *or drawn* by steam. Another trust singled out steamers by making them pay each time they passed a gate – that is, on the return as well as on the outward journey, instead of once only, as with all other traffic.

If one looks at Dance's finances, it is easy to see how even a double toll might completely ruin an already uneconomic enterprise. Dance could not, in practice, afford to pay any tolls at all; but had he decided to fight on, his outgoings would have increased by £2 4s 0d every weekday: probably as much again as his total wages bill, or more than three times his fuel bill. Simply to absorb the tolls, Dance would have had to find 72 paying passengers a day, instead of 28, and he would still have been running at a massive loss. Alternatively, he could almost treble his fares, which would delight the coachmasters and amount to commercial suicide.

In these Acts there was, therefore, plenty of evidence to support the contention of Dance, Ward and the rest that they were facing sudden, intense and countrywide hostility. There is no evidence to suggest that the Bills were brought in deliberately and solely to kill steam.[42] Nor is there any evidence of a lobby. But it is difficult to avoid the conclusion that in 1831 it became customary to use renewal Bills brought in for other purposes as an opportunity to exclude the newcomer, especially on roads it directly threatened, rather than merely to make it pay its way. The new mood was perhaps motivated by the inauguration of Dance's service – the much-vaunted replacement for the stage coach had at last thrown down its challenge. Very few of the trusts can ever actually have collected the tolls on steamers, but if one is right in thinking that exclusion, rather than income, was their objective, they served their purpose.

What had been a series of skirmishes between road steamers and public opinion, fought largely on paper, or occasionally between drivers, had become a major battle when the trusts took the field. They were armed with Acts of Parliament – their only possible legal weapon, for they had no other way of altering toll schedules.

This "escalation" meant that Gurney and his friends had to adopt the same weapons if they were to survive. Gurney did not let himself be defeated. His retreating clients said that the punitive tolls had forced them out – logically, then, capital should again become available if the tolls were withdrawn. Ward had said as much. Dance, too, retained his faith in steam on the road, and Hanning had not entirely given up his support of Gurney's schemes – no doubt because he had poured so much money into them already. They were forced to fight on the trusts' political ground, but as we shall see, Gurney and his projects – or, more accurately, the steam carriage in general – had acquired some powerful friends on that ground.

Although – as usual – the activities of Gurney and his backers were the most prominent, they formed – as usual – only part of the picture of steam carriage endeavour. To understand the events of the coming year-long battle, and the attitudes of the combatants, it is helpful to see what else was going on while Dance was running his service, and during the struggle that followed. It may safely be assumed that these events made some mark.

By 1831 Ogle and Summers had a steamer on the road again – which may have been the first one remodelled. They provided much more information about this vehicle, though how much of it is reliable is doubtful. The machine was a self-contained 3-wheeler, carrying open "treble-bodied phaeton" coachwork, and weighing about 3 tons with fuel and water. Water capacity was increased to about 84 gallons, but this still only sufficed for 40 minutes' steaming. A bigger engine was fitted, giving 20 n.h.p. There was fan-induced draught to the furnace, and drive was direct – both conventional features, but the mechanism was sprung, an unusual refinement. From now on, the centre of Ogle's activities moves away from London to the Southampton area. It was probably from this time that his vehicles were made at the Millbrook Foundry, outside Southampton.

Ogle claimed that by August, he had made experimental runs totalling over 800 miles (including those with the first steamer), mostly on the London–Southampton road, and that no "serious" breakages had occurred. Tolls were not a hindrance. Ogle had encountered none on the roads he used near Southampton, though he had to pay at Hammersmith Bridge, and on Cambridge Heath near Hackney. But it was the manner of the steamers' going, rather than the distance covered, that sounded extraordinary. According to Ogle, his machine's greed for fuel had been dramatically reduced, to only three bushels – about 150 pounds – of coke per stage. If true, this figure is more in line with the known appetites of other steamers, but it is inconsistent with a bigger engine, greater power, and with the truly remarkable speeds claimed for the vehicle.

It had actually travelled at between 32 and 35 m.p.h., said its constructors, and could cruise for hours on end at 30 m.p.h. With a full load, it would exceed 24 m.p.h. The new steamer could stop in 12 feet from 10 m.p.h. with normal braking, or in 3 feet by reversing the engine. Thanks to this, a man who fell in front of the machine on Staines Bridge escaped unharmed. Phenomenal stopping ability was claimed by most steam promoters, to illustrate the safety of their vehicles, but in their speed claims, Ogle and Summers were in a class of their own.

One cannot say outright that they were liars, but their figures were highly improbable. We are contemplating a 3-wheeled, inherently unstable vehicle, and loose-surfaced, give-and-take roads. We are asked to believe that Ogle and Summers could achieve double the speeds of most other constructors, by simply enlarging the engine of an experimental machine that had earlier run no better or faster than most. When Ogle stops making general assertions and describes particular runs in detail, he becomes much more modest and, one feels, more realistic. On one occasion, his steamer carried "about" 19 passengers for $3\frac{1}{2}$ miles through the New Forest, at an average speed of nearly 10 m.p.h. – "we have whole families of ladies, day after day, out with us in all directions." Neither is it impossible that at another time, the vehicle, with 14 or 15 aboard, climbed a 1:6 gradient at Shirley at a fast walking pace. Much would depend on the length of the hill, for one thing: any steamer was capable of delivering a short-lived burst of power. Summers's next design was to be a big 4-wheeled coach with accommodation for 8 inside and 16 outside passengers. Its adventures, too, are known in detail, and reveal a machine of exceedingly limited capabilities.

Finally, the speed claims of Ogle and Summers are surrounded by so much boasting on other topics that they inevitably become tarred with the same brush. Ogle was on the point of establishing a steam carriage factory, on the grounds that steam railways were already obsolete, and because coachmasters had ordered "a great many" of his machines. As for other constructors, "the majority of the London engineers treated our opinions with ridicule, and were amazed at witnessing the vigour of our engines."

For all their rhetoric, Ogle and Summers helped during 1831 to publicise steam on the major roads from London, and in the capital itself. In a different and altogether more businesslike way, so did Walter Hancock. Not for him jolly Pickwickian outings to New Forest glades: he was moving in on the competitive, crowded roads of London's eastern suburbs. In early February 1831 – two weeks before Dance followed suit in the west – Hancock launched a regular public passenger service between Stratford and the City, via Bow.[43] He was confident enough to use only one steamer – the *Infant*.

Hancock's bus ran in stages of eight miles, carrying about 90 gallons of water, and using around two bushels of coke – about 100 pounds – per stage. In comparison with other constructors, Hancock was impressively sober and careful both in his *modus operandi* and in his accounts of his progress in steam; and there is no reason to doubt that this machine was twice as economical of fuel as Gurney's. Like all constructors, however, Hancock claimed perfect safety for his creation. He admitted that the chambers of his boiler could rupture – and it did so, 150 times in all, on his own admission – but even when four large holes resulted, there was no noise, and the machine just stopped. He said that he could halt it in 12 feet from 8 m.p.h., or in 4 feet by reversing the engines – and was very frequently obliged to do so by children running into the road in front. Perhaps the performance was helped by the contracting metal band brakes working on his rear tyres.

Hancock was not yet competing with omnibuses on the Stratford–London road, but with stage coaches. He charged the same fares – 9d to the City from Stratford, and 8d from Bow; or 2d a mile. There were no tolls on steamers on this road while he operated on it. But for one reason or another, a 10-passenger bus was obviously uneconomic, for at some date after early August, the *Infant* was converted to a 14-seater. At one point its engines were fully enclosed, to protect them from road dirt, and present as conventional an appearance as possible.

The battle to which these events were the background began on 7 July 1831, when Gurney, Dance and Hanning, probably the most influential of the promoters, drew up a petition to Parliament praying for a Bill to place steam carriages on the same toll footing as horsedrawn coaches. Gurney, as the petitioner, asked only for equal treatment. He and his clients realised that they could not realistically proclaim that steamers would drive out the stage coaches, the trusts' biggest source of income, and in the same breath expect them to continue free of toll. Aside from the financial interests at stake, all M.P.s were aware that the trusts were the instrument, however flawed, with which the nation's major roads were kept in repair, and that they must therefore be protected until such time as a better instrument were found.

The petition was presented to the Commons on 13 July by Colonel Robert Torrens, M.P. for Ashburton. Torrens was a respected political economist and publicist of the Adam Smith school, which favoured the replacement of muscle by machines. There was a brief debate. Torrens was supported by Joseph Hume, Member for Middlesex and a leading radical reformer, by John Wilks (Boston), another radical, and by George Dawson (Harwich Borough). Stuart Wortley (Bossiney) opposed the petition, on the grounds that steamers – he meant Gurney machines – damaged the roads disproportionately, having twice as many wheels as a horsedrawn coach. There was ignorance of even well-known and accepted mechanical principles. Sir Matthew Ridley (Newcastle-on-Tyne), a coal owner, disagreed with Torrens and Hume on the more rational grounds that, unlike stage coaches, steamers still paid no duty, so if competition were to be fair, they should pay some higher toll. This was a sentiment shared by coachmasters, and no doubt by trustees as well. Also, steamers frightened horses, so causing accidents, of which Ridley had seen "several". However, when Hume moved the appointment of a select committee to consider the whole question of steam on the road, this was agreed.

A week later another petition, originating with Walter Hancock, was presented to the Commons. It asked that "no excessive and prohibitory tolls on steam carriages may be allowed to be imposed by any turnpike Acts introduced into the House". There is no evidence of particular threats to the roads where Hancock was operating his service; perhaps he simply regarded his petition, which virtually duplicated Gurney's in intent, as a reinforcement of the Cornishman's campaign. It was clearly so regarded by Parliament – it was referred to the Gurney committee in August, and never mentioned again.

This is an appropriate moment at which to pause and look briefly at the nature of the people to whom Gurney and Hancock were addressing their petitions, and the workings of the institution in which they functioned, so as to arrive at a better understanding of what transpired. Out of 658 Commons seats in 1827, the great majority were occupied by M.P.s with landed interests. Even in 1833, after the passage of the Reform Bill had increased the franchise by half, landed M.P.s accounted for at least 60 per cent of the House. About 20 per cent of M.P.s were in business, and another 20 per cent in the professions. The picture changed only very gradually thereafter – hence the fact that until the trusts went into irrevocable decline at the end of the 1830s, individual turnpike trust Bills were still passed as a matter of routine.

But the sharing of a common interest by the majority of M.P.s did not mean that they necessarily spoke, voted or otherwise acted monolithically on this or any other issue. M.P.s' characteristics and behaviour at this period constantly confound crude attempts at pigeon-holing. Torrens represented a predominantly rural constituency, where the conservative landowning interest might be expected to rule, while Ridley sat for an industrial seaport where, in theory, Adam Smith's dicta should have held sway. The fact was that the trusts in urban areas were just as likely to suffer from a decline of coaching as those in the country – or were more likely to do so, as a sizeable town with several coaching roads radiating from it would contain several tollgates.

Still less did M.P.s display solidarity as Whigs or Tories. The Lords were altogether more homogeneous. The concept of party, party interest and party discipline was feeble, and growing feebler. Nor was party a reliable pointer to occupation. There were only marginally fewer landowners among the nominal Whigs than among the nominal Tories.

The attitude of the dominant political philosophy towards Parliament was fundamentally that of the late 18th century, even after 1832. Parliament was an aggregate of disparate interests. Good government was achieved if all of Disraeli's "variety of interests" had a voice at Westminster, and if each pursued its own ends as well as those of the nation as a whole. In aggregate, the private interest was to the public good. By "interest", in this context, was of course meant propertied interest. Property was still the generally accepted badge of excellence. Measures which protected and enhanced individual or corporate property, or wealth, tended to increase the nation's wealth. The Reform Bill, though hotly disputed by the more conservative representatives of the established, landed interest, merely brought the system up to date by allowing representation of the new manufacturing interest, who were also property-owners and major contributors to national wealth. The Bill could not have been passed without support from landowners pursuing the logic of the ruling philosophy.

Because each Member was held to represent his own and his constituents' interests, "private members could promote their own measures, vote largely as they chose, and overthrow governments."[44] Parliament dealt with such special and local interests by means of private Bills presented by private members representing those interests. Most legislation was of this nature. If it had very local and limited application – for example, a measure setting up a turnpike trust or a joint stock company – the Bill was classified as private. If they affected the general public – were matters of public interest – they were public Bills. Since the different 19th century measures promoting steam on the road clearly touched the public interest, Parliament treated them as public Bills.

The public Bill brought in by the government, rather than by a private M.P., was relatively rare and was as a rule reserved for matters of major national importance. It was not the proper function of government to legislate for the nation as a whole on other topics, which were best dealt with by private initiative. In this way, the British constitution was regarded as superior to the centralised despotisms of the Continent, such as France and Prussia.

An M.P. introducing a Bill into the Commons could do so either of his own volition, or at the instance of an outside party. The latter would draw up a petition, and a friendly Member would present the petition to the House, asking leave to bring in a Bill. There was no stigma attaching to Gurney's petition – it was expected that Parliament should be a forum for promoting private material interests. Not only were individual interests pursued; by the 19th century corporate interests, too, were being increasingly promoted by members and lobbyists – most notably (in the transport field) by the "canal" members, and in the coming decade by the "railway" members. These were M.P.s who were shareholders, and sometimes officers, of the companies concerned.

The petition would next be referred to a select committee of Members for detailed consideration and possible amendment. It was generally held that the M.P.s best qualified to serve on committees were those who represented the interests at stake, or had the most knowledge of the subject in hand.[45] For this reason alone, friends of the petitioner tended to be heavily represented on a committee. Furthermore, the M.P.s who presented and supported a petition did their best to pack the committee with friendly faces, including their own, and were sometimes called as witnesses even when serving on the committee themselves. If the committee was biased in favour of the petition, the witnesses it called before it showed the same partiality.

However, in the case of a public Bill there could be a countervailing influence. Private Bills might or might not be examined in detail in the House, but in any case only by the dubious instrument of the select committee. On the other hand, public Bills, if they escaped scrutiny by a select committee, would invariably be put before either House of Parliament sitting as a committee – a committee of the whole House, which necessarily reflected a wider spectrum of interests than any select committee. Some public Bills were subjected to examination by both kinds of committee.

The narrowness of the interests of most backbench M.P.s showed in their silence, except on occasions when they saw them seriously threatened. On other subjects, they probably had no views. It is not surprising that over half rarely or ever spoke, and that the landowners in the Commons spoke least of all. This was perhaps because they were confident in their majority, and in the power of the Lords – where they were most strongly represented – to look after their joint interests.

The brief of the committee that began its deliberations on 3 August was "to enquire into and report upon the proportion of tolls which ought to be imposed upon coaches and other vehicles propelled by steam or gas upon turnpike roads; and also to enquire into and report upon the rate of toll actually levied ... and to enquire generally into the present state and future prospects of land carriage by means of such wheeled vehicles, and to report upon the probable utility which the public may derive therefrom".

The 30-strong committee was chaired by Charles Jephson, Member for Mallow, Co. Cork, who had no detectable connection with the interests of the petitioner, but became one of his supporters. Of the other members, five could be counted upon to support a Bill. They were Colonel Torrens, Joseph Hume, John Wilks, Joseph Dixon[46] and Davies Gilbert, Member for Bodmin. Gilbert was a distinguished engineer who in his time had been an associate of Telford, Trevithick and Sir Humphry Davy, and a President of the Royal Society. He sat on many committees concerned with the arts and sciences.

Reformers, whether radical or liberal, generally tended to favour steam, so likely supporters of the Bill included Henry Warburton (Bridport), the radical friend of Joseph Hume and other reformers, George Sinclair (Caithness), Edward Ruthven (Downpatrick), Thomas Lennard (Maldon), Edward Pendarves (Cornwall West), Frederick Mullins (Co. Kerry), Lord Oxmantown (King's County), Sir Richard Musgrave (Waterford), Edward Petre (Ilchester) and Samuel Bayntun (York). Politics aside, men of progressive economic, industrial and agrarian views were also more likely than not to support steam. Members of the committee under this heading included John Benett (Wiltshire), Thomas Hodges (Kent) and William Wolryche Whitmore (Bridgnorth).

John Lee Lee, member for Wells, was the son of William Hanning, which implied an acquaintance with steam on the road, if not necessarily support for it. Two committee members could be counted on for objectivity, at least. One was William Alexander Mackinnon, M.P. for Lymington. He was a conscientious committee worker whose concerns were the turnpike trusts, public health, the patent laws, and social reform in general. The other was Charles Shaw-Lefevre, Member for Hampshire, later Speaker of the House of Commons, and finally Viscount Eversley. He chaired several committees in his time. Strong of character, fair by nature, and typically a man of few words in the House, he was said to represent the best type of independent country M.P. His family name will crop up again in this account.

Sir Matthew Ridley was against a Bill. Of the rest, there were two known conservatives on the committee – Sir George Clerk, Under Secretary at the Home Office, and Sir George Staunton (Heytesbury) – as well as four "doubtfuls", including Sir Thomas Frankland Lewis, a former Secretary of the Treasury and Vice President of the Board of Trade, and Craven Fitzhardinge Berkeley, Member for Cheltenham. Berkeley was regarded as a reformer, but the fact remains that turnpike trust interests in his constituency obtained an Act hostile to Sir Charles Dance.

Nothing can be ascertained of the actual or probable opinions of the other two members of the committee; but those likely to oppose the Bill were already vastly outnumbered. If confirmation of the committee's bias were needed, it could be found in the names of the witnesses called. Among them were both Torrens and Gilbert,

Gurney, his champion Alexander Gordon, Hancock, Ogle, Summers, Dance's manager James Stone, and the engineer Joseph Gibbs, who said he was building a steam carriage. All had the most unambiguous interest in a Bill. John Farey, a steam engineer of repute, had acted as consultant to Gurney, Hancock and Heaton, while the doyen of the profession, Richard Trevithick, had been responsible for the first British road steamer, and said that he "had it in contemplation to do a great deal on common roads".

Three of the nation's most eminent highway engineers were also called. They were Thomas Telford, who came to favour steam on the road above steam on railways; John Macneil, Telford's assistant engineer on the Holyhead road; and James McAdam, John Loudon's eldest son, surveyor to part of the Holyhead road and general surveyor to the metropolis roads. All these men were believers in the doctrine of adapting roads to traffic and not vice versa, so would have no bias against steam on technical grounds. All three were officers of trusts, and McAdam was also a trustee; but all were primarily engineers, concerned with the technicalities, economics and administration of road building and repair, rather than with the more parochial, yet in a sense wider, issues that exercised the average trustee – the close relationship of a trust with the interests of the neighbouring country and people. There was no witness to put forward such a man's fears for his trust's coaching revenue and for local agriculture; nor was there any witness to represent the coachmasters, or the interests more or less dependent upon them.

Within these limitations, the committee did a painstaking job, and pursued its inquiries in great detail. It carefully investigated objections to steam on the grounds of noise, smoke, steam, sparks, danger from explosions, and controllability. Most particularly, the committee concerned itself with possible damage to roads, its members returning again and again to this point. Many were probably trustees themselves, but whatever their personal opinions, the questioners no doubt realised that the committee must be seen to have dealt fairly with objections – especially the last – if their report were to be received with favour by a House in which landowners and trusts were so heavily represented.

Although theory said that interest and specialised knowledge served a committee best, it is probable that in practice the members of this committee took a detached view of the testimony of the steam promoters. Those whose names we know were very far from fools. They are likely to have been impressed by the measured opinions of men of the calibre of Torrens, Telford, McAdam and Macneil, whose evidence, even on the printed page, comes across with far more authority than do the sometimes confused or patently inaccurate assertions of Gurney,[47] or the megalomaniac hyperbole of Ogle.

Questioned on the effect of steam carriages on road surfaces, the three highway engineers were careful to say that they had no personal experience of the subject. But all thought it likely, on balance, that less damage would result than from stage coaches. Telford added that if this turned out to be so, steamers should pay less toll, not more. Macneil considered that fears of damage were exaggerated, while McAdam said outright that he would prefer steamers to horsedrawn vehicles.

No doubt to the dismay of the promoters, Farey said that none of the steamers on the road, least of all Gurney's, was ready for commercial use; but he added that discriminatory tolls increased the chances of their eventual failure, and claimed that unlike stage coaches, they had the advantage of being as cheap to run fast as slowly.

One gets the feeling that Trevithick, old, ill, *passé*, and concerned mainly with talking about his latest steam engine design, was trundled in as a polite gesture to an ancient and revered national monument, who could hardly be ignored on such an occasion – certainly he was little questioned. But he did his best to help the petitioner by declaring that steam carriages would do all that horses could.

Torrens, the political economist, spoke last, bringing to bear arguments from the national interest that rose impressively above special and sectional concerns. He echoed and amplified the case first put forward by John Herapath in *The Times*, and since reiterated by Sir Charles Dance.[48] He concentrated, wisely, on what he claimed were the economic benefits to the nation in general, and to agriculture in particular, to be expected from steam road transport. Torrens pointed out the advantages of the greater speed and cheapness of passenger travel, confidently expected from steam; but he was concerned mainly with the economics of the carriage of goods to market. Road steamers had not yet been used for this purpose, but if they were, the reason would be their economy. The savings in fodder costs would increase farmers' profits, and thus landlords' rent rolls. This would allow hitherto unprofitable land to be exploited; and more capital and labour could be devoted to land already cultivated. This was a well-known principle of agricultural improvement – a subject in the forefront of the minds of progressive landowners country-wide.

If agricultural products were brought more cheaply to market, the whole national economy would benefit. Food prices could be reduced, real wages would go up, and trade would grow. Profits in commerce and manufacture would increase, encouraging industry, making Britain's export prices more competitive, expanding the demand for labour, and so, ultimately, creating new demand for human foodstuffs. This would outweigh the initial fall in demand for fodder, pasture and labour arising from the introduction of steam. In any case, the replacement of horses by mechanical transport would be gradual, not – as the steam promoters suggested – sudden, so early losses would be cushioned by an overlap with incoming benefits.

On the whole, the promoters of the petition had every reason to be satisfied with the committee's performance. No witness could in honesty do more than guess at the consequences of steam on the road, which was an obvious weakness of all the arguments in its favour, but the more prominent and distinguished between them said as much as could be said to placate the agricultural and turnpike interests. The possible effect of steam on stage coaches and turnpike income was successfully glossed over – this was an issue to be avoided, if possible, by steam's supporters. It is noticeable that not one of the trust officers or trustees on the committee brought it up. The tenor of the committee's report, presented to the House on 12 October, was predictable:

> These enquiries have led the committee to believe that the substitution of inanimate for animal power, in draught on common roads, is one of the most important improvements in the means of internal communication ever introduced. Its practicability they consider to have been fully established; its general adoption will take place more or less rapidly in proportion as the attention of scientific men shall be drawn by public encouragement to further improvement.

The crucial words were "by public encouragement". There were two main obstacles to the steam carriage. One was "the prejudices which have always beset a new invention", to be overcome only by "a long course of successful, though probably unprofitable, experiment". The other was excessive tolls, brought about by the determination of the trusts to obstruct steam, and their misunderstanding of its effect on the roads.

Discriminatory tolls could be justified by a reduction in the number of stage coaches resulting from steam – unlikely at present, in the committee's view – or by any additional outlay on road maintenance that it caused. The evidence suggested that, if anything, the expense would be less. "The tolls enforced on steam carriages, have, in general, far exceeded the rate which their injuriousness to roads, in comparison with other carriages, would warrant."

Steam carriages were perfectly safe – safer than horsed vehicles –

and would cause no nuisance once all were properly constructed. They were already capable of carrying 14 or more passengers at an average speed of 10 m.p.h., and would become faster and cheaper than stage coaches – but only if tolls were not set so high as to prohibit their use. The committee recommended, therefore, that "legislative protection should be extended to steam carriages with the least possible delay". Specifically, all existing unfavourable tolls on them should be suspended for three years, and a single, reasonable, universally applicable scale of tolls imposed.

In spite of the absence of what would nowadays be regarded as a fair representation of all interests involved, the committee had produced what was, in the circumstances, a reasonably balanced report. They were acutely aware of their own ignorance and that of others, and were not carried away by the over-enthusiasm of witnesses such as Gurney and Ogle. While influenced by the promoters to the extent of taking a rather rosy view of steam's existing virtues and ultimate potential, the committee was realistic and cautious as far as its immediate future was concerned, knowing that these machines were still far from perfect, and needed more time for development. In view of the then current state of the railways, they cannot, with the benefit of hindsight, be blamed for their over-optimism concerning the more distant prospects of steam on the road.

The danger of projecting a certain pattern of behaviour from a particular set of interests is well illustrated by the progress of the subsequent Toll Relief Bill, "to regulate for five years road tolls on steam carriages".[49] Drafted by Jephson, Davies Gilbert and Torrens, it was presented to the Commons by the last-named on 19 March 1832.

The drafters envisaged, by implication, private carriages or "motor cars", which had been projected but not so far built; and they took Torrens' point by allowing for goods vehicles, which with the exception of Heaton's were in the same state. The Bill proposed that all existing tolls on steam should be suspended for the period mentioned, so as to allow legislators time to gain the experience of the new vehicle that they so obviously lacked, without its being driven off the road meanwhile.

Steam passenger vehicles carrying a maximum of six people – in effect, not coaches or buses, but cabs or private carriages – should pay toll at the same rate as a 4-wheeled, 2-horse vehicle, and the rest at the rate of a 4-horse coach. No extra toll would be demanded for a passenger trailer, but the sum would be doubled if the wheels had conical instead of cylindrical bearing surfaces – the former doing more damage to roads – or if tyre width was less than $3\frac{1}{2}$ inches. A steam goods wagon with a 1-ton load would be charged the same toll as a cart drawn by one horse. For every further ton, as much again would be asked. No extra charge would be made for a single goods trailer, but 50 per cent of the toll would be payable on each additional trailer. Fines would be imposed for levying excessive tolls.

In theory, there was a large majority of M.P.s in the Commons likely to oppose the Bill. Steam carriages conflicted with agricultural, horse-breeding and trust interests; but members were now being asked to approve a measure which might damage these interests, by turning the precarious finances of the coachmasters into insolvency. It was a measure, furthermore, which would increase central government control at the expense of local and sectional authority.

Yet the Commons passed the Bill without a fight. There was no debate. It went before a committee of the whole House on 4 April, when a handful of insubstantial amendments were incorporated. On 9 April the Bill had its third reading, and went to the Lords. On account of this taciturnity, which was normal, one can only guess at the reasons. It is certain only that many M.P.s of the landed interest must have behaved so as to confound generalisations about their motivation. Respect for the committee's authority, and for that of select committees in general, may have weighed with some of them; so might the widespread lack of sympathy with the trusts' notorious inability to manage their own affairs, and a corresponding unwillingness to let any extend their influence. Perhaps some M.P.s, like some coachmasters, felt that steam carriages could never succeed, so were not worth powder and shot. Others, conversely, may have thought that steam on the road was preferable to steam on rails, and should be given a chance of pre-empting it. These would have marked the lessons of the Liverpool and Manchester Railway, which had been lethal to competing stage coaches, and the cause of far more disturbance and damage to land than any road vehicle could possibly inflict. It is possible, too, that some M.P.s were impressed with Hancock's ability to run a safe public service without, it seemed, arousing opposition from trusts or other local interests, or being harassed by discriminatory tolls.[50] Members may also have been influenced by Torrens's economic arguments, coming at a time when high food prices and unemployment were fuelling political unrest.

The Bill gave the steam carriage promoters everything they could reasonably expect. Gurney and his backers were at the high point of their achievement. But the decisive stage of this encounter between steam and the trusts was yet to come. On 27 June the Bill came before the Lords for its second reading, and was referred (together with a copy of the Commons report) to a select committee. Of its 15 members, five were known to be conservatives, or like Lord Salisbury and

Lord Wharncliffe (formerly Stuart Wortley, M.P. for Bossiney) were opponents of steam. Three were known social and political reformers, as in the case of the Earl of Radnor, or were favourably inclined towards steam carriages.[51] Goldsworthy Gurney, Walter Hancock and John Farey were called as witnesses when the committee met in July. Beyond names, nothing is known about it. No minutes of evidence or report were published. One may take it, however, that the committee's bias was against steam, for the Bill was subsequently thrown out by the Lords.

The responses of the Lords had proved much more predictable than those of the Commons. There, at least, the landowners were strong, homogeneous and conservative enough to defeat what they clearly regarded as an attack on their interests, and, perhaps, on the interests of good government.

Meanwhile Gurney's activities, manufacturing and entre-preneurial, had been frozen since the previous June, awaiting Parliament's decision. All his own money was gone. He could not move without outside finance, which would not flow while the discriminatory tolls were in force. The flood of fresh ones had not slackened. In the 1832 session – between February and early July – 52 turnpike Acts became law. Of these, an unprecedentedly high proportion – 39, or three-quarters – took cognisance of steam. All but seven Acts discriminated against it. There were no monstrous tolls, as there had been in 1831, perhaps because the experience of the Cheltenham roads trust had shown them to be unnecessary, but of the 32 discriminatory Acts, 23 charged Gurney-type vehicles between two and eight times the toll asked of stage coaches.

The *Mechanics' Magazine* reacted badly to the latest moratorium on Gurney's projects. Under the heading "Steam Travelling under a Cloud", it said: "There seems to be much mystery about this gentleman's proceedings; if half of what has been asserted of his invention had been true, our roads would by this time have been covered with self-propelled vehicles." The same old story seemed to be repeating itself.

In fact, it was being heard almost for the last time. When the reaction of the Lords was known, overturning the Commons decision, what was left of Gurney's little empire fell apart. The capitalists finally lost interest. Hanning furnished no more money. His eight part-finished vehicles were broken up, and in July the bits were auctioned off, at a loss, together with the rest of Gurney's business assets. It seems that Gurney had spent some of his own money on the Hanning machines, on top of Hanning's contribution, for he complained of the latter's failure to compensate him.

Even now, however, Gurney did not give up all hope. On 29 April 1834, he petitioned the Commons again[52] for the repeal of the discriminatory Acts. He set out in detail his work on steam carriages, and declared that if the Acts were not repealed, all the money he had spent would be irretrievably lost, and he would be ruined. Gurney claimed that between 1825 and 1832 he had spent and lost £10,000 of his own money, together with £16,000 invested by his friends, and the proceeds of the sale of licences, building contracts, and shares of his patents amounting to another £20,000. He reckoned his potential loss – the returns he could expect from mileage royalties and so forth – to be an additional £232,000.

The select committee appointed to consider the petition included men who were personal supporters of Gurney, as well as of road steamers in general. Among them was Sir William Molesworth, the radical Member for East Cornwall, who both presented the petition and chaired some meetings of the committee. On presenting the petition, he declared with more enthusiasm than accuracy that the petitioner was "the first person who succeeded in effecting locomotion by steam on common roads", and that the petition's rejection would be "an injustice which [he] confidently hoped would not be sanctioned by a reformed Parliament". Charles Jephson, who had chaired the 1831 committee and sat on the new one, said that Gurney was "a man entitled to the best consideration of the House".

Sir George Cayley, too, supported the petition. This wealthy Yorkshire squire, M.P. for Scarborough, had already evinced an interest in steam carriages. The then still-unrecognised pioneer of heavier-than-air flight was best known at this time as a brilliant, versatile and public-spirited amateur engineer and philanthropist. Any word of his on Gurney's behalf would carry weight. He was a friend of the petitioner, and the two men encouraged one another in their pursuit of technical knowledge. Cayley asserted that "by Parliament [Gurney] had been wronged, and by Parliament he ought to be redressed".

Jephson's and Cayley's words were echoed by Edward Stillingfleet Cayley, the Member for the North Riding of Yorkshire, who took a strong interest in social and economic improvements in both agriculture and industry. Furthermore, Cayley, like Molesworth, chaired some meetings of the committee, so he, too, was in a position to influence it in the petitioner's favour. William Peter, the reforming member for Bodmin, referred to the petitioner as "a man of great merit, whose public services should meet with signal encouragement". There were no dissentient voices.

But this did not save Gurney from facing some searching questions, which he did not handle well. He emphasised, as the root cause of his disasters in the summer of 1831, the dire effect on his backers of the imminence of prohibitory tolls, particularly those affecting Dance, which started the rot. To illustrate trust hostility, Gurney made much of the "filled-up" road incident, the consequent damage to the steamer, and the alleged threats of a "tickler from London".

Some, at least, of the committee were unimpressed. They did not believe that the coming tolls were responsible for Dance's retreat, and clearly regarded them as an excuse. Although the committee conceded that the trusts were hostile to steam, they called the broken axleshaft an "accident", making it obvious that as far as they were concerned, malice aforethought could be ruled out.

The committee had evidence before them to suggest that Dance had been losing money. They suggested, furthermore, that the retreating capitalists lacked confidence in Gurney's vehicles. No such sentiments were expressed by the former backers in their testimony to the committee, but Gurney himself admitted that he was no engineer. His friend Alexander Gordon said, furthermore, that he did not employ the best engineers, workmen, or tools, or have enough capital. Dr Dionysius Lardner, a well-known populariser of science for the layman, and a prolific writer on the subject at all levels, was also a Gurney supporter, but agreed with Gordon on the amateurishness of all constructors. Such criticism from such quarters may well have encouraged the committee in their surprising conclusion, even though Gurney's steamers were as reliable as most.

Perhaps, too, Gurney's customary overstatement of his case lost him sympathy. Probably in an attempt to make trust reaction appear more violent than it was, he claimed that all the discriminatory Bills of the 1831 session were brought in after Dance's service had been running for three months, which was demonstrably untrue. He said that between 1831 and the time he was speaking, 150 "prohibitory" tolls had come into force. This was a misleadingly comprehensive adjective. In fact the total of *discriminatory* Acts in the period was 132. How many of these were in practice prohibitory was a matter of conjecture, depending principally on the circumstances of individual operators of steam carriages. Running a commercial service could be uneconomic even if no tolls were imposed, as Dance had shown. In such a case, they made a losing situation intolerable, but were not by themselves prohibitory. Private, experimental journeys, on the other hand, which were far more numerous, were never stopped by tolls.

Gurney exaggerated the tolls demanded by some trusts, accusing the Teignmouth–Dawlish trust of charging £2 2s 0d for one of his carriages. It is hard to reconcile this with a toll schedule called for 6d per wheel up to one ton, and 6d per wheel per ton thereafter. He claimed that no less that £8 8s 0d was demanded by the Pucklechurch trustees; but this does not square with a toll of 1s per hundredweight. In both cases, one assumes a laden weight of 4 tons or a little over. To put it as kindly as possible, Gurney had not checked his facts.

Finally, the committee must have been impressed by the procession before them of the unfortunates, or their representatives, who had lost money in Gurney's schemes. Dance and Dobbyn were abroad, but Ward and Bulnois gave figures, as did William Hanning's solicitor (Hanning himself having died in the interim).

In their report, however, the committee were as fair to Gurney as could be expected. They distinguished between the immediate circumstances of his failure, and the significance of his work as a whole. They recognised this as fundamentally important to the steam carriage – Gurney had turned machines that had been for practical purposes useless into a new class of road traffic taken seriously by highway authorities, eminent engineers, and government ministers. They foresaw – rightly, as it turned out – that his petition, which they supported, might get nowhere. As alternatives, they recommended an extension of his patent rights, free of charge, for a further 14 years (which would be valuable if the petition succeeded and the discriminatory tolls were lifted), or purchase of the patent by the state for at least £5000 by way of compensation for his losses. It was hardly likely that they would recommend a grant of all Gurney had lost – even the great McAdam was never fully compensated for all his personal expenses, and died poor.

There is no record of Gurney receiving any money. He was in good company. The more deserving, if equally improvident George Shillibeer, who ruined himself while introducing a valuable public service, did not get a penny from the state, though promised £5000 and a place by the government of the time. Gurney may have opted for the extension of his patent, though if so, any record of this has been lost. The patent might yet regain its value, for, as will be seen, attempts to suppress discriminatory tolls continued to be made in Parliament until 1839.

No doubt for this reason, Gurney continues to be heard from, if only from the wings. In his evidence to the 1834–5 committee, he said that he wanted to take up steam carriages again, and that he had contracts to build them for the London to Exeter and Plymouth, and Bristol to Exeter and Plymouth roads; but tolls on these roads were heavy. No other details were given. In 1836 he was under contract to build carriages for the Devonport, Plymouth and Exeter Steam Carriage Company. But as the tolls remained in force, the contracts can never have been worth more than the paper they were written on; and Gurney was mentioned no more as a participant in new projects. He put no new vehicle on the road after 1831 – not even the small private carriages he was planning that summer.

The last detectable references to what appears to have been a Gurney vehicle date from 1840, and struck an appropriately melancholy note. On 21 October that year Thomas Wadeson, Sir George Cayley's chief engineer, is reported as taking a machine of Gurney type from Cayley's premises off Millbank in London on a run to Hounslow. On Vauxhall Bridge Wadeson – who was steering – swerved to avoid a fallen boy, ran on to what was probably a pile of road metal, and damaged the steering. Later, in Sloane Street, Wadeson lost control of the vehicle – no doubt because of the defective steering – and crashed through a jeweller's shop window. Wadeson's leg was trapped between the steamer and the window frame, and though the injury was slight, he died of infection five days later.

The reference to a machine of Gurney type in the lay press means nothing on its own, since Gurney was the best-known constructor, but its association with Cayley suggests that this was, indeed, a Gurney-built vehicle left over from the palmy days of 1831. Although by 1840 steamers had lost their old prominence, the inquest jury's verdict reflected enduring popular prejudice. To show their disapproval of what they regarded as dangerous vehicles on the public roads, they imposed a deodand of £10. A deodand, traditionally the proceeds of the law's confiscation and sale of an article that had caused death, by now customarily took the form of a fine on the owner in lieu.

Gurney reverted to his former role of a man of many interests, seemingly without bitterness. He concerned himself mainly with responsibility for the lighting and ventilation of the rebuilt House of Commons. A stove he designed was installed in his lifetime "in almost every cathedral, church and large building in the country".[53] He was knighted in 1863 for his services to science, and died 12 years later at the ripe age of 82. In 1892 his devoted daughter Anna unveiled a stained glass window to his memory in St Margaret's Church, Westminster, in the shadow of the Abbey.

At the time of Gurney's retirement from the steam carriage scene, there was fundamental disagreement in engineering quarters over the value of his contribution to it. Like Gurney himself, opinions went to extremes. "He has left the matter of steam travelling on common roads where he found it", claimed the *Mechanics' Magazine*, with manifest injustice. Francis Maceroni, who could at times be both offensive and misleading on the subject of other constructors, including Gurney, said that his vehicles "ran so as most satisfactorily to resolve the problem of steam carriage travelling on common roads" – an equally obvious exaggeration. The judgement of the 1834–5 committee was the most fair. Gurney was "the first man to apply steam carriages successfully to common roads". Interpreted in one way, this disregards Trevithick's work; but it rightly acknowledges Gurney's pioneer role in carrying the new vehicle beyond the realms of pure experiment. This was his achievement – to demonstrate that the road steamer was potentially, if not actually, a practical commercial proposition. Before his time, no one was justified in making such a claim. Afterwards, it was clear for all to see.

3

The End of the Steam Coach, the Beginning of the Motor Car, 1831–42

In June 1832 a battle had been lost, but for all the steam promoters except Gurney, the war was far from over. The old campaigners fought on, and new ones, undiscouraged by the Lords decision, entered the fray. During the remainder of 1832, however, activity was slow to build up. The recorded journeys were few; but one of these made up for the lack of numbers with sheer spectacle.

In their latest device, a self-contained 4-wheeled coach, Ogle and Summers set out in the summer of 1832 on an experimental trip from Southampton to London via Liverpool – the most ambitious run so far attempted by anybody. With 24 people on board at the start and luggage for 16, the vehicle weighed over 6 tons; but at least both engine and body were now sprung.

Even the most circumstantial and least prejudiced account of the journey is a chapter of accidents. The first 14 miles, from Millbrook, outside Southampton, to Winchester, were covered in good style in 67 minutes, "with steam blowing off at both the valves", which cannot have endeared the machine to the public. A hundred buckets of water were needed to refill the tank at Speenhamland, outside Newbury. Then, on a hill, the coach ran away when its shoe drag failed. The block brake with which the steamer was also fitted was seemingly of no avail. Out of control, it is alleged to have covered a mile in 70 seconds, or an average of over 51 m.p.h. for the distance. Whatever the speed actually reached, the driver for once found no pleasure in it – "the steering at that speed required from Mr Ogle the greatest attention." One can well believe it. Subsequently an axleshaft broke, and the boiler was damaged from overheating, presumably a result of tubes running dry.

At Trentham, seat of the Marquess of Stafford, that aged but enlightened nobleman's agent supplied "some good coke". Over the $3\frac{1}{2}$ miles between Knutsford and Hoo Green, the coach was said to have attained a speed of more than 38 m.p.h. – a typically improbable

Ogle-type assertion. At Liverpool, the directors of the Liverpool and Manchester Railway asked permission to examine the vehicle. There the attempt ended; the boiler was again damaged by overheating, and tubes had ruptured. Throughout, Ogle had suffered from lack of fuel and water supplies, in common with other constructors. For lack of coke, he sometimes had to burn coal, which made smoke.

Neither friends nor enemies did anything to improve Ogle's image on this occasion. A brief and incredibly naive panegyric appeared in the *Saturday Magazine* for 6 October, referring to the "Triumph of Science in Mechanics" illustrated by the vehicle, and to its ability to reach 100 m.p.h., admittedly downhill. Even Ogle must have been satisfied with that tribute; though the story also gives a normal maximum of 14 m.p.h., which is rather more convincing.

Francis Maceroni's tongue spared Ogle and Summers less than any other constructors. He said that the luckless pair had taken five or six days to reach their starting point from London–a distance of 75 miles. The trip itself occupied 10 *weeks*, and the return from Liverpool to London another 16 days. The 13 miles from Birmingham to Wolverhampton took $6\frac{1}{4}$ hours. Maceroni quoted from a letter received from a witness to the steamer's arrival at an engineering shop at Hurley, near Marlow; "A great unwieldy monster arrived in a most terribly crippled state . . . they entirely emptied our well in filling their boiler." When the coach set out at last, it stopped "every 20 yards". The witness concluded: "If this is a specimen of steam coaches, I have quite done with them." Maceroni is often so full of bile as to make him highly unreliable as a reporter, but it is clear that the expedition was a disaster for Ogle and Summers, and incidentally did nothing to enhance the road steamer's reputation. Ogle henceforth operated less ambitiously, and received little publicity: the symptom of burned fingers.

During 1832 Walter Hancock was – as usual – more successful than anyone else, and – again, as usual – made less fuss about it. There is no evidence of his running a service, but he was active in experimental work. The year 1832, furthermore, marked a new departure for him: he began to build steamers for other than his own use. The venture was unrewarding; Hancock learned lessons in 1832–3 that turned him into an outspoken apostle of independence. Unlike Gurney, he said afterwards, his practice was to use only his own capital to build his vehicles; and then he spent a mere quarter of the Cornishman's total outlay, even though each carriage cost between £700 and £1100 to construct. He also preferred to operate his own machines, rather than build them for others to work. This is hardly surprising – with a single exception, no promoters of joint stock companies interested in using his vehicles ever ran a service with them, and the exception – Hancock claimed – was a fraud.

Hancock's earliest unfortunate experience was with a flotation called the London and Brighton Steam Carriage Company, which seems never to have got off the ground. In 1832 Hancock constructed a 3½-ton vehicle called the *Era* for that company; the first time he had built a steamer for other interests. The *Era*, which carried a double body like a French *diligence*, or first-class railway carriage of the time, made some trial trips, including one to Windsor, but was never delivered. It is last heard of destined for a London–Greenwich service, also to be run by the London and Brighton company, but nothing came of that either.

In February 1833, a concern called the London and Paddington Steam Carriage Company was floated, the first serious attempt to challenge the London horse bus on its home ground. In 1832 Hancock began to build a new bus for the company. Its chequered history belongs almost entirely to the following year, for it was under construction during the whole of 1832.

Unlike the *Era*, the *Infant* omnibus did go to Brighton, as a demonstration to the London and Brighton promoters. By this time (31 October 1832) it was a much-altered design – "a thing of shreds and patches", as the *Journal of Elemental Locomotion* put it; but the same source regarded its springing as excellent. Noted also was the 40-foot rubber hose with which water was ingeniously pumped to the vehicle by the action of the engine. One mile was covered at 17 m.p.h. Some coke depots were placed in position, but not enough of them, and fuel ran short. On the return journey a wheel broke up, necessitating a halt at Salford Mill, 22 miles from home. These were routine troubles.

Less normal and more ominous was the later discovery of a 50-yard stretch of Streatham Hill covered 6 inches deep in road metal, "to prevent the return of the steam carriage". The reporter knew the name of the person responsible, and quoted his actual words, though did not identify him. The attempt was not successful. No one made a great to-do about it, presumably because (unlike in 1831) there were no major material interests or moral issues at stake at this time and place. It seems that at some time in the year, the *Infant* was also run on the Harrow Road.

Steam activity had been so muted in the second half of 1832 that it was being said in October that "there does not exist at this moment in Great Britain a single public road upon which a conveyance is carried on by steam at even the ordinary moderate velocities." Perhaps this was because most constructors were absorbing the shock of their Parliamentary defeat, and gathering their strength.

This strength was far from negligible. Indeed, rather than being weakened, steam was in some ways stronger in 1833–4 than it had been before its setback. These were years of unprecedented activity on the part of constructors, with three operators running scheduled services at different times, on roads unencumbered by crippling tolls, and joint stock companies constantly being floated to raise capital. It was estimated that, by the end of 1833, 19 road steamers were already in existence or were being built in London and its vicinity alone, 14 of them experimental. If true, this is a remarkable picture, in view of the 1832 Lords decision, and deserves investigation.

The partisans of steam could draw encouragement from three quarters. In the first place, road steamers had found sympathisers in the government, even before the Commons were reformed, and even with the Lords (from which the administration was largely drawn) hostile to them as a body. These well-wishers did not regard steam with sufficient favour to bring in a government Bill to rescue it – this would have been wholly out of character with the dominant philosophy of government – but the Toll Relief Bill having been defeated, they tried to give alternative support in a practical way.

The Stage Coaches Bill before Parliament in June 1832 proposed to abolish existing taxes on stage coaches and impose new ones, at the same time taxing the new railways and steam carriages. In July, Joseph Dixon presented a petition from the Glasgow and Garnkirk Railway Company to exempt all steam from the proposed tax, which as far as stage coaches and steam carriages were concerned, would comprise a licence fee and a mileage duty. Other supporters of steam rallied round – Charles Jephson and Joseph Hume both favoured the petition, saying that such a tax would be ruinous, and should at least be deferred for four or five years. Another supporter was the radical Henry Warburton.

The opposition made no distinction between steam on the road and on the railway, either. Sir Charles Burrell, Member for Shoreham and a supporter of the stage coach interest, declared that if a tax were levied on horse coaches, steam should be taxed as well – and anyway, steam carriages were "very dangerous". Thomas Spring Rice, Member for Cambridge, and a popular moderate reformer, feared that if steam drove out the stage coach, as had happened on the Liverpool to Manchester line of road, and it was not taxed, the lost revenue would not be replaced. These financial arguments were plausible. Lord Althorp, the reforming Chancellor of the Exchequer, said that he had corresponded with steam carriage proprietors, and that they did not oppose a tax. This would have been in line with their policy of not seeking favoured treatment; though it is hard to see how, in practice, they could have contemplated further financial burdens that included duty of 1d to 4d per mile according to capacity.

Dixon and Hume returned to the fray when the Stage Coaches Bill was debated in August. Dixon proposed an amendment exempting steam carriages from tax. That redoubtable eccentric Colonel Charles Sibthorp, Member for Lincoln, saw rural unemployment resulting from steam, and therefore an increased burden of poor rates on his constituents: "The use of vehicles impelled by steam ... would throw greater obstacles than at present in the way of the landed interest."

Dixon's amendment was defeated by the impressive margin of 48 votes to two; but on the following day Lord Althorp surprisingly announced that he had decided to exempt steam carriages from all taxes under the Bill: "This was not much but it would be found advantageous in promoting these ingenious and useful inventions." Althorp added that he was "not ... very sanguine as to their being speedily brought to answer". Significantly, he made no such concession to the railways, which were actually and potentially a much richer source of revenue. But still, by this action the government had admitted that steam carriages were deserving of special encouragement.

The road steamer's position was further strengthened by the fact that the original constructors and company promoters, usually people of little consequence with a well-deserved reputation for amateurishness, no longer held the fort alone. There are indications that the struggle for the Toll Relief Bill brought together and activated an altogether more serious, professional element. Politicians and established engineers of repute joined forces to promote steam on the road, for the usual mixture of disinterested and mercenary motives. Steam suddenly acquired heavyweight, "respectable" backing. These were men who could not be suspected of starry-eyed idealism. They would be quickly on to a promising "investment", and would as quickly drop it if it did not yield results. They had considered the railway, and had come to the conclusion that the future lay with steam on the road, not on the track. "There is not at the moment, in this country or any other, a single instance of regular land communication satisfactorily sustained by the agency of steam"[1] – the Liverpool and Manchester Railway, open for two years, was still running uneconomically and inefficiently. So spoke the young, so far little-known engineer John Scott Russell in October 1832, before he built a road steamer himself.

In the same month appeared the first issue of the *Journal of Elemental Locomotion*, "or monthly advocate of the advantages to arise from the substitution of inanimate for animate power." Edited by

Alexander Gordon, it picked up the arguments of John Herapath, Sir Charles Dance and Robert Torrens. Inadequate food supplies led to higher prices; in fact the country produced enough food for its people, but used it to support its draught animals. This was intolerable, in view of "the tumultuous hurricane of political excitement which is sweeping over us".[2] Experiments had been made with steam ploughs since Trevithick's time. With a prescient eye, the *Journal* advocated the development of a multi-purpose tractor plough, adaptable to haulage, harrowing and threshing, which would be able to work at twice the speed of a horse plough. But with the exception of the steam-driven threshing machine, pioneered by Trevithick and gaining ground – particularly, it seems, in Scotland – steam on the land was still in the future. The brightest and nearest prospect, the *Journal* held, was for the steam coach, which "is about to open up commercial, financial, moral and political results which will change the entire form of society". Such elevated sentiments were not regarded as inconsistent with commercial interests. It was acknowledged that the *Journal* was founded in order to create a climate of opinion favourable to the formation of a joint stock company running steam carriages.

The *Journal* devoted most of the space in its six issues to specifically promoting steam carriages and attacking railways. Such specialisation, at a time when public attention was focused on railways, must have told against it. It became bi-monthly after January 1833, and its last issue was dated April–May that year. However, neither the *Journal* nor its aims were dead yet. In April, Alexander Gordon called a meeting to form "a society for ameliorating the distress of the country by means of steam transport and agriculture". Henry Handley, M.P. for Kesteven and Holland, who four years earlier had offered a prize for a steam plough, took the chair. Those present included Sir Charles Dance, Walter Hancock's brother Thomas, Colonel Torrens, and two other M.P.s.

The National Institution of Locomotion for Steam Transport and Agriculture was duly inaugurated. Of its founder-membership of 39, no fewer than 29 were M.P.s, among them Sir George Cayley, Lord Oxmantown, Charles Shaw-Lefevre, Colonel Torrens, William Mackinnon and Charles Jephson, all former members of the Gurney committee of 1831 and most known supporters of steam on the road. It had the hallmarks of an organised pressure group. In December 1833 it was reinforced by the first (and only) issue of the *Journal of Steam Transport and Husbandry*, the designated successor of the defunct *Journal of Elemental Locomotion*. There was a new editor, R. Cort, but its editorial policy was unchanged, except in that it fostered even more strongly the objects and beliefs of its predecessor. It concentrated on three topics: promoting steam on the road; proving to its own satisfaction that railways could never compete with canals or stage coaches, let alone steam carriages; and publicising the foundation of the National Institution.

A strong presumptive connection appears between the new journal and the National Institution, and the commercial enterprise fostered by the first journal. Referring to members of the institution, Maceroni said that "some of the above gentlemen have since merged into a company". This was the London, Holyhead and Liverpool Steam Coach and Road Company. The Institution, like the *Journal of Elemental Locomotion* before it, was clearly being used as a power base for commercial operations. Its heavy preponderance of M.P.s could as easily be used to support an Act setting up a joint stock company as to promote any other measure.

The London–Holyhead road, the first major trunk highway engineering project to be completed in Britain since the departure of the Romans, was under serious siege by steam almost as soon as it was finished in 1830. Sir Charles Dance and John Ward had stakes in operating steamers on parts of it, but had not yet run any. The commercial prospects were enticing. The London–Birmingham stretch of the road was thronged by the manufacturers of Birmingham and the surrounding towns on their way to and from the capital, and by all the traffic created by the expansion of Midlands industry. It was no coincidence that Britain's first trunk railway was built between the two cities. In 1833, before the railway had been built and had taken away their business, the coachmasters ran 61 coaches and 3050 horses on the road, involving an investment of £120,000. They carried 550 passengers daily, and cleared a 10 per cent profit. Another estimate – 480,000 passengers a year – was quoted in the prospectus of a proposed London and Birmingham Steam Carriage Company. In 1829 there were 34 daily coaches. Competition between them was intense, with the result that the country's fastest coaches operated on this route. Any successful competition would have to match their performance. The London-Birmingham coaches regularly did the journey in 12 or 13 hours (an overall speed of $8\frac{1}{2}$–9 m.p.h.), and could go a lot faster on occasion. This inconvenient point was not mentioned by the road steamer's protagonists. They reserved most of their fire for the railways. The confrontation they now sought was with an opponent that had yet to prove itself on a trunk route. They may have regarded the railway as therefore being in a weaker position than the stage coach; or it may have been that steam carriage entrepreneurs were more wary now of open attacks on trust interests.

In May 1832 the London and Birmingham Steam Carriage

Company issued a prospectus soliciting £200,000 in £20 shares. It aimed to establish a service with steam carriages to be built by William Church, an American mechanical engineer and inventor who had settled in Birmingham. There was no doubt of the ultimate success of steam carriages, said the prospectus. Railways – including the planned London–Birmingham line – demanded huge quantities of capital, massive and unsightly excavations, and much valuable land. Lines had to avoid town centres, which was inconvenient, and all but the most negligible gradients. Finally, the prospectus alleged that rail travel was monotonous. Road steamers incurred none of these disadvantages. There was news in June of a Birmingham–London service due to start that month, operated by a tractor with a water-tube boiler towing an omnibus and a baggage trailer. Forty passengers could be accommodated, it was said, and the outfit had run experimentally. There was then a long silence.

The London and Holyhead Company was next in the field. The new concern invited applications for 350,000 £1 shares, and fielded a uniquely high-powered array of "names". Among the company's officers were Thomas Telford, engineer to the Holyhead road commission, described as consulting engineer and company secretary, and Telford's assistant on the Holyhead road, John Macneil, as "acting engineer". Charles Jephson was on the company's committee, or board. So were three M.P.s with constituencies straddling the Birming-ham road – William Cartwright (Northampton), Sir Charles Knight-ley, noted agriculturist (Northants South), and William Stuart (Bedfordshire). The fifth director was the most impressive of all – Sir Henry Parnell, M.P. for Dundee since 1833. He had been the inspirer and head since its inception of the Holyhead road commission – effectively, Telford's chief – and was himself a leading expert on road construction.[3] He was a reformer and free-trader, an economist and a writer on finance with a considerable reputation, though a political maverick. Very obviously, the powers behind the prestigious Holyhead road had thrown their weight behind steam on that road. It is not unreasonable to suppose that they were alarmed at the prospect of the planned railway rendering "their" road obsolete almost as soon as it had been finished, and depriving it of the toll income necessary to keep it up.

Apart from Jephson, the company and the National Institution shared two other names – Henry Handley and Sir Andrew Agnew, Member for Wigtownshire, another reformer. They were members of the Institution, and trustees of the company. According to the prospectus, the company would hire, not buy, the steam carriages. Even so, the operation would entail an investment of £350,000 to transport 500 passengers a day. Charging 23s instead of 40s for an inside seat, and 13s instead of 20s outside, the steamers would replace virtually all the London–Birmingham stage coaches, and make a clear 20 per cent profit. The projected London to Birmingham railway, on the other hand, would cost £3½ million, carry 424 passengers a day, and show only 8⅜ per cent profit. Some of these very speculative figures, making steam carriages sound more attractive than either stage coaches or railways, were quoted in both the prospectus and (unacknowledged) in the *Journal of Steam Transport and Husbandry*. No attempt is made to justify them; it is clear only that an unprecedentedly ambitious scheme, orchestrating business, the press, Parliament and the impressive-sounding National Institution, was under way to dish the railway.

The enthusiasm of Sir Charles Dance for steam had survived the rejection of the Toll Relief Bill in 1832. He had retained one of his Gurney tractors, and early in 1833 sent it to the eminent marine engineers, Maudslay, Sons & Field, to be modified. Dance was not an engineer; the work was superintended by Thomas Bailey, a former Gurney employee, who went to work for Maudslay's at Dance's instance. This was the beginning of a close involvement on the part of Maudslay, Sons & Field, and more particularly Joshua Field, in steam carriages. It would be pleasant to think that James Nasmyth might have sparked off their interest in the subject before he left them in 1831.

The boilers of Gurney's tractors had been fitted with his "separators", the function of which was to separate water in suspension (the priming) from the steam before it passed into the cylinders, then return it to the boiler tubes. If not returned to the boiler, priming in the steam meant less water in the tubes, which were that much more likely to burn out and burst. Also priming, if not excluded from the cylinder, was exhausted with the steam, wasting water and depositing a dirty spray all around. Dance's redesign, which he patented, involved removing the separators. We do not know why he did so; since Gurney's boilers used a lot of water and frequently burst, the separator was not, perhaps, noticeably good at its job.

On 11 March 1833 Dance ran his altered machine from Stanmore to London, covering 13½ miles of very soft roads in 80 minutes. On the following day he drove through the West End to Westminster. However, an attempt to reach Brighton in the third week of August ended badly after 34 miles, when an ill-judged reversing of the engine to reduce speed on a descent broke a connecting-rod. It was particularly unfortunate that Dance should have so eminent a company on board. It included Joseph Maudslay, Joshua Field,

William Boulnois (Gurney's former client), Alexander Gordon, Sir Henry Watson (a member of the National Institution), and the distinguished civil engineer William Carpmael. No less portentous was the presence of the great coachmasters William Chaplin and Edward Sherman, whom Dance no doubt hoped to win over to steam, and who probably came out of curiosity. They must have gone home laughing; but the converted of the party announced that "the great difficulties of steam carriages in common roads are now overcome". This was justified, to them, by the 34 miles being covered in three hours, plus $26\frac{1}{2}$ minutes for taking on fuel and water.

Dance tried again, successfully, on 20 September, when he towed 15 passengers to Brighton in an omnibus behind the tractor. Among the company, once more, were Joseph Maudslay and Joshua Field. The running time was 5 hours 16 minutes, plus 1 hour 6 minutes spent at stops. Dance returned the following day, and reported no mechanical failures.[4] He was baulked by a stage coach, and the firebars of the grate clinkered-up – a common result of unskilled stoking. There were no other incidents.

Dance may have felt encouraged by his trouble-free if slow progress to Brighton, or perhaps by an expression of interest in steam services addressed to one of his connections by the French government. At all events, a long propaganda letter extolling steam carriages in general and his own in particular appeared in *The Times* on 26 September; and on 12 October he began his second attempt to operate a regular service, this time out of London – possibly in emulation of Walter Hancock. The tractor and its omnibus trailer ran three times daily between Wellington Street, Waterloo and Greenwich, a distance of 5 miles. The fare asked was 2s 6d one way, which proved that this was not intended as a commercially viable long-term operation. It was in fact described as a "demonstration". No doubt the high fare was designed to discourage the vulgarly curious from taking seats that might be more profitably occupied by influential and moneyed persons. Reports of what happened are contradictory. An account probably written by Dance says that the machine ran on 8 successive days at an overall speed of 10 m.p.h., with an average load of 14 passengers. The *Journal of Steam Transport and Husbandry*, on the other hand, reported that "on the fifth or sixth day, [Dance] withdrew his carriage, totally disabled" with burst tubes.

However, on account of the success of the Brighton trip, it was this machine that was used for a trial run from London to Birmingham. It was hired for the occasion by a committee of distinguished engineers anxious to see for themselves, by personal participation, whether steam carriages were a practicable proposition. Two of them, Telford and Macneil, were officers of the London and Holyhead company; no doubt the occasion was also intended as a test run on behalf of that concern, and a means of gaining publicity and backing for it through the eminence of the committee. This also included Alexander Gordon, the noted engineers Joshua Field, Bryan Donkin and Timothy Bramah (to be remembered for his construction of the Griffith vehicle), and William Cubitt, speculative builder, and constructor of canals, river works, docks and, later, railways. Another member was John Rickman, friend of Telford and Southey, Clerk to the House of Commons – a distinguished statistician and administrator responsible for Parliamentary reports on the census and other topics, and secretary to the commissioners for roads and bridges in Scotland and for the Caledonian Canal. Colonel Charles William Pasley, another friend of Telford's, was director of the Royal Engineers establishment at Chatham and a partisan of progress and innovation in military technology. The rest of the committee consisted of William Carpmael, who had accompanied Dance to Brighton, and two other civil engineers.

Macneil, Donkin and Cubitt, who were in charge, did all they could to make the expedition a success. Supplies of coke and water were laid on at 5-mile intervals. The roads were expected to be extremely bad, because of the season, so horses were made ready at the bottom of steep hills. This was rather ominous, but the all-up weight of the *ensemble* was six tons, including the tractor, the omnibus, their passengers, fuel and water. The outfit set out from Maudslay's works at 3.30 a.m. on 1 November, with Thomas Bailey at the helm. Not all members of the committee were present at the start; some joined at St Albans. It was 11 a.m. before they reached Stony Stratford, $52\frac{1}{2}$ miles from London. The reasons given were soft roads, due to rain, newly laid gravel, and a burst boiler tube, with which they had limped along for all but six miles of the distance. The object had been to reach Birmingham by nightfall; this was now out of the question. The next morning the tube was found to be still defective, and the expedition was called off.

In view of the complete failure of the trip, the report drawn up by the committee was remarkably mild in tone, possibly reflecting the influence of its "Company" members: "It was clear that the engine was not adequate, in the horrible state of the roads, to reach Birmingham with anything like *éclat*." The committee was satisfied that steam transportation was practical in principle – only the Dance vehicle was wrong, lacking the power to cope with really atrocious surfaces: "With a well-constructed engine of greater power, a steam carriage conveyance between London and Birmingham at a velocity unattainable by horses, and limited only by safety, might be maintained." A 7 m.p.h. average fell far short of that ideal.

Early December found Dance back in London, trying to run a daily service from "The Steam Coach Office, Waterloo Bridge", to Clapham: a more modest ambition than London to Greenwich. There was more trouble with burst tubes, and by about the fifth, the attempt had been abandoned. During the same month Dance was crossing swords with the *Mechanics' Magazine* and with Maceroni, and boosting his own efforts; but although he retained an interest in steam carriages, he thereafter abandoned independent enterprises. Thomas Bailey did not regard his removal of the Gurney separator as an improvement, and indeed, the tractor was going no better without it. Gurney commented, without a blush, that "Sir Charles Dance is no engineer, and is constantly changing his opinions".

The London and Holyhead company failed to apply for an Act in the 1834 session. The fact was noted, and attributed to a failure to raise capital. It was clear that however distinguished the names behind the company, not one of them knew anything about building steam carriages, and none with the exception of Dance had had any experience of running them. Dance's latest failure seemed to illustrate the proposition. Gordon, however, blamed the defeat of the company on the death in September 1834 of the man he regarded as its moving spirit, Thomas Telford. For his part, Gurney believed that the lack of a uniform and equitable toll on the London-Holyhead road was responsible. He described how tentative feelers to the House of Lords had met with a refusal to countenance the lifting of existing tolls on the road, for fear of jeopardising the interests of the trusts concerned. There is irony here, in view of the effect on these same trusts of the railway that the London and Holyhead company had sought to forestall. Nor was any more heard of the *Journal of Steam Transport and Husbandry*, or of the National Institution – further evidence, if any were needed, of the links between company, journal and institution.

Plans for a service continued to preoccupy Macneil into 1834. By the summer, he was no longer linked with the London and Holyhead company. He had transferred his allegiance to the London and Birmingham Steam Carriage Company, of which he was engineer. He said that he had meetings with the trustees of all the trusts on the Holyhead road, on behalf of the London and Birmingham company. According to Macneil, they said that they would support a Bill legalising a joint stock company to run steam carriages on the road, so long as sufficient tolls were laid on steam to pay for the repair of any damage it caused, and to pay the interest on loans raised for improving the road for steamers. The toll would be about the same as for a four horse stage coach. It is difficult to reconcile this with Gurney's account of the failure of the London and Holyhead company, and in any case, no more was heard of a Bill. As we shall see, Macneil had yet another string to his bow at this time: a group of engineers, of which he was a member, had commissioned Maudslays to build a new steam carriage, unconnected with either company and intended for a different route.

The supporters of steam may well have found a third source of encouragement in the voluntary disarming of the trusts. This did not take place until 1834. In 1833 two-thirds of the 64 turnpike Acts passed took cognisance of steam. Of these 42 Acts, all but three went out of their way to discriminate against tractor-trailer outfits in particular – either an already penal toll was made still heavier, or a toll equal to that for a stage coach was increased if a trailer were towed. Gurney was no longer operating, but most vehicles were of his type. All but 11 of the 42 Acts penalised every form of steam carriage regardless of type. Five tolls were so high as obviously to be intended as exclusive, though again, none attained the levels of 1831. Interestingly, one of the discriminatory tolls was imposed by the Monk Bridge–New Malton–Scarborough trust, of which both Sir George and Edward Stillingfleet Cayley were trustees. This happened in March 1833 – the month before Sir George joined the committee of the National Institution, the main aim of which was to foster steam carriages.

This was the picture as before, but in the 1834 session it altered radically. This change must be seen against a background of continuing deterioration in both the financial condition of the trusts, and in the regard in which they were held by the legislature. The great number of trusts, each of limited extent and jurisdiction, was uneconomic and led to anomalies in toll charges; and there was still need for "more competent and skilful officers". So said the Lords select committee on turnpike returns in 1833. Like other committees before it, it recommended the consolidation of adjoining trusts. The case in favour of this was now the stronger for the manifest success of the metropolitan roads consolidation. Economies of scale would lead to the removal of toll anomalies, and – more important – to reduced expenditure. This should enable tolls to be cut, which would benefit both the coachmasters and the general travelling public; but the Lords' main concern was for the financial wellbeing of the trusts' creditors. The overall debt of the trusts was "great and increasing", even though their total mileage and toll income were also going up.

Parliament was stirred to action. By an Act of 1834, all those turnpike Acts due to expire in that or the following session would be automatically renewed for two years. The measure had the double effect of saving the trusts concerned the cost of renewal, and discouraging them from raising their tolls, building new roads, or otherwise extending their powers – all activities which would require a new Act. The result was a dramatic drop in new Acts in 1834. Only 14 passed Parliament, of which 11 mentioned steam. Ten of these discriminated against it. There was a special significance in the decline as far as steam was concerned. It furnished proof that antipathy to steam had never been the prime mover of Act renewals in the past. Had it been otherwise, Acts would still have been sought after 1834; existing legislation that ignored steam would have been as unacceptable as ever. In 1835, 21 Acts became law, 16 in 1836. The change was permanent; although existing anti-steam tolls remained as controversial as ever, new tolls ceased to be an issue. Indeed, from 1836, as will be seen, they would be explicitly discouraged by the legislature.

So, in 1833–4, the steam enterprises multiplied; nowhere more prolifically than in the Birmingham area, already the objective of the great gentlemen of the London and Holyhead company. In October 1833 the *Birmingham Advertiser* carried a plug for the London and Birmingham Steam Carriage Company in the guise of a news item, and in May 1834 there is at last evidence of the Church machine running on the road. It was an extraordinary-sounding vehicle; a coach in the form of "a very large and wide van"[5] on three wheels. It carried 40 passengers at 15–20 m.p.h. for a short distance, hit a kerb and had to be towed back to its factory by workmen. It also suffered from an "imperfect" boiler. This was not an auspicious beginning.

The extensive Heaton family did much better. Tolls were a discouragement, but they did not give up on that account. A company to be capitalised at a modest £10,000 was floated, and took up the Heaton patent. The brothers undertook to build carriages for it at £500 a time. One, a $2\frac{1}{2}$-ton, fully sprung tractor with a fire-tube boiler of single-chamber locomotive type, went for short experimental runs in the Birmingham neighbourhood, towing a trailer. The laden weight including passengers, was 4 tons 12 hundredweight. The steamer's most advanced feature was a change-speed mechanism.

Several trips from Birmingham to Wolverhampton are also recorded. In July 1833 the vehicle covered the 13 miles in 1 hour 56 minutes, with three people on the tractor and 22 in the trailer, but twisted an axleshaft *en route*. It went again on 1 August, attaining 12 m.p.h. on the level. The Heaton machine's most impressive achievements were its last. On 2 August it steamed from Birmingham to Wolverhampton and back three times in the day, a total distance of 84 miles in 14 hours, while carrying up to 34 passengers. This was the highest day's mileage so far recorded by a steam carriage. Then, on 28 August, towing a coach and carrying a total of 20 passengers, the steamer travelled from Shadwell Street, Birmingham, to Bromsgrove and back. On the way it climbed Lickey Hill, which had an average gradient of 1:9 for nearly half a mile, and had a soft, sandy surface. Coke consumption for the 29 miles was 11 bushels, at the local price of $2\frac{1}{2}$d to 3d a bushel. The Heaton machine appears to have used as little fuel as Hancock's *Infant*, and the fuel cost – 1d a mile – was smaller, with coke at half the London price. It was also obviously very reliable and powerful. The Heaton brothers might safely be regarded as the Hancocks of the Midlands, except that they never achieved a service. By the spring of 1834 they had built another steamer, but then came to the conclusion that no commercial operation could be economic, and retired from construction.

For Walter Hancock, too, 1833 and 1834 were years of increasing activity, though they began badly. On New Year's Day 1833 the *Kent and Essex Mercury* reported the inquest on Richard Outridge, one of Hancock's engineers. Three days before Christmas he had wired down a safety valve on Hancock's new bus, building for the London and Paddington Steam Carriage Company at the Stratford works. The subsequent boiler explosion killed him. The coroner ruled that Outridge's death was accidental, caused by his own negligence, but any fatal explosion was bad news to a steam carriage constructor. It helped their image even less when steam promoters blamed one another for dangerous design, as Gordon did Hancock.

Trials of the new bus – called the *Enterprise* – began on 26 January, but the service was not inaugurated for another four months. Starting on 22 April, the *Enterprise* plied for 16 successive days between the City and Paddington, along the City Road and New Road.[6] The fare was 1s, the same as on the horse buses. During this period occurred the incidents involving horse bus drivers, and their temporarily satisfactory sequel. The reaction of the competition had been immediate and unambiguous.

Even his colleagues gave Hancock trouble. After taking delivery, the company failed to pay him in full for the carriage. They tried to avoid responsibility for doing so by claiming that the vehicle was unsatisfactory, while at the same time praising it to the travelling public, and refusing to return it to Hancock's works for overhaul and modifications. Later the company asked Hancock to take the *Enterprise* back, and reimburse the money they had paid him for it so far. Finally the business was wound up, and the *Enterprise* came back into Hancock's hands.

David Redmund, the promoter and engineer of the company, was a tricky customer on all counts. He kept *Enterprise* in his yard in Charles Street, City Road, for a length of time that could not be explained merely by the need to apply its company livery. It later transpired that Redmund was building a steamer of his own that bore a close resemblance to the *Enterprise*. The boiler differed in detail, to avoid infringement of Hancock's patent, and this was said to have accounted for the fact that the machine never ran satisfactorily. The Redmund project also differed from the *Enterprise* – and from every other steamer of the time – in its steering arrangements, which were on Ackermann principles, a system so far seen only on horse carriages. Even so, Hancock regarded Redmund as an unscrupulous pirate.

Towards the end of 1833 another new omnibus, the *Autopsy*, was completed. It undertook an uneventful expedition to Brighton at about the same time. On 11 September Hancock took the *Infant* down the same road again, and was not so lucky. It covered the 57 miles from Stratford in 9 hours 40 minutes including stops for water, coke and two meals. The average running speed was 12 m.p.h. Two days were spent in Brighton, where a clutch broke in the street. On the return, speed was reduced by the accumulation of clinkers on the firebars.

In October *Autopsy* plied for hire daily for nearly four weeks along the City Road between Finsbury Square and Pentonville. It was withdrawn partly because of lack of depots and vehicle accommodation on the route, and partly because of the demands made on Hancock's time by new construction at Stratford. He was now on his own again, running a service himself. In the spring of 1834 the British self-propelled vehicle industry received its first export order, from a Viennese gentleman. He collected the tractor built to his order, drove it with a fully loaded trailer from Stratford to the City without incident, and shipped it to Rotterdam on 26 July. By September the machine was running in Vienna.

Hancock launched his next public service on 18 August 1834. It ran from Moorfields, north of the Bank, to Paddington. Hancock used the *Autopsy* and the old reliable *Infant*, which were joined in September by a just-completed machine, a new *Era*. This looked very much like its eponymous predecessor, apart from its single coach body with room for eight inside and six outside passengers. The latest machine had a two-speed change-speed mechanism, a feature that, by this time, had also been fitted to the *Infant*. Support from press and public was good, and the service was a success. Ten to twelve passengers per vehicle was a normal load, and by the time the service was wound up by the end of November, nearly 4000 passengers had been carried. The *Morning Chronicle* of 19 August reported completing the 5-mile journey in half an hour, including stops for picking up and setting down passengers. The running speed was 12 m.p.h. There was no disagreeable noise – the report's only complaint was that "a considerable amount of steam was allowed to escape". Horse vehicle drivers were now more friendly, and Hancock announced his intention of hiring them to man his buses.

On the Edgware Road some time that autumn, the new *Era* ran into freshly laid macadam 4 to 5 inches deep – an "unusual depth", but beyond this observation no suggestion of malice was made. At any event, the *Era* passed through the gravel easily, while a horse bus stopped in it and had to be pulled out with the aid of an extra horse.

The experience gathered in these busy years resulted in only two major amendments to Hancock's carriages. He had been plagued as much as any constructor by clinkers blocking his firebars, causing delays and loss of power. In July 1833 he patented his removable firebars, which could be wound out with a crank, complete with their clinkers, and swiftly replaced with a clean set. Hancock's other improvement was not so much an invention as an adaptation of an existing idea. During 1834 he designed new wheels for his steamers. Of composite construction – cast-iron naves and very strong spokes – they provided great robustness without excessive weight. This was the earliest recorded use of artillery-type wheels on a self-propelled vehicle. They were peculiarly suited to steam carriages. These were heavy, fast machines with driven wheels, which were subjected to unprecedentedly severe stresses.

Meanwhile Ogle and Summers had shifted the centre of their activity back to London, but were operating on a less ambitious scale than hitherto. In December 1832 they had driven from Portman Street to Stamford Hill, a distance of seven miles, in 31 minutes, and were still making short runs in London in the summer of 1833.

New constructors, too, were busy on the roads in and around London. Francis Maceroni had so far confined himself to gaining experience of other aspects of the steam carriage business. He was an amateur engineer who, as we have seen, had taken space in Gurney's establishment for his own experiments on steam, but had become more deeply involved with Gurney's projects, working on them and promoting them to financiers. At this period he gives the impression of being a salesman and publicist at heart, rather than a constructor.

After Gurney ceased his activities in 1831, Maceroni was approached by another constructor in need of finance. This was John Squire, an ex-Gurney engineer who had built a carriage of his own. It primed badly, and in order to develop a better vehicle, Maceroni obtained finance and engaged Squire as foreman engineer. Discarding Squire's boiler, Maceroni designed another. Capital ran out, and

Maceroni found more; but the days of easy money were over. Sir Charles Dance was offered an interest in the patent, but refused it on the grounds that he was developing a boiler of his own at the time: the modified Gurney apparatus. Hanning, too, declined to support Maceroni's new venture, having burned his fingers so badly on the old. As a result of his steam operations, Maceroni was usually insolvent. He was driven to pawning his personal possessions; and once his carriage was completed, it was frequently limited to short runs because its constructor could not afford the fuel for longer ones.

Maceroni had to contend not only with the consequences of the Gurney defeat, but also with his own feckless nature. In politics he was a Bonapartist radical, romantic to the point of eccentricity. He had campaigned for South American independence from Spain – which was socially acceptable in the 1820s – but in 1828 he offered his services to the Turks against the Russians, in spite of their recent attempt to suppress Greek nationalism. This was, however, consistent with his dedicated Bonapartism. Worst of all, in 1831–2, in support of the Reform Bill agitation, he wrote a pamphlet entitled *Defensive Instructions to the People*. This advocated armed revolution by the masses, and gave detailed advice on street-fighting, including an admonition to shoot officers first. At this very time, he was soliciting cash from investors. The reaction of the moneyed classes may be imagined. Here was a half-foreign Bonapartist, who still consorted with the Imperial family, doubly dangerous as a professional soldier, teaching armed revolution to the mob. The kindest adjective applied to Maceroni was "irresponsible".

By the summer of 1832 the Maceroni and Squire vehicle was on the road, and by January 1833 it was running "almost daily" in the vicinity of the Paddington works. During one of these early excursions, Squire "nearly demolished" a house in Paddington Green.[7] The machine was self-contained, with a pleasure carriage body variously described as a chariot or a barouche, and as accommodating nine or 16 passengers; presumably different bodies were fitted at different times. In its early days, the steamer was said to weigh $2\frac{1}{2}$ tons with fuel and water, but without passengers. Its range between fuel and water stops at this time was 12 miles,[8] and the highest recorded speed was just under 10 m.p.h. Alexander Gordon – who had become a Maceroni supporter since Gurney retired – estimated a coke consumption of one-half to three-quarters of a bushel per mile, which was heavy even for the day.[9] The first boiler fitted, allegedly "entirely different in principle and arrangement"[10] from Gurney's, was in fact also a water-tube boiler, though more similar to Ogle's than to Gurney's in layout. It was soon altered, for fear of infringing Ogle's patent rights. Normal working pressure, in amended form, was 150 p.s.i. The engine was said to be noisy, and the jolting worse than that of a stage coach.

It will be seen that a fog of controversy, entirely characteristic of the man, surrounded Maceroni's machine and its performance. His own words tend merely to compound the confusion. He claimed at one time that the carriage went 1700 miles without repairs to machinery or boiler, yet his own descriptions, let alone those of others, of runs in the autumn and winter of 1833–4 tell another story. With 15 passengers, including Gordon, Maceroni and Squire drove from Paddington to Windsor and back early in September 1833. Nathaniel Ogle accompanied the party briefly on horseback, but dropped back to save exhausting his horse. The average rate excluding stops was 12 m.p.h.; including halts, it fell to under 8 m.p.h. There were plenty of what Maceroni described as "little accidents, chiefly owing to a want of care on the part of the workmen" – that is, his employees. One delay was "in consequence of the fireman having burnt his hand when thoughtlessly putting coke on the fire without his shovel". The machine often ran out of steam – refuelling was left too long, and then too much coke was fed in. Near Colnbrook, on the outward journey, the steamer bogged down in 4 inches of new gravel, and had to be pushed out. An axleshaft broke at Hammersmith on the return. Steam was let off after this breakdown, scaring the locals, and "some few" horses shied. On a different occasion, coal was burned for lack of coke, and volumes of black smoke resulted. The vehicle and the way it was handled seem to have been as anti-social as most. Another journey to Windsor was made in October.

The steamer went to Harrow at least twice, breaking down on each occasion but ascending Harrow Hill at between 6 and 7 m.p.h. – faster than a stage coach with extra horses. The *Morning Chronicle* was full of praise: "There can now be no reasonable doubt but steam carriages will answer on common roads". On a later run up the Harrow Road, Daniel Gaskell, M.P. for Wakefield, was a passenger. Regular trips on the Edgware Road were also made, though not always as far as Edgware. One, undertaken on 4 October 1833, must have been less eventful than earlier runs, as an average speed of 15 m.p.h. exclusive of stops was recorded. The *Observer* commented on this occasion that the vehicle was "as easily managed as a child's cart". A journey as far as the Welsh Harp, in the following May, sounds more exciting. Among the passengers was – not surprisingly, in view of Maceroni's sympathies – Prince Jerome Bonaparte, one-time King of Westphalia under Napoleon; and a stage coach was passed at a rousing 18 m.p.h.

In order to attract press notices and orders, Maceroni took journalists and public figures for rides more often even than did

Gurney; but although his press was just as uncritical, his "catches" were less useful and spectacular. The last slice of financial good luck came his way in January 1834, when he was able to raise enough capital to buy out Squire for £1100.

In the same month the Maceroni machine went from Regent's Circus, Oxford Street, to Uxbridge. On board was the Marquess of Tweeddale, who was later to become interested in steam ploughing. On the return journey the Oxford coach passed them while they were taking on water at the bottom of Notting Hill, to the cheers of the undergraduates on board; but the steamer overtook the coach before it reached Oxford Street. The Marquess said that there was no noise or smoke, so perhaps the machine was well managed on that occasion. On this or another journey to Uxbridge – there were two – the running speed was 11–12 m.p.h., but the overall average, including stops, fell to little more than half this figure, mainly because of the length of time taken to replenish the water supply – up to 20 minutes on each occasion.

At the end of April 1834 John Macneil, Alexander Gordon and others were to be seen taking a 10-mile run up the Edgware Road. Macneil's interest was undoubtedly professional; he was engineer of the London and Birmingham company at about this time, and he promised to arrange coke depots for a run to Birmingham that Maceroni planned. It is possible that Macneil was looking about for an alternative to William Church's carriage, which was not a success, as we have seen; but the Birmingham trip never happened.

Robert Wallace, M.P. for Greenock, said when supporting Gurney's petition at the end of April 1834 that he "had travelled often in the steam carriage on Mr Gurney's principle [sic], the property of Colonel Maceroni, and such was its smoothness and easiness of motion, though going at the rate of 16 miles and a half an hour, he could shoot a pigeon flying from the coach, though somewhat out of the knack". Charles Hullmandel made the remarkable assertion that, over a period of four or five months when he had ridden on the steamer, there was never any steam, smoke, noise or breakdown, and that no horses were frightened. At the time he said this – 1839 – Hullmandel was a director of a company recently launched in an attempt to put the Maceroni design into commercial operation. Earlier, he had supported Maceroni's enterprises with cash.

Runs continued through May, June and July 1834. In that year *Turner's Annual Tour* – a volume of travel essays written by the novelist and journalist Leitch Ritchie and illustrated by J. M. W. Turner – contained an exciting account of a ride to Watford. Ritchie met Maceroni – "an old acquaintance" – on Bushey Heath. On its way to

Watford the carriage had already climbed the very bad, steep road from Edgware. The descent to Watford was worse. The drag not being put on soon enough, the machine ran away down Clay Hill at 30 m.p.h., flashing unstoppable through Bushey village. On the way back, Clay Hill was ascended at the same speed achieved by stage coaches with five horses in harness.

That summer Maceroni was building a second steamer, said to be for export to Germany. This weighed four tons with 15 passengers, baggage, fuel and water. It had a maximum speed of about 15 m.p.h., and coke consumption was around a bushel every three miles. Faster, and with a fuel economy comparable with the best, this carriage was a clear improvement on Maceroni's first.[11] Sadly, though, his fortunes were about to take a down-turn from which they never recovered. He still owed Gurney the £150 advance on mileage charges paid more than six years earlier. Early in June, at Gurney's instigation, an attempt was made to arrest Maceroni for the debt. He managed to evade the officers, and continued to demonstrate his steamer unmolested, so the prosecution cannot have been very determined; but the fact that it was instituted, and by a former colleague, is an indication of his plight.

At about this time an Italian named Asda rode on the second carriage, and interested Maceroni in the prospect of selling his patent in Belgium and France. But it would be of no validity, said Asda, and hence of no commercial value, unless a Maceroni vehicle actually ran in those countries. He offered to see that this was done, in return for a share in the Maceroni patent. What clinched Maceroni's acceptance was Asda's offer of £1500 cash. In view of Asda's subsequent behaviour, it may in fact have been an outright payment for the Belgian and French licences; but Maceroni afterwards implied that he should have received more. At the time, the matter was not in question – the only alternative was losing the vehicles and all he possessed to his creditors.

In September 1834 Asda shipped both the Maceroni carriages to Antwerp, under the superintendence of the mechanic James Wearn. In the same month "one of the locomotive machines" at Antwerp performed creditably on the Brussels road. Major stage coach proprietors were among the passengers, and horses showed no fear. In early December the carriages were in Brussels, exciting still more favourable comment.

By early February 1835 both vehicles were in Paris, having been driven there – so it was said – all the way from Brussels, a distance of 225 miles. They enjoyed a very friendly reception from press and public, and none other than King Louis Philippe was among the passengers. Runs were made to Versailles and Saint-Germain, and a

Paris-Rouen service was contemplated.

By May 1835 Asda was behaving as if the vehicles were entirely his property. A French source referred to "the steam carriage of M. Asda, constructed in England by Colonel Maceroni". Asda sold the patent for £16,000, of which sum Maceroni saw nothing. He would have got more, said Maceroni, but for the fact that railway projects were already pre-empting steam carriages in France. Another factor may have been the unsuitability of the vehicle for French roads. A steam pipe fractured on one occasion, and the French authorities criticised the springing as being too weak. Times had changed since the days of Trésaguet.

Whatever the reason, no more was heard of the Maceroni machines in France; and for reasons which will appear, it is probable that they found their way back to England, if not back to Maceroni.

It is possible that Maceroni was encouraged to demonstrate his machine in Belgium and France by the contemporary endeavours of Jean-Christian Dietz and his son Charles in those countries. Abroad, there were no steam activities on the British scale, but at intervals throughout the 1830s, reports appeared in the British press concerning the Dietz enterprises. Dietz *père* was a German engineer who had settled in Brussels. By September 1833 he was testing a 3-wheeled, 8-ton steam tractor with a water-tube boiler near Brussels. This was his prototype. By 1834 Dietz was running a similar design with twin front wheels and a shock-absorbing layer of wood blocks in tarred felt between the wheel rims and the iron tyres. In July 1834 this machine, in the hands of Charles, made an experimental trip from Paris to Vincennes, towing an omnibus, at an average speed of 9 m.p.h. The machine then drew between 60 and 70 passengers in two omnibuses. In September it ran between Paris and Saint-Germain. A regular Paris-Versailles service was planned, and started on 1 December 1835, only to be abandoned after a few weeks. It was said that the opposition of the railway interests on the same route was responsible, but mechanical problems may have contributed: on a run to Nogent, a boiler tube burst. [12]

It is interesting that railways were seen as a common factor in the downfall of both Dietz and Asda in the summer of 1835. They were seldom quoted as a factor in the downfall of British ventures.

In a pamphlet he published in the spring of 1835, after his activities had ceased, Maceroni wallowed in self-pity, at the same time finally admitting that his first machine had been less than perfect. Axleshafts had broken four times, and the carriage was frequently off the road for long periods awaiting repair because he could not afford to keep it running.

There now ensued an interesting episode that may have had a connection with Maceroni's withdrawal. The facts are these. First, in March 1835 Andrew Nash, a former convict who had made good as an innkeeper at Parramatta, near Sydney, set sail for England. When Nash left to return to Australia in February 1836, he took with him one (or, according to some reports, two) steam coaches. Nash and his vehicles arrived in Sydney in July 1836. There were several local newspaper references to them, and talk of the establishment of a Sydney-Parramatta steam service. The Steam Locomotive Company was projected by Nash to this end. After that, nothing. The newspaper coverage did not consist only of reports of Nash's activities. A great deal more space was given to Maceroni's. Leitch Ritchie's piece in *Turner's Annual Tour* was quoted at length, as were letters from Robert Wallace to the *Glasgow Free Press* and the *Scotsman*, and accounts from the Antwerp and Paris newspapers. Without exception, the material that did not concern Nash concerned Maceroni's machines; it was all published at the same period, which was around the time of Nash's return; and none of it had topical news value on its own. There is no positive evidence that Nash had bought Maceroni's carriages, but given the facts, the inference is not unreasonable. It is easy to envisage the innkeeper Nash arranging for the reports to go to the Sydney newspapers as part of a campaign for promoting his enterprise. If he did not buy the Maceroni vehicles, returned to England from France, why were the voluminous accounts of British steam activity concerned only with those machines?

Maceroni gave two reasons for his failure: the "theft" of his carriages by Asda; and the diversion of investors' capital from road steamers to railways, a theory prompted, no doubt, by Asda's experience. He explicitly discounted inequitable tolls as a cause of his withdrawal. Like Hancock, he paid tolls only to the Metropolitan roads trust, at the same rate as for a 4-horse coach. Unlike Hancock, he had no objections to this; but then he was not trying to run a service on a commercial basis. Trusts on the other roads he used took nothing – "there is no Act to enable them to take it." He was clever in confining himself to such roads, but it was neither accurate nor fair to add that turnpike hostility was "a perfect fiction of Mr Gurney and his friends".

On 1 July 1834 another new vehicle appeared in London. This was the steam carriage of Yates and Smith, capable of carrying 20 passengers, and said to be intended for the Brighton road. It ran through the streets of Whitechapel at 10–12 m.p.h., but burst a steam pipe on the rough paving.

Two other newcomers to the steam carriage field came, and went, during 1834 – both, one might say, with a bang. One was the machine of Sharp and Roberts, which had made an experimental run in Manchester in December 1833, and another in March 1834. Its last outing took place on 4 April, when in blew up in the Oxford Road after the pumps between water tank and boiler failed and the boiler ran dry. It had a single-chamber, locomotive-type boiler; indeed, these manufacturers were better known for locomotives. They had built an unsuccessful engine for the Liverpool and Manchester Railway in 1831, and three years later provided a locomotive for the new Dublin and Kingstown Railway. Considering that between 40 and 50 passengers were on board at the time of the explosion, the casualty list was small – according to different accounts, two or three passers-by injured, a shop-front destroyed and some windows smashed. Richard Roberts's steam carriage patent of 1832 had included a form of split-shaft bevel-gear differential. If the carriage as built incorporated it, this was the first appearance in Britain of the modern differential as a substitute for crude wheel-declutching mechanisms.

Like James Nasmyth, John Scott Russell, a fellow-Scot and engineer, was interested in steam on the road when young, before he became famous in other fields. Russell was only 26 in 1834, and virtually unknown, although he was already a student of the design of ships' hulls. He had been building steam carriages for about 18 months when, at the end of March 1834, he started running them between Glasgow and Paisley.

In some respects, Russell's machines were of advanced and efficient design. Built at the Grove House Engine Works, Edinburgh, they were fully sprung – engine, boiler and body. The driving axle was gear-driven from a separate crankshaft, and steering was by rack and pinion. A tender containing fuel and water – also sprung – was towed behind. Water could be fed direct to the boiler from the tender by means of rubber hoses. All the machinery was out of sight, below the stage-coach-type body, making for a compact and tidy appearance. The tender also had accommodation, permitting a total of six inside and 20 outside passengers to be carried.

Normal boiler pressure was only 20 to 25 p.s.i.; but on the other hand the boiler (which could raise steam in 20 minutes from cold) was of single-chamber, fire-tube type, like that of Sharp and Roberts, so an explosion would be far more destructive than in a water-tube or Hancock-type boiler. Also, the boiler was made of unusually thin iron, reinforced with slender rods. The machines cannot have been easy to drive, since the task was divided between three operators. The helmsman, who did nothing but steer, sat at the front, but the engineer who controlled the steam was at the back with the stoker.

The Steam Carriage Company of Scotland was promoted to run the vehicles, which operated intermittently in the first instance. During April six trips were made in one day, in an average time of 41 minutes for the $7\frac{1}{2}$-mile distance; but early in May Russell is reported to have stopped running. A regular public service is first referred to early in July, when six Russell steamers were making hourly departures; tenders filled and waiting to be picked up had been stationed along the route, and there was heavy press coverage by the *Glasgow Courier, Glasgow Herald* and *Edinburgh Observer*. The elapsed time was improved to between 30 and 35 minutes – the Russell steamers were clearly both fast and reliable. The service was very well patronised – so much so that up to 34 passengers found their way on to each vehicle.

After less than a month, this most promising of all the commercial steam carriage operations came to an untimely end. It had dismayed the proprietors of the Paisley and Ardrossan Canal, who had recently introduced a passage boat service alongside the Glasgow-Paisley road to take passenger traffic away from the stage coaches. Much more important, it was altogether too successful for the trustees administering that road. Their Act imposed no tolls on steam, so the stage coaches, their main source of income, were now faced with a competitor armed with loaded dice – this on top of the passage boat threat. The fact that Russell's guards voluntarily gave the gatekeeper 2s 6d (more than the coach toll) on passing was clearly not thought to balance the odds. Interestingly, Russell reported no trouble with the coachmasters – it was the trustees who were worried. This squares with the experience of most other steam operators. Russell claimed, nearly 40 years afterwards, that there had been plenty of traffic for both steamers and stage coaches, and that the future of horse-based industries in general was the trustees' sole concern, but this is too unspecific to be convincing, given the circumstances, and the violence of trust reaction. The Gloucester–Cheltenham trustees may or may not have laid gravel maliciously three years before, but when heaps of road metal appeared on the Glasgow–Paisley road, and accusations were levelled both by Russell's company and by the press, there was none of the scepticism recorded in 1831. If, as seems likely in this case, the trust surveyor had obstructed the road deliberately, it may have been because the trustees doubted their chances of getting a prohibitory toll out of a Parliament increasingly averse to enlarging trust powers. They may also have felt under threat from the passage boats on the canal.

When on 29 July the inevitable accident happened, it was much worse than anything that had befallen Dance. Already, wagons and other traffic had been damaged or forced off the road by the piles of gravel. Then, at Half Way House, between Glasgow and Paisley, one of Russell's coaches broke a wheel negotiating one of these obstructions, and turned over. Its frail boiler burst with the shock, and five people were killed. The Court of Session promptly stopped the service, and the trustees had achieved their purpose. The Steam Carriage Company of Scotland subsequently sued the trustees for damages to the extent of £30,000, but no more was heard of its activities. The venture had come to an end after about £40,000 had been poured into it by Russell and his backers. Russell's vehicles later reappeared briefly in London – whether still owned by him is not known – and thereafter no more was heard of him in this context. He found real fame as a marine engineer, building the *Great Eastern* for Isambard Kingdom Brunel, and later designing the *Warrior*, the Royal Navy's first major iron ship. Russell was also one of the organisers of the Great Exhibition of 1851. But although his was an original and versatile mind, he, like Gurney, was a very poor businessman. This fault lay at the root of the financial troubles that beset the *Great Eastern* during its construction.

A curious episode in the love-hate relationship between Maceroni and Gurney casts a little more light on Russell's activities. During 1835, while attacking the Ward–Gurney failure in Scotland four years earlier, Maceroni used as ammunition against Gurney incidents which cannot have involved the latter's vehicles, and must have concerned those of Russell. According to Maceroni, Gurney's project failed in spite of the fact that tolls on steam on part of the Glasgow–Paisley road had been lifted – this thanks to the good offices of Robert Wallace, who was M.P. for Greenock. There were in fact no tolls on the Paisley road, south-west of Glasgow, and even if there had been, their waiving could not have helped the Ward–Gurney operation, which was destined for the Glasgow–Edinburgh road to the east of the city. Furthermore, Wallace did not represent Greenock until the 1833 Parliament. This was probably the most blatant piece of misrepresentation attributable to Maceroni – transferring events of 1834 into a context three years removed in time and involving other people. Maceroni was without doubt the least reliable and attractive of contemporary chroniclers of the steam carriage scene, none of whom could be described as objective.

If one accepts this interpretation of Maceroni's 1835 remarks, it follows that it was Russell who benefited from Wallace's intervention in the matter of tolls on the Paisley road, since no one else ran a service on it. This would account for a contemporary remark to the effect that "the question of tolls was a trivial matter" – "trivial" was not an adjective that could be applied to the Bathgate road toll of 1831.

The remarks concerning the tolls and Wallace's intervention, communicated to Maceroni by Ward, originated with Angus McLeod, whom Maceroni described as his agent and Ward's in Scotland. Maceroni's involvement north of the Border was abortive. In 1831 McLeod had been responsible to Ward for finding potential investors in the Scottish rights in the Gurney patent. Apparently undeterred by fiasco on that occasion, McLeod now performed the same function for Maceroni, to equally little avail.

Another Scottish enterprise of the period was less ambitious than Russell's, or anyway shorter-lived. All that is known of it is that in the summer of 1833 a vehicle built by a group of local men made an experimental trip from Aberdeen into the surrounding country.

It was against this background that Goldsworthy Gurney's new petition for the repeal of the discriminatory Acts was presented at the end of April 1834. One can only guess at his reasons for choosing this moment. No doubt it seemed auspicious. There was a new situation, seemingly far more favourable to him than at any time since his failure in 1832. Steam had recently attracted a flock of powerful and influential new friends, in and out of government, the spread of discriminatory tolls was being sharply checked, and experimental and commercial activity was more intense than ever before.

Technically, the 1834 petition was intended to compensate Gurney for his losses, but in practice the question of repeal involved every steam carriage constructor and promoter. Although there was no evidence this time that the petitioner was backed by such interests, they were as deeply concerned now as they had been at the time of Gurney's 1831 petition. The debate on the petition had brought this out. Lord Althorp, with his entirely objective attitude to steam, was in favour of sending the petition to a select committee, no doubt so that its more general implications could be explored, as in 1831. This wider approach was reflected, too, in the committee's brief. This was to "enquire into the case of Mr Goldsworthy Gurney", but as Gurney was so intimately involved in "the origin and subsequent progress" of steam carriages, the first could not be investigated without going into the second.

In the second session, some committee members were dropped and new ones added. The analysis that follows considers all together. Apart from the personal supporters of Gurney, who had declared themselves when the petition was presented – Molesworth, Jephson, the two Cayleys, Peter – the committee included known and committed supporters of steam in general, in the shape of Henry Handley and Robert Wallace. The radicals Robert Gordon (Cricklade) and Thomas Wakley (Finsbury), the liberals Thornhill Baring (Portsmouth) and Sir Charles Lemon (Cornwall West), and the reforming Earl of Euston (Thetford) and Charles Buller (Liskeard) could also be expected to sympathise with steam. Edward Pendarves and John Benett had both sat on the pro-steam 1831 committee. Dudley Ryder, Lord Sandon (Member for Liverpool) was a moderately liberal man, had scientific interests, and was a member of the National Institution of Locomotion. Sir Henry Hardinge (Launceston), an eminent soldier and former Secretary at War and Irish Secretary, was conservative by conviction but later, as we shall see, rode in a steam carriage.

The Earl of Darlington, though a reformer, had opposed the first Stockton and Darlington Railway Bill, so could not be counted on. Support for measures of political and social reform were an indication of progressive ideas in other fields, but by no means a guarantee of them. Thomas Pemberton, Member for Ripon, was a known conservative; so were Hall Dare (Essex South) and Sir William Miles (Somerset East). Nothing is known of the predilections of the remaining eight members of the committee, but its bias is already clear. The two chairmen that it had at different times – Molesworth, and Edward Stillingfleet Cayley – were both Gurney and "steam" men. If more signals were needed, they could be found in the character of the witnesses called. The committee were more strongly in favour of steam in general than of Gurney in particular, but even he received his due, as we have seen.

The witnesses called spoke for a narrower band of interests than those of 1831, unrepresentative though that body had been. Thomas Bailey, David Dady, William Bulnois, John Ward and three minor characters had all been closely concerned with Gurney three or more years earlier as employees, as business associates, or as the latters' advisers and representatives. Their evidence related only to Gurney's personal claims, and all, by definition, were on the side of steam if not necessarily on the side of Gurney. Gurney himself was also called as a witness. In the circumstances, his testimony naturally took the form of self-justification, but it was a case for steam in general as well.

Of the witnesses not linked to Gurney professionally, Alexander Gordon and Dionysius Lardner were his supporters, John Macneil was nowadays a strong partisan of road steamers, and both he and Henry Handley[13] had a business interest in them. Only two witnesses could be regarded as uncommitted. The great scientist Michael Faraday could be counted on for objectivity, and his status guaranteed him a respectful hearing. William Poole of the Patent Office was called upon solely to confirm the dates of Gurney's patents. As in 1831, there were no representatives of anti-steam opinion among the witnesses; and the comparative lack of neutral voices meant that this time the proceedings were even more heavily loaded in favour of steam.

The two men whose views probably carried most weight, on account of their reputations, were the noted highway engineer Macneil, and Faraday the famous physicist. Macneil had lost his caution of 4 years earlier. He spoke with an enthusiasm born of his new-found experience of, and professional interest in, steam carriages. Since 1831 he had, he said, travelled in almost every steam carriage on the road, and had studied the comparative effects of those vehicles and of stage coaches on road surfaces. "It steam carriages ran, generally, upon the turnpike roads of the kingdom, one-half of the annual expense of the repairs ... would be saved." They frightened very few horses. At 15 m.p.h. they were safer than stage coaches at 10 or 11 m.p.h., because the latter's horses were unmanageable at such speeds. So much for the trustees, and the timid traveller. Macneil felt, too, that prejudice had waned since 1831 – specifically, there was less fear among agriculturalists for the future of the draught horse. It was generally held, he added, that Parliament would not pass any more turnpike Bills incorporating prohibitory tolls. He presumably based his first assertion on his talks with trustees on the Holyhead road, and his second on the mood of Parliament as reflected in the renewal Act it passed that session.

For his part, Faraday, too, came down on the side of steam carriages, to the extent of admitting that the engineers who had thought them impractical 10 years before had been proved wrong. He agreed that public opinion was changing in their favour.

The committee's questions, too, were more restricted in scope than those of the 1831 committee. Perhaps naturally, they were concerned exclusively with the activities of Gurney and his associates, with his vehicles and patents, and with comparisons of all these with the doings and inventions of other contractors. The committee began to call witnesses on 7 July. The end of the 1834 session came before it had finished hearing evidence, so it resumed in May 1835. In its recommendations that affected steam in general, the report that it produced in that month was more predictable even than that of 1831: "The prohibitory tolls should be repealed, and a general Act passed, fixing tolls on steam carriages." So as to give Gurney a chance of recouping his losses, these tolls should place steamers on an equal footing with horsed vehicles. The committee's alternative recommendations for compensating Gurney have already been noted.

For over a year, no action was taken on the committee's report. Since current events naturally coloured the conduct of Parliament, it is advisable – at the risk of losing continuity – to interrupt the story of the petition's progress here to look at the activities of the interested parties in 1835 and 1836.

In January 1835, William Church of Birmingham is reported as running his coach six miles out on the Coventry road and back. The going was very muddy, yet the unwieldy machine is said to have covered a mile at 24 m.p.h. No more is heard of Church's activities. In June the London and Birmingham Steam Carriage Company's shareholders met to be told that unspecified problems had so far prevented the launching of a service, but that "the difficulties in the way of running steam carriages on gravel roads are entirely obviated".

In mid-April the last positive news was heard of Nathaniel Ogle's operations, when his coach covered the 16 miles between Tonbridge and Farnborough in Kent in 3 hours. This was not a performance he would have liked to see quoted, even though the route was extremely hilly, and included the notorious 1:12 gradient of River Hill. There was a passing suggestion that Ogle was running on the New Road in London in 1836, but no real evidence.

By the time Ogle ceased his activities, at a date unknown, he claimed to have run 3000 miles with one carriage alone, and to have experienced mechanical mishaps only, except for a fatal accident near Hammersmith when a workman fell under his wheels. His achievements included, he said, a run with 26 people on board from Tonbridge to Maidstone – 13 miles – in 40 minutes, and a trip with 30 passengers from London to Ascot in $2\frac{1}{4}$ hours. The speeds, though very high, were less fantastical than some of the others to which he had laid claim. Neither of these trips can be dated, or otherwise documented.

In 1834 Ogle had floated a company and issued a prospectus. Four thousand shares were subscribed for, but only one gambler paid money over. This, a mere £20 deposit, was returned to him. Ogle said he lost £3800 on this venture alone, and by 1839, $10\frac{1}{2}$ years after entering the field, had gone through £47,000. In that year he said that he still had "several" steamers standing ready (there is no evidence that he ever built more than two, or at most three), as well as two others "oxidising away". No doubt this fate overtook them all, for they were never called upon to run thereafter.

One of the reasons Ogle later gave for the failure of road steamers in general suggested that with experience, he had grown more honest with himself and others. Like other critics, he blamed constructors for working alone and not pooling their knowledge. No other constructor admitted as much. Apart from that, prohibitive tolls, and public ignorance of and prejudice towards steamers were to blame. The reasons particular to Ogle obviously included the fact that he had spent a great deal of money, and had less to show for it than any other prominent constructor.

In the early summer of 1834, or perhaps before, William Cubitt, one of the committee that had arranged the abortive London to Birmingham run in Dance's vehicle, issued a challenge to his fellow-engineers, to join him in paying for the building of a new steamer. It is known that Dance and Macneil were among the acceptors, and Maudslay, Sons & Field were duly commissioned to do the work. Cubitt was clearly undiscouraged by his experience with the Maudslay-modified Dance machine of 1833. The new vehicle, a tractor, cost £1100 and was complete by October 1834. It had a water-tube boiler, and weighed a massive 6 tons with fuel and water – this apparently without the omnibus it was to tow. An unnamed ex-Dance employee now working for Maudslay – still, perhaps, Thomas Bailey – was the driver of the vehicle, which was intended for a proposed London to Bath service.

For some reason, the Cubitt-inspired machine is not heard of again until the summer of 1835, when it undertook a trial trip from Maudslay's Lambeth works to Denmark Hill, a distance of $9\frac{3}{4}$ miles. Its patronage seems to have been every bit as distinguished as that of Maudslay's first excursion into road steamers, for on board, among other notables, were Sir Henry Parnell and Sir Henry Hardinge. The new machine also visited Slough, went to Reading five or six times – once with Parnell as a passenger – and on another occasion travelled as far west as Marlborough. Its maximum speed was 18–20 m.p.h., and its average time between London and Reading was 3 hours 10 minutes. An average speed of 15–16 m.p.h. was claimed, but this must have been exclusive of stops for fuel, water and repairs. Cubitt himself rode in the outfit on six or seven occasions. It was easily controlled, but horses shied at it more than they did at coaches, and flying sparks were a problem, for the fire burned coal, not coke.

The main difficulty, and by implication the cause of the abandonment of the project, was that the vehicle was clearly going to be uneconomic to run in service, compared with coaches and railways. The capital costs would be huge, for the service proposed, which was going to be on a scale comparable to that of the equally abortive London and Holyhead company, would involve not only workshops and depots, but also 100 tractors. This was the first and only direct admission ever made by a steam carriage promoter that his vehicles could not compete with either existing or future alternative means of transport. It may have had a wider effect than its authors anticipated.[14]

In December 1834 two of John Scott Russell's coaches were shipped to London, and in February of 1835 were noted as running on the Hammersmith Road, preparatory (it was said) to launching a London to Windsor service. No more was heard of this. There is a suggestion – no more – that Russell vehicles were running in London that summer, but then there was silence.

A similar fate – and the usual one, when he entrusted his vehicles to other operators – overtook a Hancock venture early in the year. Late in 1834 he had rebuilt the new *Era*, which was renamed *Erin* and dispatched to Ireland in November for a demonstration to the promoters of the Hibernian Steam Coach Company. (Hancock gave the withdrawal of the *Era* as the reason for the cessation of his 1834 City to Paddington service.) The *Erin* arrived in Dublin on 6 January 1835, and ran about the streets; the first self-propelled road vehicle to be seen beyond the Irish Sea. At the end of eight days, the *Erin* was shipped back to Stratford.

Also in 1835, Hancock built another, entirely new vehicle, to the order of the Hibernian company. Called the Irish or Dublin drag – though it seems never to have gone to Ireland – it was a powerful tractor that hauled an omnibus-load of 18 people – including M.P.s – on a demonstration run to Brentford and back at 14 m.p.h. Hancock took the *ensemble* to Reading on 18 July. Early in August the *Erin* coach travelled from Stratford to Marlborough and back. This was not such a satisfactory run. The fan draught was not working, and there were no regular water supplies – Hancock had to refill his tank by buckets from pumps, ponds and streams, like everyone else. For both these reasons, the fire frequently sank low, and power and time were lost. One imagines that Hancock missed his London arrangements, which from long experience must have been more efficient. During the outward journey, $7\frac{1}{2}$ hours were spent running, as against $4\frac{1}{2}$ hours on adjustments and replenishments, almost all of it filling up with water.

On 28 August the *Erin* went to Birmingham on behalf of the London and Birmingham Steam Carriage Company, which was still in being on paper, and whose promoters were now sensibly considering a Hancock vehicle. The trip, completed at an average speed of 10 m.p.h., was entirely successful, but more power was considered necessary for such long hauls. The *Erin* had been built for shorter runs. Nevertheless, the company wrote off their potential rivals without more ado. The *Coventry Mercury* said: "We hear that it is the intention of the company to employ the present coachmen and guards as directors of the steam carriages." This sort of talk, designed no doubt to lure investors, was turned by an irony of fate against its originators when, instead, it was the railways that gave work to those whose livelihoods had been destroyed by steam. Neither the *Erin* nor any other steamer went to work for the London and Birmingham Steam Carriage Company, of which nothing more is heard.

Hancock surfaces next on 11 May 1836, when he launched a new service. This generally ran between the Bank and Paddington, but occasionally covered the whole distance between Stratford and

Paddington via the Bank. It employed all Hancock's existing vehicles – *Erin, Enterprise* and *Infant*. There is no mention of the *Autopsy*, which had presumably been broken up or sold, but Hancock converted the "Irish drag" of 1835 into a new omnibus, which he christened *Automaton* and added to the working fleet. With accommodation for 22, it was bigger than the rest, none of which was designed for more than 14 passengers, and the engine was larger and more powerful. The *Automaton* once reached 21 m.p.h. on the Bow Road with 20 passengers on board, and could average 12–15 m.p.h. The service ended in mid-September, though *Automaton* went on to make some expeditions to Epping in October.

This, Hancock's last commercial operation, was the most intensive, prolonged and successful that he or anyone else ran. His machines covered 4200 miles between them, and carried 12,761 passengers. Their maximum capacity over the same period was 20,420 passengers. On average, each carriage ran for 5 hours $17\frac{1}{2}$ minutes every working day. During the four months there were, Hancock claimed, only four mechanical breakages, and a single accident. There is evidence of one other mishap, in May, when some coach horses ran away from a steamer, damaging the coach and themselves.

Summing up his 1836 achievement, Hancock stated that when he introduced steamers on to the Stratford–Paddington route, the horse buses (by now running the whole distance) took 2 hours 20 minutes to cover the distance, which was nearly 10 miles long. Hancock started by cutting an hour or more off this time, whereupon the horse buses accelerated greatly. By July they were averaging 8–9 m.p.h. over the distance, compared with Hancock's 9–10 m.p.h., taking all his vehicles together. In other words, Hancock had performed a major public service on behalf of the London commuter. This was accomplished against a background of renewed hostility from omnibus drivers, but "general civility" from the public at large.[15]

Even so, this was the end of Hancock's public commercial services. The reasons can only be guessed at. Nathaniel Ogle said that Hancock failed because the nature of the services he ran – short hauls punctuated by numerous halts – rendered them uneconomic. This is plausible – the same argument holds good for any form of powered transport – but Ogle seems only to have been guessing, too. He provided no figures to back up his assertions. This goes for any other argument over the economics of Hancock's services – the only factors that can be assessed at all accurately are fuel costs and tolls, which by themselves convey nothing in Hancock's case. Yet Hancock built no more public steamers, and ran no more commercial services at his own expense. When as we shall see, he eventually contemplated a return to the field, he clearly had no more money of his own to spend, or if he had, did not intend to spend it. The inference is that, in 1836, he withdrew because his services were uneconomic, and he was losing money.

In September 1836 the editor of the *Mechanics' Magazine* said that "Mr Hancock is now the only engineer with a steam carriage on any road". How was it that the number of active constructors and entrepreneurs had been reduced from at least nine in 1834 to five in 1835, to a single man in 1836, and to none at all by the autumn of that year? Turnover had always been high, and the particular reasons for the disappearance of individual constructors are in most cases known, or can be inferred. The point is that before 1835 fresh protagonists had always arrived to replace the casualties, and veterans had made comebacks. This constant renewal of impetus had ceased. Eighteen thirty-four had been the last year for newcomers. In 1835 only more or less scarred veterans remained. By late 1836 even they had gone.

As is so often the case at this time, questions must be answered partly with guesses. The fall in numbers may have been due to the depressingly uniform failure of the company promotions with which predecessors or their business associates had tried to raise working capital. The unprecedented rash of company promotions in 1832–4 showed that the public's money was now regarded as a necessity – private fortunes had proved unable to bear the strain. Successful railway promotions, on the other hand, were increasing and were becoming more dramatic, ambitious and promising. In 1831–4 five new steam lines were opened. Work on the London to Birmingham railway began in 1833, and on the Great Western Railway two years later. Capital was pouring more heavily than ever into railways, while steam carriages remained starved of it. It was estimated that by 1839 over £20 millions had been invested in railways.[16] There was nothing, as yet, to show that the great trunk lines would be economic when built, but they seized the imagination. Also, the steam locomotive worked. In every way, it was potentially the complete answer to long-distance land travel requirements. The struggles of the steam carriage, in most cases handicapped by technical difficulties and discriminatory tolls, must have seemed puny in comparison. The London–Holyhead and London–Birmingham company promoters, like others, were swimming against an increasingly strong tide.

Worse, at least two constructors – the Heaton brothers and William Cubitt – had come publicly to the conclusion that a steam carriage service could not be economic even if capital were forthcoming. Cubitt's view – that steamers could not operate economically in competition with either railways or stage coaches on one

of the nation's most heavily travelled highways – was a direct contra-
diction of the optimistic stance adopted by the London and
Holyhead promoters in 1833, According to Cubitt and the
Heatons, steam carriages were defeated before they began to fight.
Perhaps other intending constructors and promoters came to the
same conclusion. Gurney was no longer active, but in 1835 he saw
the trend: "The railroads are now cutting also on the great roads,
which affects steam on common roads." For his part, Cubitt may have
been influenced by his growing involvement as a railway engineer.

Up to July of the latter year, there were no other discouragements
peculiar to 1835 and 1836. We are left, unsatisfactorily, with these
alone to account for the decline in activity, and – to confuse the issue
further – with a dramatic drop in hostile turnpike legislation, which
should, on the contrary, have encouraged such enterprise.

After July 1836, however, any would-be constructors or company
promoters who might have been planning activity faced a fresh
discouragement. Here we must return to the leisurely proceedings at
Westminster that had begun against such a different background in
April 1834. At last, on 8 May 1836, a "Bill to repeal such portions of all
Acts as impose prohibitory tolls on steam carriages", drawn up by
Edward Cayley and Sir William Molesworth, was presented in the
Commons by the former.

The uniform scale of tolls to be imposed on all turnpike roads
catered for small private steamers – of which one had by now actually
appeared[17] – as well as bigger public vehicles. Up to a weight of $1\frac{1}{2}$
tons unladen, the same toll as for a two-horse carriage would be
demanded. Steamers of up to 3 tons were equated with a four-horse
coach. Above that weight, or if tyres were less than $3\frac{1}{2}$ inches wide, the
toll was doubled; as it was if the wheels had conical instead of
cylindrical bearing surfaces. Thus, trustees afraid of damage were to
be pacified. As a further gesture to the trusts, public-service or other
commercial vehicles would be charged at each time of passing, while
private machines would return toll-free. Thus a trust would be
compensated if the larger steamers caused more damage to its roads,
or reduced its income from stage coaches.

In the end, the Bill's toll provisions were as fair to all interests as
those of 1831; and there was no time limit on them – steam would be
protected indefinitely. The main difference lay in the presence in the
1836 Bill of precautions against explosions – which was hardly
surprising, in view of the fact that in the four years 1831–4, four steam
carriages, or about one in five of those running, had blown up,
sometimes with loss of life. A maximum permissible diameter was set
on the water vessels of boilers, so as to eliminate single-chamber

boilers. Small was safe. Also, all boilers had to be tested to double their normal working pressure, or to at least 100 p.s.i. A steam carriage operator would have to satisfy two Justices of the Peace that this test had been carried out without explosion, and also declare the weight of the vehicles on oath. The Justices would then issue a certificate, without which no steamer could run. Amendments to give effect to these precautions were incorporated on the two occasions in June when the whole House sat in committee on the Bill.

As with the 1832 Bill, the new measure passed the Commons without debate, but when on 28 June it was brought to the Lords, its reception was chilly. The Marquess of Salisbury, a member of the Lords committee on the 1832 Bill, insisted that it should be referred to a select committee. If the subject were not aired further, "to secure the public against the occurrence of accident", he for one would vote against the Bill. His words made two things clear. First, he regarded the conduct and findings of the Commons committee of 1834–5 as inadequate. They were in truth one-sided, even by the standards of the day, so this reaction was to be expected. Second, the dangers of steam carriages were in the forefront of his mind, in spite of the Bill's safeguards. This, too, cannot be wondered at.

In reply, the reforming Earl of Radnor, who presented the Bill and had also sat on the 1832 committee, did his best to deflect Lord Salisbury's aim. The intention of the Bill, he said, was to remove the financial burden incurred by Gurney in his pioneering efforts. This, after all, had been the purpose of the 1834 petition. What he described as Gurney's invention had been brought to "a state of great perfection", in which the public was "secured from accident by the peculiar construction of the boiler". But Lord Salisbury was not to be distracted from the Bill's wider implications. Lord Lyndhurst, the Lord Chancellor, supported him, and the measure was duly referred to a select committee of peers on 18 July.

The 22 members of the committee were chaired by Lord Salisbury, which did not presage well for the Bill. The influential Lord Chancellor was with him. There were in addition four known conservatives, including Lord Wharncliffe and the Dukes of Cumberland and Richmond, who probably agreed with Salisbury and Lyndhurst. Wharncliffe, furthermore, was now the Chairman of the Great Western Railway – an additional reason for him to oppose steam on the road. On the other hand, there were at least five peers of reforming views, including a former prime minister, the Earl of Ripon. There is no evidence of the witnesses being weighted against the Bill, although they represented a much broaded cross-section of interests than those called before the Commons committee. Gurney, Hancock and Alexander Gordon were all produced. Joshua Field, William Cubitt and Thomas Harris, one of Sir Charles Dance's former engineers, could also be assumed, on their past form, to favour road steamers. So could a clergyman called Williams, of whom nothing is ascertainable except that he claimed to have ridden in steam carriages more than anyone else. On the other hand, two railway engineers were called – George Stephenson and John Braithwaite – and they could not be expected to favour a potential competitor. Neither could Benjamin Worthy Horne, the noted coachmaster, nor William Palmer, a coachman. Thus all the major land-going passenger-carrying interests were represented. The only other witness called was William Alexander Provis, engineer of the Menai Bridge and assistant to Telford, who pleaded lack of qualifications to speak on steam carriages, and was excused.

The committee's questions reflected Lord Salisbury's fears. They concentrated on asking about the perils, accident-proneness and general unpleasantness of steam carriages – the danger of explosions and of spark-induced fires, the noise, smoke, and letting-off of steam, and the frightening of horses. Only incidentally were other issues, such as possible damage to roads, brought up.

The steam carriage promoters, their associates and supporters were reasonably honest in their replies, being guilty of *suppressio veri* at worst. They were much more outspoken when it came to accidents suffered not by themselves but by other constructors. As usual, they were the worst enemies of their own cause.

Gurney made no mention of explosions, or of any other kind of accident, in connection with his own vehicles. He would concede only that the fan-induced draught of his early vehicles had been noisy. Instead, he drew attention gratuitously to the exploding single-chamber boilers of Burstall and Hill, Sharp and Roberts, and Russell, so as to emphasise the superiority of his boiler design over theirs. He did not seem to understand the drift of the questions being asked – that steam carriages as a whole, not just his, were on trial, before a court unappreciative of technicalities, and (as the events of the 1832 had shown) of proven hostility to steam on the road.

On this occasion, Hancock's behaviour was not much better. He admitted that horses were frightened by his carriages, as they were by other traffic, and he confessed to one accident; that already noted. But he was quick to attribute another to Maceroni; and he had already further divided the ranks of steam by petitioning the Lords on 11 July to delete the clause in the Bill that prescribed maximum boiler diameters. Since the clause was designed to exclude single-chamber boilers, and his own water vessels were only two inches in diameter

– only a quarter of the maximum laid down – there was no obvious reason why Hancock should oppose it, other than, perhaps, a belief that technical matters should not be decided by legislation. In part, no doubt, Hancock's behaviour was intended simply as a show of his independence of other steam constructors. It will be remembered that he had presented his own petition at the time of Gurney's appeal to Parliament in 1831. Rather surprisingly, the clause was deleted – perhaps because it was considered a mistake to restrict boiler design to one type (the water tube) only.

Thomas Harris and the clergyman Williams, more honest, or without an axe to grind, made up for Gurney's omissions by mentioning the overturning of the phaeton by Dance's tractor in 1831, and the explosion in Edinburgh in the same year. Joshua Field admitted that horses were more frightened of his 1834–5 machine than of coaches. Hancock, Harris, Field and Cubitt all conceded that the machines with which they had been associated had at one time or another thrown out sparks, which, as we have seen, were much feared for their fire-raising possibilities.

The witnesses most likely to be hostile to steam carriages were in fact extremely objective and honest. Benjamin Worthy Horne claimed that steamers were noisy, but they did not frighten his horses, and he could not defend with evidence his assumption that they were dangerous. The coachman William Palmer agreed that steamers were noisy, and claimed that a Hancock vehicle *did* frighten his horses, causing them to run away. But Palmer then declared that no horses were wholly predictable or safe – in other words, there was nothing specially alarming about steamers.

George Stephenson was against steam carriages mainly on technical grounds. They had to be uneconomic, relative to railways, because of the higher rolling resistance of roads compared with smooth rails. If they used the steam blast or jet, they would be as noisy as locomotives with the same device. Furthermore, water-tube boilers were more, not less, likely to explode than single-chamber boilers because their tubes contained very little water. Braithwaite agreed that steam carriages could not be economic to run, and added that they smelt. One gains the impression that the evidence of the railway interest was deliberately hostile, even if most of its arguments were justified.

By concentrating on the steamers' actual and potential liability to accident, the committee had of course got plenty of material. The evidence was there and undeniable, provided more eagerly by the supporters of steam than by its opponents. The point that the committee ignored in its report of 4 August 1836 was that this evidence was open to more than one interpretation. Steamers had blown up because of poor design or mismanagement, which were not universal failings and might be rectified. This was not taken into account – the fact was that they *had* blown up. The Lords' lack of interest in technicalities is, perhaps, reflected in their agreeing to delete the clause limiting the diameter of boiler vessels. The far-sighted report and recommendations of the 1831 Commons committee was ignored.

For every witness who swore that horses were more frightened by steamers than by other traffic, mainly because of their noise, there was another who absolved steam from any greater responsibility. This, too, was not considered – no one could deny that steamers frightened horses, so contributing to accidents. Spark emission, like noise, was a nuisance that might be abated by research and development, but this was of no interest to the committee: there was no present remedy. This attitude may be explained, and to some extent justified, by the destructive fires that had been caused by sparks from railway locomotives. Although it admitted that "very considerable progress had been made towards [the steamer's] perfection", to the committee steam was still dangerous, in more than one way. There was no more to be said: Lord Salisbury's views had won the day. Furthermore, as the evidence of William Cubitt on his own operation and that of the clergyman Williams on Russell's showed, the encouragement of steam carriages led not only to "dangerous experiments", but also to "wild speculations".

These were the "serious objections" entertained against the Bill, not "counterbalanced by the prospect of any great public advantage". The committee recommended that the Bill be thrown out.

The most interesting, because unexpected, feature of the Lords' questions and of their report is a negative one. Although the report recommended that the size and weight of steamers be controlled, to avoid damage to roads, there was no longer any direct reference to a need to protect the trusts and their creditors. Defending them, right or wrong, was no longer fashionable. It followed that the possible loss of trust income from a decline in coaching caused by steam carriages was no longer an issue, if it had ever been one. Furthermore, while the committee rejected a relaxation of existing tolls on steam, it specifically declared itself against any further prohibitive tolls. No reason was given. It cannot have been because steam on the road was no longer thought significant – the uncompromising tone of the report made that clear. One is left with the presumption that discriminatory tolls came under the heading of toll anomalies between adjoining trusts, to which Parliament had already shown itself hostile.

The increasing coolness of the Upper House, traditionally the firmest supporters of trust interests, becomes more striking when seen against the trusts' rapidly accelerating decline. The Highways Act of 1835 had abolished statute labour, but in practice the trusts had for long preferred to take financial composition from the parishes in lieu of the share of labour to which they were entitled. The end of statute labour meant the end of compounding, and hence a heavy financial loss which the trusts could ill afford. The Act was worst than a half-measure. It removed an abuse, but left only the discredited parish rate system in its place. It substituted no reformed system of road maintenance, and struck a heavy blow against the most efficient existing means of keeping up the roads. The spread of railways was about to deal the shaken edifice an even harder blow.

Owing to the length of time that had elapsed between the presentation of Gurney's petition and the Lords' decision, the latter had no identifiable effect. As we have seen, it was a blow that landed on air. During 1836 only one constructor, Hancock, was running steam carriages. He had comparatively reliable vehicles, he ran on roads heavily frequently by potential paying customers, and he was not unduly incommoded by tolls. The rest had been driven out, probably by lack of capital – a condition attributable in part to a Lords' decision, but that of 1832, not 1836. The latter would have been discouraging, but given money, there is no reason to suppose that constructors and promoters would have been crushed by the 1836 decision, any more than they had been by that of 1832.

The Lords' rejection of steam carriages in 1832 was the decisive Act of the two. If the Toll Relief Bill had become law at that time, the steam carriage might have attracted the capital it needed for development. By 1836 the railway was a hungrier and lustier child, demanding, and justifiably receiving, the capital it needed for nourishment, and the chances of the public passenger-carrying road steamer were that much poorer. It comes as a surprise to learn that its day was not yet quite done, as we shall see.

Meanwhile, the sudden growth of interest in road steamers in general since 1827 had given rise to suggestions for every sort of vehicle, not just competitors in the field of public passenger-carrying. In a letter dated 15 September 1827 Robert Southey, the poet and friend of Telford, wrote to the Bristol surgeon John King: "I live in hope of having a steam carriage which will enable me to transport myself and my family at a reasonable cost. We will mount the vehicle some day when the water boils, and steer for my native city."

The satirists foresaw private steamers in their caricatures at this time, and in 1827 and 1828 at least two were designed. One, its inventor unknown, had chain drive. The other, a steam phaeton, was patented by William Harland of Scarborough. Neither machine seems to have been built. At this date, the road steamer was seen mainly as competition for stage coaches. Only when commercial steamers began to fail did their makers turn to private machines.

By early August 1831 Goldsworthy Gurney was seriously considering an alternative to commercial road steamers. This was natural enough, since Sir Charles Dance's service had just failed, and the future of any commercial service was in doubt. Gurney said that "private carriages will also be used. Under this opinion, I have given directions for building a small one." In the same context,[18] he announced that "I have a carriage now building which I do not expect will weigh above 5 hundredweight, which I expect to do the work of about 1 horse, and carry 2 or 3 people: speed is a particular object, and it is not intended to carry anything more than light parcels." This could almost be the recipe for the first sports car. Private carriages, added Gurney, would be in use within five years, if no impediment were put in their way.

But there is no evidence that Gurney's vehicle was completed or ran. By 1832, in any case, all his manufacturing activities had ceased. Given, too, the lack of any evidence that George Medhurst's steamers of 1819–27 were purpose-built as private vehicles, the credit for the earliest "motor car" built in Britain must go to Walter Hancock. The date of 1835 which he gives in one place for the completion of a three-passenger gig, his first private steamer, is significant. Like Gurney before him, Hancock thought of building a private vehicle at a point when the commercial steamer was in trouble on most fronts.

There is much fuller documentation for another Hancock vehicle – or perhaps it was the first, still in existence. This was on the road in the spring and summer of 1838, well after Hancock's last successful venture was over. Around the end of April Hancock and two friends drove in a 4-wheeled "steam gig" from Stratford through the City, and on 22 June he demonstrated "a newly commissioned steam cab" in Hyde Park. It was tractable, could cruise at 12 m.p.h., and in three or four hours' running through a great crowd of fashionable onlookers frightened no horses. In a postscript to his book, dated 4 July, Hancock writes:

I have brought out the steam phaeton shown on the title page, intended for my private use. It has seats for three persons, independent of the one steering . . . it has run principally in the City, and upon the roads in the east of London, but within the last few days, I have occasionally run it in several parts of the west end of the town, principally in Hyde Park, amongst the throng of carriages and horses . . . on fine afternoons.

The carriage was lower-powered than the commercial vehicles, but was of course lighter.

From the description, it seems that the "cab" and the "phaeton" were the same machine. A description in the *Mechanics' Magazine* refers to it indifferently as a gig and a phaeton, which reinforces the feeling that in 1838, at least, there was only one private Hancock steamer. In any case, the three terms were not used in a mutually exclusive sense, except by coachbuilders. Most commonly the gig and the private cab, or cabriolet, were both light, open, 2-passenger, 2-wheeled vehicles drawn by a single horse, while the phaeton was usually a 4-wheeled cab. The Hancock machine most resembled a phaeton, but unlike any of the named vehicles, was ill-proportioned and heavy-looking. The writers describing the Hancock carriage had only the three most common types of smart, popular, private carriage as standards of comparison, and as the steamer was an entirely new concept, none of them exactly fitted it.

Whatever their number, one hears the last of Hancock's private steamers in 1839. George Dacre, clerk to the trustees of the consolidated Middlesex and Essex trusts, complains of "a person of the name of Hancock", who "travels about continuously by locomotive engines upon the road, and with smaller ones which he calls gigs . . . and they frighten the horses to such an extent that I have often been requested to interfere on the subject . . . I see him every day: he first alters one part of his machinery, and then another . . . it is merely as an experiment." Like every other constructor, Hancock was tinkering to the end.

Gurney may have been contemplating private steamers for sale, but produced none; it seems that Hancock never even thought of doing so, practical though his machine obviously was. In varying degrees, the same disabilities would have afflicted private steamers as afflicted commercial vehicles. It was probably true that discriminatory tolls would have been less discouraging to private owners, by definition well-to-do, than to a commercially run enterprise, and they, like their sporting descendants the first motorists, might have been more tolerant of unreliability and danger than the fare-paying general public. Lack of capital would, however, have inhibited manufacture in this field as badly as it did that of commercial vehicles.

Other objections common to all steamers were more potent in the case of private vehicles. William Bridges Adams, a historian of the horsedrawn carriage, drew a discouraging, if fanciful, picture of the private steamers: "His travelling garb is rough and rude, his breath is sulphureous, his voice is hissing, his joints creak, the anointing of his limbs gives forth an unpleasing gaseous odour, he carries with him a kitchen and a fuel chamber, and his whole appearance is black and unsightly"[19] – a prospect not to be compared with the horse carriages of the discerning wealthy, so light and elegant now that Obadiah Elliott's elliptical springs had done away with the perch. Also, the private steamer was an impersonal thing, lacking the character of other vehicles. Furthermore, suggested this critic, the carriage builders were already expressing hostility to the idea of private steamers, in case they should supersede the horse. Adams added, unhelpfully, that to realise a profit, operators of steamers would need to carry fare-paying passengers.

So were the first "motor cars" aborted: more quickly, even, than the first self-propelled coaches and omnibuses. But the disappearance of the steam carriage constructors was only part of a larger picture – one of general desertion of the main trunk roads by through public (if not local or private) traffic, traditional as well as new. No sooner had the steamer gone than the vehicle it tried to replace, the stage coach, was (in cases where it ran parallel) swept from Britain's trunk roads by the railway, a much more dangerous challenger.

Six hammer-blows descended on the trunk road stage coach in four years. In 1838 the London to Birmingham railway was opened throughout; by 1839, the Eastern Counties Railway was working to Chelmsford. The Great Western Railway was finished as far as Reading in the following year, as was the entire London to Portsmouth and Southampton line. In 1841 the London and Brighton Railway was open, and the Great Western was completed to Bath and Bristol. The forecasts of Torrens and the rest came true. By 1839 it was being admitted that "whenever mechanical power has been substituted for animal power, the result has hitherto been that the labour is performed at a cheaper rate".

The effects were immediate and calamitous for the through stage coaches involved. Henry Gray, a jobmaster, reported in April 1839 that three-quarters of the London–Birmingham business had been lost; business to the north as a whole had declined by half. Forty-two coaches had been taken off the London–Birmingham road already. Edward Sherman, the coachmaster, told how he alone had had to discontinue 15 of his daily northbound coaches. On the London–Birmingham run, only two of his nine daily coaches survived. None was a day coach. By the summer, Sherman expected all his coaches to be off the route.

Cost was one factor in the change of public allegiance. The normal rail fare from London to Birmingham was £1, as compared with £1 inside a coach and 12s outside, and there were few cheap trains; but the additional element of tips for coachman and guard, which accounted for a substantial proportion of the cost of a coach journey, was absent. Furthermore, said Sherman, although most travellers were still too timid to travel by rail, the numbers of the fearful were daily declining. Curiously, no mention is made by the sufferers of the railway's main advantage – an average speed of 20 m.p.h. or more, double that of stage coaches as a whole.

The decline in trunk road stage coaching was illustrated by the falling tax revenue from this source. Receipts from mileage duty dropped from £523,856 in 1837 to £314,000 in 1841, Revenue from licences fell even more drastically, from £498,497 in 1835 to £73,000 in 1854, but the latter figure also reflected reduced licence charges, designed to aid coachmasters. In the former year, Benjamin Worthy Horne alone had paid nearly £27,000 in duty and licences.

With the exception of Horne, the coachmasters had shown no early signs of alarm, but as soon as the enemy was confronting them, some prudently changed sides. William Chaplin joined forces with Horne, then helped the London to Birmingham railway by withdrawing coach competition and providing feeder coaches. With Pickfords & Company, he acquired a share in the railway company's freight-carrying agency, then sold most of his coaches before his assets vanished, and invested the return in the railway. He was deputy chairman by 1839, and chairman four years later. Chaplin was by then already Chairman of the London and South Western Railway, after having helped it out of financial trouble. Edward Sherman undertook much of the London carrying business of the Great Western Railway. Another coachmaster, Joseph Baxendale, became Chairman of the South Eastern Railway.

There was no such escape for the turnpike trusts on the coaching routes parallel to railways. In 1836 Sir James McAdam had warned them of what would happen to them,[20] but whether they believed him or not, there was nothing they could have done to avert disaster, for they were tied to the roads. In 1838 the trusts were at their greatest extent – 1116 trusts controlled 22,000 miles of road. But a year later their liabilities, too, had reached unprecedented proportions – £1032 millions in unpaid interest, and a total debt of over £9 millions. Weakened already by mismanagement, and by the abolition of statute labour (which by 1839 had cost the trusts as a whole £200,000), the trusts on these roads were crippled by the railways. The effect on the trusts between London and Birmingham has already been noted. In 1839 the clerk to the New Cross trust stated that in the first full year of its operation, 1837–8, the London to Greenwich railway – though open only as far as Deptford – had caused a drop in trust income from £15,375 to £12,920. An estimated one-third of the coaches on the route had been taken off. No less a figure than Sir James McAdam confirmed the general trend.

There was some compensation for the trusts in feeder and construction traffic. As early as 1832 it was noted that the loss in stage coach duty caused by the withdrawal of coaches between Liverpool and Manchester was being offset by "an increased communication of stage coaches on other branches of the roads" leading to the two cities. By 1839 it was being said that "nearly all roads leading to stations or termini have increased in their traffic". The clerk to the Middlesex and Essex trust noted an actual increase of toll income, contributed by construction traffic involved in the building of the Eastern Counties Railway. But a trust that benefited from the railway was a rare exception, and anyway, construction traffic was by its nature impermanent. The total income of all the trusts in England and Wales grew from £1.43 million in 1834 to £1.53 million in 1839, but income from feeder and construction traffic did not make up for the loss of the main road stage coaches as far as the local trusts directly affected were concerned.

It was already clear, however, that the horse-breeding interest need not have worried about steam on the road or on the railway. The horse trade was described as flourishing, providing animals for feeder coaches and for the new city cabs and omnibuses. The total number of stage coaches (including those on feeder roads) declined little, from 3874 in 1834 to 3632 in 1839. The number of licensees of post horses actually grew, from 9388 in 1837 to 9762 in 1839. In addition, the number of 2-wheeled carriages had increased from 2625 in 1832 to 3691 in 1839. "Carriage folk" – whether they owned vehicles or hired them – were on the increase.

Contractors were called upon to hire out draught horses in large numbers to help in railway construction. During excavations in May 1838 for the Great Western Railway at Sonning in Berkshire, Robert Lovegrove furnished between 146 and 176 animals daily over one period of six days – and he was not the only contractor involved. During the building of the Stafford – Tamworth section of the Trent Valley Railway in 1846, the number of horses employed daily from May to October varied between 109 and 195. Once their lines were operating, some railway companies bought horses, as well as hiring them, for their freight and passenger feeder traffic. The London and North Western Railway alone owned 612 animals by 1848. In the same year, Pickford & Company, the largest carriers, handled 850 tons of goods daily for the L.N.W.R. at their Camden Town depot. They owned 400 horses, with their own stabling and veterinary service.

The sudden and rapid decline of the trusts from 1835, becoming particularly pronounced after 1838, drew a very quick reaction from Parliament, no doubt because of the extent of the interests at stake. In March 1839 a Commons select committee was appointed "for the purpose of ascertaining how the formation of railroads may affect the interest of turnpike trusts and the creditors of such trusts". It sat at intervals from late March to early June.

The committee was chaired by William Alexander Mackinnon, M.P. for Lymington, and a member of the 1831 committee that had considered Gurney's first petition. The turnpike trusts were one of Mackinnon's major interests. The witnesses fell into three categories. Those with an interest in trusts included creditors, trustees, trust officers and the prominent toll farmer Louis Levy. The trust officers called were Sir James McAdam, general surveyor of the Metropolitan roads, John Lawrence Bicknell, clerk to the New Cross trust, and George Dacre, clerk to the Middlesex and Essex trust. All spoke for local highway authorities of major importance in and around London. Bicknell and Dacre respectively administered trusts controlling 39 and 36 miles of heavily frequented road.

The coaching interest, on whose tolls the trusts so much depended, were represented directly by Edward Sherman, the coachmaster, and Henry Gray, jobmaster and chairman of the society of postmasters. Indirectly, coaching was also represented by the trust officers, for their interests were basically the same. The evidence of these two groups, which has already been quoted, harped on the disaster that had been visited upon trust finances by the withdrawal of coach traffic from roads parallel to the railways.

The third category of witness, more heavily represented than any of the others, comprised partisans of the steam carriage. At first sight, it is extraordinary to find old constructors, their fingers well burned, and new joining battle again when all the signs indicated that the day had finally been lost three years earlier. Their testimony – fully orchestrated to private interest, and ringing with confidence – was poignantly reminiscent of earlier committees sitting in happier times.

In fact, the presence of these men before the committee of 1839 becomes less strange on reflection. Mackinnon must have called them out of the depth of his concern for the trusts, and the bleakness of their situation. As for the supporters of steam, they had nothing to lose by trying once more. Either they had no vehicles in being, or like Ogle, they did have a machine or machines, the cost of which must long since have been written off. In either case, they doubtless hoped to recoup earlier losses. Their evidence made it clear that all further capital was going to have to come from the pockets of the investing public or of the taxpayer, not from their own. If the money could be found, past defeats might be erased. No mention was made in their evidence of a need to remove discriminatory tolls – that would follow inevitably, if steam became the mainstay of the trusts.

This was the promise, and main theme, of the steam partisans. Alexander Gordon, Francis Maceroni and Nathaniel Ogle all came forward to plead, once more, for the steam carriage. Maceroni presented it as the potential saviour of the trusts, of the inns that depended on coach traffic, and indeed of the coachmasters themselves if only they would at last be converted to the new vehicle. The inns would be used as depots, as well as places of refreshment. Maceroni told how he had floated a new company with all these objects in mind.

Gordon emphasised the need for adequate capitalisation – as on the railways, a number of vehicles would be needed to sustain a service, for example six or seven on a London–Brighton route. For his part, Ogle advocated the establishment of an experimental steam carriage route subsidised by public funds. Gordon later supported the idea of a state subsidy, in the form of a prize of up to £10,000 for the first long-distance service established, to be offered in conjunction with repeal of the discriminatory tolls. Such suggestions really amounted to an admission of defeat – the railways had needed no such help.

Other witnesses backed up the steam promoters, or rather, Maceroni and his company in particular. Much of the evidence was clearly planned to this end. Leitch Ritchie, the journalist, Charles Hullmandel, a director of the new company, Captain George Fitzgerald, a Middlesex magistrate, and Gordon himself had all ridden in Maceroni's machine in 1833–4, and spoke in its favour. George Concanen, probably an associate of Maceroni, told of a conversation with a man called Benningfield, "a late coach proprietor, now a wholesale tobacconist", who was in favour of Maceroni's scheme. Several other coachmasters and innkeepers supported it too, said Concanen.

There is no doubt that the steam partisans made the intended impression on the committee. They were helped, no doubt, by the presence on it of William Mackinnon, by now a supporter of steam, of Sir Henry Parnell, and of Charles Shaw-Lefevre, another veteran of the 1831 Commons committee. The weight of Sir James McAdam's approval probably told as well – he favoured steamer's broad wheels, and the absence of damaging horses' hooves. While principally concerned with unoriginal recommendations for the improvement of the condition of the trusts, the committee's report added that "the use of steam carriages on turnpike roads might be encouraged by lessening the tolls payable on such carriages, which in some cases are equal to a prohibition, although such carriages are considered to cause less injury to roads than those of less weight drawn by horses".

The supporters of steam had, perhaps, something to gain from a renewal of effort. Gordon, Maceroni and Ogle could even now see a future in trunk road steamers, in spite of the triumph of railways, and because of the failure of the stage coaches. This must have seemed an illusory prospect to most people; but there might well be other ways in which road steamers could earn their keep. Ideas had been prompted by the very success of the railway – why not take advantage of it, and also make good its deficiencies? This thought must have become more attractive still after the 1839 committee reaffirmed the twice-expressed support of the Commons for steamers, even though, as before, its recommendations were not carried into effect. Whatever the reasons for the new optimism, there was a new rash of company promotions, and even a few steamers on the road again.

In May 1838 Sir James Anderson popped up after nine years' absence from the field, as a promoter of the Steam Carriage and Waggon Company. In the interim, he had designed a steam plough. This time, he was the designer rather than the backer of a steam carriage, "now nearly completed", according to the prospectus. This gave the names of Anderson and four M.P.s among the directors. It revived the tired old arguments as to the expense of railways and the cheapness of road transport, but there were also new arguments, more relevant to the times. In the prospectus, the road steamer was seen as a feeder to the railways, furnishing "a tributary stream of passengers and goods to the grand lines" – very much the new role of the stage coach. The idea was not new, having been proposed at least as early as 1835.[21]

Anderson claimed to have spent over £30,000 experimenting on his own steam carriages and those of others. The first fruit of his own labours was a tractor with a boiler of Hancock type – which was so close to the original that when Hancock drove his gig through the City of London, it carried a notice on the back disclaiming any connection with Anderson's company. Other information of a reliable sort is very difficult to come by. All of it originally emanated from newspapers in the vehicle's country of origin, Ireland, and was implausible, contradictory, or both. It was clear only that the machine was very long and large, and unusual in form. One of the most circumstantial and least improbable descriptions refers to 16 inside and 14 outside passengers in two compartments with interconnecting doors, rather like a corridor train, the tractor and trailer no doubt each carrying one compartment. It was reported in October 1838 that the vehicle was finished, and would proceed from Sir James Anderson's seat at

Buttevant to Limerick in two weeks' time. It was destined for London, but did not actually arrive there until July 1839. Much was promised for the expedition to England, but nothing was accomplished.

Thereafter, Anderson seems to have concentrated his activities in Ireland. By 1841 two tractors were in being, one for hauling passengers and the other for freight. Anderson had been trying to establish his vehicles' credibility in competition with stage coaches on the Dublin–Galway road; but if one reads between the lines of a company report presented in November 1841, it is clear that he had failed to do so. One of his tractors took two days to cover the 48 miles from Dublin to Meldrum, then retired, defeated by mud, floods, filthy feed water and bad coke. By this time the amount invested by Anderson and his partner, Jasper W. Rogers, had reached £60,000. The report has a valedictory air, and it is not surprising that no more is heard of Anderson's steamers.

By May 1839 Maceroni's new concern, the Common Road Steam Conveyance Company, had been floated. It sought capital of £200,000 in £5 shares. The company's engineer was to be Alexander Gordon, and its carriages would be built to Maceroni's design. They would be hired out to coachmasters at 2s 2d a mile for them to operate. The company, Maceroni declared, could expect a profit of 100 per cent on its capital. But Maceroni, despite the publicity he achieved in testimony before the 1839 committee, got nowhere with this last fling. In October 1841 he wrote a plaintive letter to the *Mechanics' Magazine*, telling how the manufacturer of the steam carriage had tried to overcharge the company. The latter had refused to pay, and the project had foundered, taking the last of Maceroni's worldly goods with it. The epilogue is sadder still. Two months later Maceroni again writes to his old adversary, the *Mechanics' Magazine*, begging it to print what he admits amounts to an advertisement free of charge – he is offering his boiler patent for sale, although it has only seven years to run. One of steam's most energetic and publicity-conscious promoters, who had done as much as anyone to keep it before the public eye, had been defeated at last.

The General Steam Carriage Company was projected at about the same time. Like Anderson's concern, it saw the road steamer as a feeder, offsetting the admitted "great advantage of railways" as a trunk route carrier. Feeders were needed where there was no stage coach communication, and where local traffic was insufficient to "repay the enormous outlay of constructing a railway". Nothing more is known of this company promotion.

The Patent Steam Carriage Company's prospectus was optimistic to the point of sounding simple-minded. It solicited applications for

10,000 £5 shares, "half to be paid upon subscription, and the remaining half upon proof of the propelment of a carriage". Of the £25,000 subscription required, £5000 was for building the vehicle. The other £20,000 would be refunded to subscribers "in case of failure of the carriage". In other words, investors were being invited to subsidise experiments, rather than capitalise a company lacking only money to permit take-off. One suspects that the directors were too honest for their own good: the vehicles of most of the other companies were probably no further advanced.

Three other attempts to revive steam made more progress. One was made by Walter Hancock, who raised steam in *Automaton* for the first time in two years. On this occasion, however, he did not intend to spend his own money in establishing a service. In April 1839 he was seeking contracts from operators to run *Automaton*, which was described as ready for the road, and a few months later was also trying to raise capital. To back his appeals, he took the steamer on several demonstration runs. In mid-June *Automaton* went from Stratford to Ilford, and back as far as the City, without incident. Another, much longer trip to Cambridge and Newmarket and back in early October was less successful. A lot of minor disorders, probably resulting from its long immobility, plagued the steamer. Fuel consumption – about a bushel a mile – was extremely heavy. Speed was lost, but as far as Cambridge the average was still over 10 m.p.h., and between Tottenham and Walton it was said that nearly 25 m.p.h. was attained. Everywhere, *Automaton* was very well received.

Afterwards, Hancock confined himself to shorter journeys, on the road from Stratford to the City and from there north to Barnet. On 11 November a trip up the Barnet road was made "under the patronage of the directors and clerk of the Highgate Archway trust",[22] during which Highgate Archway Hill was climbed at between 6 and 7 m.p.h. It sounds as though Hancock, like Maceroni and Ogle, may have seen steamers as the new support of the turnpike trusts, and that at least one trust was thinking on the same lines. Unfortunately, *Automaton* broke down on the outward journey; but two more expeditions to Barnet and back in March 1840 were without incident. The best time for the 13 miles was 1 hour 10 minutes. A distinguished passenger on several occasions was Sir James Gardiner, a former Secretary at War and Irish Secretary.

This was the last occasion on which any Hancock steamer is recorded as having run. Hancock had obviously failed to raise capital, so after 16 years finally desisted from his efforts to establish steamers as an acceptable alternative to other forms of roads transport. Thanks to efficient, rational design that produced relatively reliable, economical and fast vehicles, and a concentration on roads with plenty of passenger traffic and insignificant tolls, Hancock came closer than any other constructor to success. The respect which this limited achievement gained him is constantly reflected in the admiration of his contemporaries – even other constructors were constrained to give grudging praise, in print and in person before select committees. It is possible that herein lies Hancock's real achievement – without his reflected glory, the first road steamers might not have received the encouragement they got from press, Parliament, government and eminent engineers, and so may not have survived as long or developed as far as they did. As for Hancock himself, in 1841 he patented an automatic braking and signalling system for railways; thereafter the technology of rubber absorbed his interest. He made machinery for the factories of his brothers Thomas and Charles, but like his contemporaries in the world of steam road vehicles, he was an engineer first and a businessman second. By 1851 he was ruined, and a year later he died.

When Hancock went to Cambridge in October 1839, it was noted that one of his passengers was "a new steam carriage constructor" – Frank Hills, a manufacturing chemist of Deptford. He had taken out a patent for a carriage that January. The vehicle was complete by the summer of 1840 or earlier, for at that time it ran to Blackheath and Bromley. It turned out to be an attractive, civilised and in some ways advanced machine. With its smart open *britzka* body, a fashionable style, it was a purpose-built private steamer like Hancock's phaeton, but larger and better-looking. There was room for six passengers inside and three on the box. The machinery was fully enclosed, and it and the body were sprung. There was a change-speed mechanism.

The *ensemble* was a compact 16 feet long, and weighed about 4 tons fully laden with passengers, fuel and water. It had cost £800 to build, which made it very much a rich man's toy. The engine developed 12 n.h.p., from a tubular boiler with a normal pressure of 60–70 p.s.i. Water was used up at the rate of 10–12 gallons per mile, which was a lot. This might have been accounted for by the speed at which the carriage was driven. There is no reason to doubt the claimed maximum speed of 25 m.p.h. and cruising pace of 16 m.p.h., for this machine put up the most remarkable performance so far recorded. In August 1841 it went from Deptford to Hastings and back – a total distance of 128 miles – in a single day, despite the necessity of climbing River Hill on the return. This was half the time needed by the stage coaches. On a subsequent fast run from Deptford, the carriage covered the 21 miles to Sevenoaks at an average running speed of 14–15 m.p.h., exclusive of three stops for fuel and water, and delays due to poor stoking and defective pumps. Hills undertook other expeditions as well, to Brighton and to Windsor.

An unidentified steamer ran down from Camberwell, in London's southern suburbs, to Brighton in May 1840 in the excellent time of three hours exclusive of stops. There were six halts to take on water, each occupying up to 20 minutes. Given the speed implied here, and the fact that there were no other steamers recorded south of London at the time, this may have been an early achievement of the Hills carriage.[23] There is no suggestion that Hills intended the machine for anything more than his own private use, and it drops from sight after September 1841. Hills went on to patent improvements to steam carriages in 1843, including differential gearing, rack-and-pinion steering and a condenser. If he had built another vehicle, it would no doubt have been a notable advance, in most respects, on all its predecessors, but that was not to be.

At about the time that Hills's carriage was making its last recorded excursions, another was taking to the roads. John Squire had much experience of construction, on his own account, for Gurney and for Maceroni. He now reappeared as engineer for the General Steam Coach Company. The company's prospectus had none of the slightly defensive tone of others published at the time; there was talk not of supplementing the railway, but of supplanting it. Railways were notorious for their accidents; and they could not penetrate the centre of towns as easily as road traffic, so were less convenient. The prospectus ventured on to more dangerous ground when it claimed that the railway mania had subsided, that stage coaches were being revived, and that "the successful substitution of steam for animal power on turnpike roads is now no longer doubtful" – a remark that is a brave echo of the heady days of 1831.

Such talk was strictly for the more than usually gullible investor. For his part, Squire did his energetic and by no means negligible best to justify the spirit, if not the promise, of the promoters' pronouncements. No doubt he had learned a great deal from his previous employers, but one wonders how far he would have gone in those earlier, more propitious times if he had not been burdened by two such improvident, impractical amateurs.

In mid-April 1841 Squire's machine, a self-contained coach with a water-tube boiler, began running daily between Regent's Park and Tottenham, a distance of $8\frac{1}{2}$ miles, which it is said to have covered in half an hour or less. It is not known if this was a public service, but the inference is that it was. The speed sounds improbably high, especially in view of a later remark to the effect that the normal running pace was 12–15 m.p.h. The schedule was kept up for at least two weeks.

Sixteen passengers were carried on occasion, including several M.P.s. There was, it was claimed, hardly any noise, smoke or steam. Control was easy, as was illustrated when a cow ran across the road in front of the coach as it was descending the hill from Camden Villas at full speed. Flocks of sheep were also liable to get in the way, but the steersman threaded his way through them without mishap.

From Gurney's day to that of Hills, constructors yielded regularly to the temptation to drive a new steamer to Windsor, in the hope of exciting royal interest and the publicity that would bring. John Squire was no exception. During September 1841 he demonstrated his coach on two successive days to Prince Albert, then made trouble-free runs around Windsor and to Datchet and Frogmore with local notables on board. It seems to have been altogether a successful public relations exercise.

Then no more is heard until Easter Monday 1842, when the coach, now named *Albert* in honour of the Prince, started to ply on alternate days between Regent's Park and the villages east and north of London, including Ilford and Barnet. As before, there is no proof that this was a commercial service, but the report reads as if it was. A few days after the runs began, when the *Albert* was on its way to Barnet with 16 passengers, a tube or a joint blew. The passengers "precipitately left the coach", three ladies bruising themselves in the process, and began walking back towards London. The coach was repaired and turned around. It caught up with the passengers, who decided to board it again – no doubt weariness had got the better of fright. It is not known how long the service – if that is what it was – survived thereafter, but the omens were not good. In any case, no more was heard of this, or of any other road steamer of its generation, whether working a service or not.

The picture of passengers trailing disconsolately away from a broken-down steam coach somehow provides an appropriate close to the first age of steam on the road. What had put an end to it? In attempting an answer, it is important to differentiate between the factors applicable at a particular time to particular vehicles and their operations, or those quoted by particular individuals, and those factors which contributed more or less to the downfall of all or most constructors and entrepreneurs. Many contemporary chroniclers, whose words are nowadays taken out of context as the truth, did not make such a distinction, either because they were being highly subjective, or because they could not look back over an era that had ended. For instance, in 1832 John Scott Russell launched a wholesale attack on existing steam carriages, at a time when he himself as yet had no vehicle on the road, and when the first age of steam had not reached its peak. His main point – that "imperfect suspension has been the ruin of every machine" – was not true of every steamer; it was only a part-truth, and it was quite misleading by itself. This was recognised by the *Journal of Elemental Locomotion* even at the time.

Five major factors, some or all of which were common to all enterprises, can be identified as elements of a complete picture. All affected private as well as commercial steamers, to a greater or lesser degree. Hindsight enables the modern historian to allocate priorities differently, but these, too, were the factors accorded the most significance by the commentators who looked back at road steamers immediately after their demise.

The factors were inextricably interrelated, but the facts point plainly to one, whose absence might have allowed steam on to the road in spite of the others. This was trust hostility, which was never universal, and which was not always an obvious consideration – and indeed was sometimes discounted by constructors such as Maceroni and Ogle. But it undoubtedly held back steam at its critical and most promising moment, 1831–2. The reasons for it are largely a matter of hints and inferences – potential unproven damage to roads and reduction of other traffic; arguable danger to other road users; the real risk of fire in roadside crops; the simple, generalised conservatism. The effect, on the other hand, was all too clear – discriminatory tolls, and support for them from the legal authority of last resort, the House of Lords.

Alexander Mackinnon, chairman of the 1839 committee and member of that of 1831, was quoted as saying that "the innkeepers, turnpike trustees and stage coach proprietors had done all in their power to oppose the steam carriages . . . the trustees were like the man in the fable, who killed the goose for the sake of the egg". There is little solid evidence that innkeepers and coachmasters actively opposed steam, but Mackinnon was right about the most important interest of the three, the trustees.

Without the discriminatory tolls, other steam carriage services would probably have been established in 1831, or as soon as Gurney delivered more vehicles, or at any time up to 1834; though no one can say whether they would have succeeded. Without the tolls, the capital to establish and sustain such services might have been forthcoming before railways provided the complete answer to long-distance land travel, and attracted so much investment. Without the tolls, capital for development, for overcoming technical problems, might have been furnished.

Lack of capital left individuals to finance operations which, in terms of "rolling stock", were nearly as expensive to establish as railways, and less economic to run. The public's money went into the form of conveyance which seemed likely to supersede road transport of all sorts. It might be said, indeed, that if the trusts and the Lords had been instrumental in discouraging road steamers in 1831–2, the railways were in a sense responsible for putting them down a second time in 1835–6 by offering a greater prospect of profit, in spite of their massive first costs. Nathaniel Ogle went further, suggesting that the proprietors of the Liverpool and Manchester Railway induced trustees near Warrington to impose prohibitory tolls. But Ogle was Ogle; and nowhere else is it implied that the railways played more than a passive and indirect part in the defeat of the steam carriage. Alexander Gordon was in no doubt of their true role: "A few years ago, when the Liverpool–Manchester railway was in progress, particularly when it was opened, the public mind was seized with a sort of mania for railway communication, and the spare capital of the country was all required for railway pursuits." Maceroni agreed with him, as we have seen. Gordon pre-dated the beginning of the mania, but in essence he was right.

Shortage of capital had its effect on the third factor – the real drawbacks that affected the road steamer. These included much greater weight at the wheels than a stage coach; loose and sometimes rough road surfaces; and lack of experience in making mechanisms able to withstand a combination of weight, jolting and power stresses. These were problems afflicting every constructor. In most machines they were complicated by inadequate suspension, and a combined axle and drive shaft. In some vehicles they were compounded by unnecessarily enormous weight, and other design features that were unwise, or constantly altered and therefore never developed, or both. All this, together with such minor factors as the difficulty of keeping grates clear, led to a greater or lesser degree of unreliability, both in absolute terms and in relation to the railway.

Even more noticeable was the road steamer's lack of sustained speed capability compared with that of a passenger train. Its average speeds were in fact little if any greater than those of stage coaches. This drawback was attributable to two causes. One was lack of fuel and water supplies *en route*, which led to loss of steam as well as time. The other was the surface on which the steam carriage had to run, which was not only uneven, but also shared with other road users. Although many of the steam vehicles of the 1830s had excellent power-to-weight ratios compared with railway locomotives, they (unlike locomotives) were still underpowered in relation to the surface beneath their wheels. Gravel, mud and hills saw to that. Even if any steam carriage was theoretically capable of emulating the speed of a train – and here one disregards Ogle's claims – it would certainly have been knocked to pieces or ditched before such a speed was attained.

Steam carriages had further disadvantages too. The noise, smoke, steam and smell which, to some extent, they all emitted were anti-social. When produced by the railway locomotive, on its permanent way relatively isolated from the public, these were less objectionable. The railway engine enjoyed other advantages arising from having a relatively straight and level road to itself. It needed no steering mechanism, nor a differential action between its driving wheels. It could haul far heavier loads faster with the same power. It did not need to vary its power output and the loading on its mechanical components nearly so frequently, as when stopping and starting, or climbing gradients. In other words, the locomotive could be simpler and less highly stressed.

No steam carriage could honestly be described as totally safe, while they frightened some horses, threw out sparks, and blew up; though in this sense they were at no disadvantage compared with either the stage coach or the railway.

William Bridges Adams felt that these technical drawbacks were the road steamer's foremost enemy. His highly coloured picture of its disagreeable features has already been quoted. Writing in 1839, the anonymous author of *The Roads and Railroads, Vehicles and Modes of Travelling of Ancient and Modern Countries*, etc., agreed: "The principal obstacles to the introduction of locomotive carriages on common roads were considered to be the weight of these carriages themselves, and the mode of propulsion" – that is, driven wheels. The damage so caused to roads, said the author, kept steam carriages from being protected by law against discriminatory tolls.

If capital had been available, some of these drawbacks might have been rectified in time, placing the steam carriage at less of a disadvantage. As it was, they helped to antagonise trustees, and may have put off the public from patronising services when they were established.

With more passengers, the effect of the fourth factor – high running costs – would have been alleviated. We have seen that Dance was losing money heavily even before a toll was imposed on him, though he did not admit it. Cubitt and the Heaton brothers saw that services were going to be uneconomic before they were started. For all the promoters' insistence that steam road services would be cheaper to run than any other – an insistence that suggests that the assertion was often queried – it is probable that the other services, too, were found to be uneconomic in practice. Again, given more capital for development, means might have been found of reducing fuel consumption. High running costs were also undoubtedly related to uneven road surfaces, and to repair and maintenance expenses arising from unreliability.

Lastly, the steam carriage failed because of the personality defects of the constructors and entrepreneurs. The gathering before the Commons committee of 1831 epitomised the fact that, by then, constructors had no excuse to be ignorant of one another's activities. But for the most part they refused, or were unable, to learn from one another's failures and successes. This was due only in part to the need to protect patents; it was a reflection also of a degree of conceit, and a corresponding dislike of and contempt for rivals, exceptional even among inventors. In Maceroni it verged on the paranoid; Ogle and Gurney were little better, and even Hancock was not above the occasional lapse. With few exceptions, too, the constructors were unbusinesslike – bad not so much at obtaining money (Gurney was a genius at this) as at using it to the best advantage. They were improvident, and were obsessive tinkerers and experimenters. In this they were typical inventors; but together with the obduracy of the trusts and the Lords, it lost them the support of their backers. Finally, many were dedicated but clumsy and irresponsible publicists. This is shown by the cavalier way in which they treated the susceptibilities of their most dangerous opponents, the turnpike trusts, which might almost have been calculated to antagonise. Such behaviour arose from a combination of arrogance and over-confidence.

The charge of amateurishness that was levelled frequently at constructors was based on their lack of professional engineering and business skills. Few, indeed, were by training either mechanical engineers or businessmen, but one cannot help feeling that their conduct as much as their lack of qualifications branded them as amateurs. Perhaps the first was to some extent a reflection of the second. The behaviour of most of the prominent steam carriage constructors must have horrified the professional engineers, such as Timothy Bramah, James Nasmyth, David Napier, Joshua Field, Joseph Maudslay, William Cubitt and Thomas Telford. It is significant, perhaps, that, in general, the more knowledgeable and professional the engineer, the sooner he withdrew from steam carriage activities.

Gordon and Adams agreed on the dire effects of amateurism. "Really very few engineers, practical men, have paid any attention whatever to the subject," said Gordon, with some exaggeration. Adams did not find this surprising: "Mechanical men in regular business rarely embark in speculation." A little later, Gordon waded mercilessly into the other sort of constructor: "They have exhibited the partial efforts of men who underrate the defects and magnify the merits of their own invention, and are disinclined to adopt any improvement, however good, which did not originate with themselves." The years in close association with Goldsworthy Gurney, then Francis Maceroni, must have been enough to embitter any man; but even so, Gordon had been too sanguine in expecting "hearty and combined operation in the various endeavours" – a form of behaviour that had never been typical of inventors.

Of course, some steamers suffered less than others from these drawbacks. Those that were least susceptible, such as Hancock's machines, ran better and for longer than any others. At the other extreme, Ogle and Summers had nothing at all in their favour except persistence, which every constructor needed.

But the history of Hancock's endeavours leads one inevitably to the conclusion that since he failed, none of the others could possibly have succeeded. The problems which seem to have defeated him – high running costs and lack of capital – must have afflicted most constructors more severely still; while the majority also had to contend with more or less hostile trusts, and with more offensive and less safe, practical and dependable machines.

What did these road steamers leave behind them? The answer, sadly, is almost nothing detectable. When a new generation of steamers arose, they owed hardly anything, it seemed, to the experience so bitterly gained by the pioneers. It was as if the latter had never been. The newcomers hardly ever referred to their predecessors, and little in the new designs visibly reflected earlier work on steam carriages. This was forgotten or disregarded, or passed unnoticed. For instance, the advanced and efficient boiler design of Walter Hancock was lost. Features of the modern motor car, including change-speed gears, Ackermann steering operated by rack and pinion, and differential gearing had to be rediscovered. Even the personalities were largely different. This was partly accounted for, no doubt, by the passage of time, but the extent to which not only the partisans but also the opponents of steam had changed is remarkable.

The reason was almost complete lack of continuity between the first and second generations. The commercial passenger-carrying road steamer stayed dead because its context – long-distance road traffic – had died with it, or very shortly thereafter. The next generation of road steamers originated in a totally different context – different needs, different solutions, different people. The emphasis would be on power for agriculture and on goods haulage, and to a greater extent than before, on private "motor cars". These would form a tiny proportion of the self-propelled vehicles on the road, but they were made in larger numbers than their predecessors, and survived much longer. This time, the private vehicle would be a more independent growth, springing up beside its big commercial brothers. It was not built as second-best because commercial vehicles had failed.

Notes

PART 1

1   As in the case of Papin's model, and the engine which introduced James Watt to steam power at Glasgow University.
2   Indeed, the low-pressure engine flourished for half a century after the high-pressure engine "arrived".
3   Each cylinder with its mechanism was commonly described as a separate "engine" by early steam carriage constructors.
4   A considerable investment. In 1785 a single 4 pounder field artillery piece cost only 250–300 francs to manufacture. A franc at both dates had the same value as one livre.
5   It is possible that the average speed required was that expected of draught animals towing heavy artillery on a road. This is supported by a letter from the Musée de l'Armée, Paris, 5 September 1974. Experiments conducted on the London-Holyhead road in 1830 by John Macneil, the road's assistant engineer, as described in evidence to the 1831 House of Commons Select Committee on Steam Carriages, showed that a laden 6-horse wagon with an all-up weight of $4\frac{1}{2}$ tons (10,080 lbs), comparable with the weight of the Cugnot tractor with a 5000-lb load, averaged $2\frac{1}{2}$–3 m.p.h. – 4 k.p.h. or a little over.
6   In Robert Stuart, *Historical and Descriptive Anecdotes of Steam Engines*, ii, 208–9, published in 1829, appears the earliest traceable description in English of Cugnot's work.
7   The idea may have derived from toll bridges, which had existed since the Middle Ages.
8   Malachy Postlethwayt, *Universal Dictionary of Trade and Commerce* (1751) 616.
9   W. Albert, *The Turnpike Road System in England and Wales*, 189.
10   Proof that the low-pressure engine at its best was no longer always Newcomen's lethargic monster is provided by the success of the first working steamboats. Those of the Marquis Jouffroy d'Abbans in 1783, of John Fitch in 1787, and of Patrick Miller in 1788 all had condensing engines. See Marquis Achille de Jouffroy d'Abbans, *Mémoitr*, read to Académie des Sciences, 1839.
11   The cylinder of the oil-fired, high-pressure double-acting engine was recessed into the boiler to keep it hot. Drive was by crankshaft. Double action was normal on road steamers, since it was not only efficient, but also improved smoothness and starting torque.
12   A basically similar specification to that attributed to Papin's model of nearly a century earlier. Other reasons why Symington may have dropped the project could have been the realisation that a condensing engine lacked the power-to-weight ratio needed to propel a full-scale road steamer, and that it would, in any case, have been in violation of Watt's patents.
13   Ironically, Watt's determination and success in protecting his low-pressure and high-pressure patents brought about a revolution in the judicial approach to patents in Britain. Until the eighteenth century, the law gave too much protection

to the patentee and not enough encouragement to innovators. The 1624 Statute of Monopolies had, *inter alia*, confirmed the Crown's right to grant letters patent in new inventions for 14 years. If, through no fault of his own, the patentee had not reaped his reward in that period, the patent could be extended by Act of Parliament. Watt took advantage of this. A patent could be granted in the first instance without a full specification, which had to be submitted within six months. In practice, patents could be vague, all-embracing and still valid.

By Watt's time, however, the legal requirements were being tightened up. In Lord Mansfield's judgement in 1778, a patent was declared voidable on the grounds of insufficient specification. From the Watt litigation against infringers, which was frequent and well publicised, arose the recognition that fresh patents could be granted for improvements to a known machine, such as the steam engine, and even for ideas or principles, so long as the specification showed that they had been developed far enough to be practical in an industrial or commercial application. It would no longer be possible for one man to stifle progress with a "blanket" patent whose terminology covered every possible development regardless of the likelihood of its working, or getting beyond the paper stage.

Watt's was the first patent applicable to steam carriages. Only two more followed between 1784 and 1802. There is, comparatively speaking, a rash of railway locomotive patents between 1811 and 1815, but no more road steamer patents until 1821. Between then and the end of 1830, no fewer than 23 were lodged. This pattern faithfully reflects the changing conditions facing the road steamer – when the auspices become favourable, and not before, the patents multiplied.

14 Francis Trevithick, *Life of Richard Trevithick*, i, 160–2.

15 New in execution but not in theory; the idea was incorporated in Fourness and Ashworth's patent of 1788, as was recessing the cylinder into the boiler, and crankshaft drive.

16 Watt's steam carriage patent of 1784 had specified change-speed gears.

17 According to a letter in the *Mining Journal* (2 Oct. 1858) Captain Andrew Vivian, one of Trevithick's partners, recalled in old age how cab drivers and omnibus men had pelted the carriage with cabbage stumps, rotten onions and eggs. This account is suspect, since there were no London omnibuses as such until 1829. The account suggests, much more clearly, an encounter of the sort common when the buses and coaches of Hancock and others were running in London 30 years later.

18 London's population almost doubled between 1780 and 1820, inevitably leading to traffic congestion and road wear. Albert, op. cit., 65.

19 When a machine was a novelty and made few public appearances, this was usual. Britain's pioneer "motorists" from the 1820s onwards were regarded with a mixture of amazement, condescension and amusement. Serious attention, and hostility, came only with an increase in numbers, and the clear likelihood that they were going to make themselves felt.

20 George Granville Leveson-Gower, second Marquess of Stafford and later first Duke of Sutherland, is best know to history as an "improving landlord" associated with the notorious Highland Clearances. He built 450 miles of Highland roads at his own expense, between 1812 and his death in 1833, and, like his grandson, took a strong interest in modern technology. Britain's biggest landowner and richest man – Greville's "leviathan of wealth" – he held a 20 per cent interest in the Liverpool and Manchester Railway, and was the majority shareholder in the Liverpool–Birmingham Canal.

21 A generation later, it was estimated that the resistance to carriage wheels even of a

good road was 12 times that of railway track, all other things being equal. See N.W. Cundy, *Inland Transit* (1833) 65.

22 As late as 1833, it was difficult to find even a tilt hammer in London. See Francis Maceroni, *A Few Facts Concerning Elementary Locomotion* (1834) 22.

23 Industry on a scale to encourage steam, as existed in Britain, had not yet come to the United States, which was still basically a nation of farmers and merchants. The American colonies had not seen their first Newcomen engine until 1753.

24 G. and D. Bathe, *Oliver Evans: A Chronicle of Early American Engineering*, 109–11. Evans referred to his creation as "a heavy flat-bottomed boat", and as "a machine for clearing docks". Its Greek name, *Orukter Amphibolos*, meant "amphibious digger". See also *Mechanics' Magazine* (25 Sept. 1830) 73.

25 F. Trevithick, op. cit., i, 138. Trevithick envisaged using treads of one sort or another, but nothing more protruberant.

26 Walter Hancock, *A Narrative Of Twelve Years' Experiments*, 18. Hancock does not clearly specify "legs", but seems to mean some such device.

27 Alternatively, the foundations might be of rubble, and if stones were not available for the surface, gravel might be substituted.

28 Prematurely, William Blakey patented a water-tube boiler in 1766. The type could get nowhere in Britain until the Watt patents expired. Dallery took out a patent for a water-tube boiler in 1803, though he is reported to have used it 23 years earlier. In Britain in the same year of 1803, the American John Stevens issued a similar patent for a boiler with a large number of small-diameter tubes; so, too, did Arthur Woolf. Woolf's boiler was supplied with his compound engines, so by 1820 the type was known.

29 Possibly this was the vehicle built by "an ingenious cotton spinner of Ardwick" for goods or passengers; it was said to be capable of 9–10 m.p.h. See *Gentleman's Magazine* (Nov. 1821) 452; from *Manchester Guardian*.

30 *Mechanics' Magazine* (3 June 1826) 79. The ignition of coal gas inside the cylinders created a vacuum. This drove the pistons, not the force of the explosion, as in the modern motor vehicle. Brown worked a gas-engined boat on the Thames in January 1827. The Brown carriage may have reappeared in September 1828, when a gas vacuum vehicle was reported proceeding along the Hammersmith road at 7 m.p.h.

31 The major design problems affecting both rail and road were set out clearly, if wordily, by the *London Journal of Arts and Sciences* in February 1826 (no. 65, 142). Boilers were too heavy and cumbersome, or else too small in generating capacity. The power produced, on its way to rail or road, was either dissipated by inefficient mechanisms or used up in wasteful friction.

32 *Observations on Railways with Locomotive High-Pressure Steam Engines* (Mar. 1825).

PART 2

1 But see p. 21: Trevithick claimed that his vehicles did not suffer from wheelspin.
2 British Parliamentary Papers [henceforth B.P.P.], Report and Minutes, Select Committee of the House of Commons on Steam Carriages (1831) 49.
3 *London Journal of Arts and Sciences*, no. 79, 164.
4 *Observer* (9 Dec. 1827).
5 A German Prince [Ludwig von Puckler-Muskau], *Tour in England, Ireland and France*, letter (16 Jan. 1828).
6 B.P.P., Report and Minutes, Select Committee of the House of Commons on Mr Goldsworthy Gurney's Case (1834–5) 42. Gurney mentioned, but did not

describe, a third type of brake. This was presumably a block brake, applied to a tyre rim or nave by lever or screw. It was in use by 1831 on Walter Hancock's steam omnibus *Infant*, in the form of a metal band on the tyre. But although they were being used on railways, block brakes were as yet rare on the road. They were first fitted to mail coaches about 1838–9 (John Philipson, *The Art and Craft of Coachbuilding*, 45), and were also introduced on horse omnibuses. They were not in general use until about the 1860s.

7   At the other extreme, George Stephenson thought that a steam carriage took as long to stop as a stage coach – in his estimation, 150 ft from 14 m.p.h.

8   They were also harmful to roads, as Gurney admitted and his champion Alexander Gordon confirmed: Alexander Gordon, *A Historical and Practical Treatise upon Elemental Locomotion*, 74.

9   B.P.P., Select Committee (1834–5; 1835 session) 24–9.

10 William Bridges Adams, *English Pleasure Carriages* (1837) 191. The expense of carrying the Liverpool and Manchester Railway across Chat Moss caused widespread dismay at the time. Railways could costs £30,000–£40,000 a mile to build.

11 *Courier* (10 Sept. 1827). Speeds quoted at this period must be treated with reserve, in the absence of speedometers or even odometers. Informed and objective estimates become impossible as the speeds to be judged rose beyond the familiar. Until the spread of the railways, the only fast vehicles commonly seen, with which useful and valid comparisons could be made, were the stage coaches. Their absolute, theoretical maximum speed would be 30 m.p.h., or less – a full gallop. Such a velocity would be seen, if at all, only briefly and under the most favourable conditions, for the sake of both horses and passengers. The top speed regularly achieved by the fastest coaches would be between 15 and 20 m.p.h.; at least this would be necessary for the averages they achieved.

12 This in spite of Gurney's specific claim to the contrary, first made 32 years later. It is significant, too, that the 1831 Gurney vehicles are the first to be called noisy, and that the steam blast was blamed for that noise.

13 B.P.P., Select Committee (1834–5) 11. Ross knew Gurney through their mutual interest in steam propulsion for ships.

14 Herapath published a pamphlet embodying his case, in the form of *A Letter to the Duke of Wellington upon Mr Gurney's Steam Carriage*. Its frontispiece was a print of the Duke riding in the Gurney machine's trailer at Hounslow; but no other evidence that he did so can be found.

15 B.P.P., Select Committee (1831) 69–73. Ogle and Summers had been working on steamers since 1829.

16 In fact the title of Hancock's memoirs – *A Narrative of Twelve Years' Experiments* – shows that he regarded all his vehicles as experimental. This did not stop him from putting them into public service; a risk justified by their performance.

17 B.P.P., Select Committee (1831) 32 *ff*. In 1826, 14 trusts in London north of the Thames had been consolidated under one authority, the Metropolis Roads Trust. It administered 125 miles of crowded roads, and had the biggest annual revenue (£60,000–£70,000) of any trust in the nation.

18 *Manchester Guardian* (26 June 1830); from *Halifax Chronicle*.

19 In 1836, at the peak of the coaching boom, the total income of the trusts was £1.77 millions, and their expenditure was £1.78 millions. See B.P.P., Report and Minutes, Select Committee on Turnpike Trusts (1839), Sir James McAdam's evidence.

20 J.E. Bradfield, *The Public Carriages of Great Britain* (1855) 20 *ff*. The first cost of

the horses was higher than the value given here.

21 B.P.P., Report and Minutes, Select Committee of the House of Lords on the Tolls on Steam Carriages Bill (1836) 8. Given this figure, and 4000 coaches, at least another £800,000 must be added to the sum of the industry's investments, which probably approached £5 millions in 1836. This figure disregards posting activities, and the coachmasters' investments in hotels and inns. By comparison, over the whole period the canal system's growth, between the 1750s and the 1830s, about £20 millions had been invested. (Phyllis Deane, "Capital Formation in Great Britain before the Railway Age", in *Economic Development and Cultural Change*, ix, 302). Woollen manufacture – after cotton, Britain's most important textile industry – employed 55,000 operatives in 1835 (B.R. Mitchell, *Abstract of British Historical Statistics*, 199.) By any standards, coaching was a major industry.

22 R.C. and J.M. Anderson, *Quicksilver: A Hundred Years of Coaching 1750–1850*, 119. Another source puts Chaplin's turnover at double this figure.

23 B.P.P., Select Committee (1831) 56. The average speed of stage coaches overall was 9–10 m.p.h. in 1834, at which time the *malle-poste* of France averaged only 6 m.p.h. The nation foremost in Europe for the quality of its roads 50 years before had taken second place.

24 L.T.C. Rolt, *The Inland Waterways of England*, 145–9; Alexander Gordon, op. cit., 241–6. There is no mention of passage boats in Priestley's *Navigable Rivers* etc. (1831).

25 See p. 108.

26 Quoted in *Mechanics' Magazine* (31 Oct. 1829). This open letter was probably that which was subsequently published as a pamphlet: see p. 160, *n.* 14.

27 For example, Francis Maceroni, op. cit., 34.

28 John Cary, *Cary's New Itinerary* (1828); Stanley Harris, *The Coaching Age*, 141. By 1836, the number had risen to 30.

29 J.E. Bradfield, op. cit. The figure Bradfield gave for stage and mail coaches together was 1.25 million miles weekly. This may have been an exaggeration – the Stamp Office put the annual figure at 25 million miles, around the end of the 1830s.

30 B.P.P., Select Committee (1836) 21, 64. These figures must relate to the most heavily used roads: the average expenditure per mile on turnpike roads countrywide was only about £33. See B.P.P., Abstracts, Income and Expenditure of Turnpike Trusts (1834).

31 B.P.P., Select Committee (1834–5) 57.

32 Goldsworthy Gurney, *Observations on Steam Carriages* (1832) 41.

33 Maceroni, op. cit.

34 Different sources tell of different frequencies. This was the original schedule.

35 Gurney, op. cit., tables pp. 36–9. These figures cover the period to 1 June.

36 It went into considerable detail; it was published; and a copy was later sent to Lord Althorp, Chancellor of the Exchequer, in an attempt to convince him that road steamers were practical, and deserving of fiscal support. These are not the characteristics of a fraudulent document.

37 A claim that a bushel of coke could last two miles was probably a slight exaggeration. Neither had water consumption improved; 10 gallons a mile was admitted. See B.P.P., Select Committee (1831) 18.

38 It is impossible to be certain which trust was responsible, as the locations given vary widely.

39 See pp. 48–9; also *Mechanics' Magazine* (1 Oct. 1831) 16.

40 Hanning's growing disgruntlement was recorded, at second hand; so was Dobbyn's resentment at Maceroni for involving him with Gurney. See *Mechanics'*

Magazine (23 May 1835) 141.

41 A gatekeeper who – according to Nathaniel Ogle – was entitled to ask 2s 6d per horsepower later charged him 7s 6d, having estimated his carriage's output to be 3 h.p. Ogle believed the man should have demanded £6 5s 0d. Whether this was true or not, Ogle felt that he had got the better of the trust. It may be that some gatekeepers simply looked at a steamer and guessed how many horses would be needed to draw it. See B.P.P., Report, Select Committee on Turnpike Trusts, (1839).

42 Thirteen Acts passed between 1829 and 1831 were named as notorious at the time, or were otherwise exceptionally punitive. In no instance is there a case for saying that the suppression of steam was the principal object of the Act. One was a consolidation Act; one was the trust's initial, embodying Act. Seven were renewals, after 21 years or more. As for the other four, the existing Acts did not yet need renewal; a new Act was obtained in order to increase tolls across the board, and/or to make new roads. This was a frequent occurrence. In all 13 cases, it would be natural to impose a toll on a newcomer at the same time.

43 In his evidence before the 1831 Committee, Hancock says that the *Infant* had been running for hire since about the beginning of July, but elsewhere gives a February date, as do other contemporary authorities. It is possible that both dates are correct, for like other steamers, Hancock's tended to operate for a period, stop, and later restart.

44 J.K. Glynn, *The Private M.P. 1833–68*, University of London Ph.D. thesis (1949) 30 *ff*.

45 S.H. Beer, *Modern British Politics*, 25. The first check on interest did not come until 1844, and then, as we shall see, it was limited in scope.

46 Dixon, Member for Dumbarton, revealed himself as a partisan of stem carriages that same summer, when opposing the Turnpike Tolls (Scotland) Bill.

47 For example, Gurney stated before the committee that the tolls on steamers on the Metropolis roads were the most favourable of any, which was not so. He also claimed that 54 Bills discriminating against his steamers were brought in during the 1831 session; the true number was 42.

48 In a letter to Gurney dated 8 February 1832, Dance claimed that a general conversion from horse to steam coaches would benefit all classes. The proprietors would gain from smaller capital outlay, and win more custom because they could ask lower fares. The working class would benefit because new jobs would be created – more men, especially skilled artificers, were needed to run steam coaches.

49 B.P.P., Bills (1831–2) iv. The promoters had been able to persuade the drafters of the Bill that three years was not enough.

50 Hancock was not yet, of course, competing with horse omnibuses.

51 Lord Radnor and Lord Salisbury were respectively for and against the 1836 Bill.

52 See p. 125 for those proceedings of the subsequent select committee that affected the state of steam in general, rather than Gurney personally.

53 *The Times* (8 Mar. 1875).

PART 3

1 *Foreign Quarterly Review*, x, 481. The anonymous article was attributed to Russell by Alexander Gordon, op. cit., 117.

2 *Journal of Elemental Locomotion* (Oct. 1832) 6. The Reform Bill had become law in June, but this did not signal the end of agitation.

3 Author of *A Treatise on Roads* (1833); later Lord Congleton.
4 Anon., *A Concise History of Steam Carriages on Common Turnpike Roads*, 21–5. This work, which favours Gurney and concentrates on the work of Dance, suggests that the latter was the author. See also Gordon, op. cit., 89–93.
5 B.P.P., Select Committee (1834–5) 86. Modern histories have thrown doubts on the existence of the vehicle, because of its unlikely appearance as depicted in a contemporary print, but these are unjustified.
6 Hancock, op. cit. Some details of the 1833–4 Hancock vehicles appear in the captions accompanying an Ackermann print of the *Enterprise*, dated June 1833, and in another, without publisher or date, showing three machines, and describing a fourth – the *Era* of 1832, awaiting an owner. From internal evidence, the print appears to have been published in the autumn of 1834. Both these prints are straight publicity for Hancock, not satire.
7 *Mechanics' Magazine* (29 Aug. 1835) 404.
8 Five miles out and 5 miles back on the Harrow road was a "one-fire trip", according to the *True Sun* (16 July 1834).
9 Gordon said that the cost of coke was 3d–4d per mile; coke cost 6d a bushel in London. See B.P.P., Select Committee (1839) 35.
10 Prospectus, Common Road Steam Conveyance Company (1839).
11 *Mechanics' Magazine* (9 Oct. 1841) 292. The description of 1835 quoted here does not make clear which Maceroni carriage was involved, but the greatly improved performance, noted by an unbiased authority, suggests the later one.
12 *Mechanics' Magazine* (14 Sept. 1833) 445; ibid. (5 July 1834) 240; *Gentleman's Magazine* (Aug. 1834) 193; J.C. Dietz, *Charles Dietz, Précurseur Oublié*. In October 1838 there was more news of Dietz *père*, whose tractor towed a train of vehicles from Brussels to Ghent. This was probably the third Dietz design, a complicated machine dating from 1836 that had six steering road wheels and two central driving wheels, and which ran from Brussels to Antwerp.
13 Handley was asked only to identify Dance's handwriting on a letter to Gurney.
14 Maudslay, Sons and Field built another steamer at about this time – an ordinary railway locomotive, with plain instead of flanged wheels. It was an experiment, abandoned because the "steam blast", tolerable on a railway, was too noisy for the road.
15 Hancock, op. cit., *passim*; B.P.P., Select Committee (1836) 20–7; Institution of Civil Engineers, *Proceedings* (1876–7) 47–8.
16 B.P.P., Select Committee (1839) 27, 31. The figure already equalled the total sum invested in canals from the start of the "canal age".
17 See p. 139.
18 B.P.P., Select Committee (1831) 18, 31.
19 William Bridges Adams, op. cit., 197 *ff*. Adams was best known as an engineer. He was a prolific, though financially unsuccessful patentee of improvements to railways, notably the fishplate joint for rails. He opened a works at Bow, and it is ironic that in the 1850s, a steam railcar he had built there was, as we shall see, converted into a road vehicle.
20 B.P.P., Select Committee of the House of Commons on Turnpike Trusts and Tolls, 1836, Report, vi; Minutes, 125.
21 *Mechanics' Magazine* (22 Aug. 1835) 389. This journal had always been sceptical of the long-distance trunk route ambitions of steam coach promoters.
22 *Mechanics' Magazine* (22 June 1839) 201.
23 *The Times* (23 May 1840). Nothing more can be found concerning the excursions of Hills's vehicle.

Index